S0-FIY-409

PELICAN BOOKS

A 620

A HISTORY OF LATIN AMERICA

GEORGE PENDLE

George Pendle was born in London in 1906 and educated at
Merchiston Castle School and Corpus Christi College,
Oxford, later attending the Sorbonne and Madrid University.
He first visited Latin America on business in 1930–1, and in
1932 published his first book, *Much Sky: Impressions of
South America*. From 1942 to 1944 he was British Council
representative in Paraguay and is particularly fond of that
country; the following year he was general manager for Latin
America of the Book Export Scheme. He was B.B.C. special
correspondent to Brazil and Argentina in 1955.

Since the war he was written a number of books and studies
about Latin America and these include *Chile, Paraguay and
Uruguay; Argentina;* and *South America*. He collects early
travel books on Latin America. George Pendle, who is
married to a grand-daughter of the principal founder of the
Welsh colony in Patagonia and has two sons and a daughter,
lives at Frinton-on-Sea without belonging to either the golf or
tennis club. He gets his exercise by vegetable-gardening and
sawing up driftwood.

A HISTORY
OF LATIN AMERICA

GEORGE PENDLE

PENGUIN BOOKS
BALTIMORE · MARYLAND

Penguin Books Ltd, Harmondsworth, Middlesex, England
Penguin Books Inc., 3300 Clipper Mill Road, Baltimore 11, Md, U.S.A.
Penguin Books Pty Ltd, Ringwood, Victoria, Australia

—

First published 1963
Reprinted 1965

—

Copyright © George Pendle, 1963

—

Made and printed in Great Britain
by C. Nicholls & Company Ltd
Set in Monotype Times

Contents

Contents

Contents

List of Maps

Preface

THIS is an essay in the history of Latin America. It is not a collection of the separate histories of the twenty republics. I have given special attention to events and characteristics which will help the reader to understand what is happening in Latin America today.

The author of such a book must of course be indebted to many others who have studied Latin America. My chief debt is to the works of R. A. Humphreys and John Lynch, Preston E. James and Pedro Henríquez Ureña. On the long journey from the days of the Aztecs and Incas to those of Fidel Castro and Betancourt I have found many helpful signposts in Hubert Herring's *History of Latin America*, which seems to me to be the best of the mammoth histories published in the United States of America. Other acknowledgements appear in the footnotes.

I thank Dieter Pevsner and Miss M. B. James for their valuable advice and patience during the past four years, and Stephen Clissold for a last-minute reading.

G.P.

1

Introduction

LATIN AMERICA – the geographical area – extends from the southern border of the United States of America to Cape Horn, and embraces the wide arc of the Caribbean islands. In general usage, however, 'Latin America' means the twenty independent republics which arose in the territories in this area that once belonged to the Spanish and Portuguese empires, and the old French colony of Haiti.

The population of the twenty republics is about 208 million.

Mountains dominate the physical map. Even on the Atlantic side of South America there are no extensive coastal plains. The rivers that rise in south-eastern Brazil flow inland, because mountains obstruct their passage to the ocean. Only one of the countries of modern Latin America (Uruguay) lies wholly outside the tropics and sub-tropics. Elsewhere, however, mountains have enabled man to escape tropical conditions. Quito, the capital of Ecuador, is only fifteen miles south of the Equator, but it is at an altitude of 9,300 ft and its climate consequently is temperate.

At the time of the Spanish conquest the principal Indian civilizations were on the plateaux and in the high valleys among mountains. The Spanish invaders fought their way to those remote altitudes because it was there that they could find the stores of gold that they coveted and the labourers that they needed; and for centuries the mountains determined to a considerable extent the pattern of human settlement, just as they have affected the course of history in other ways. In Venezuela, for example, the mountains have produced the nation's *caudillos* – tough and wily highlanders who have come down to dominate the more easygoing inhabitants of the coast. It was the same before the Spaniards' arrival. The Indians in the Venezuelan highlands 'were superior in every way to those of the lowlands. Perhaps the cooler

13

air of the mountains was more conducive to active life.' Or the difference may have been the result of 'better water, better diet, steep slopes on which to keep the muscles hard, and a relative freedom from the mosquitoes and other insects of the lowlands'. The highland Indians were tall and warlike. The tribes on the Orinoco delta and the shores of Lake Maracaibo 'were shorter, were subject to rickets, had pot bellies and bad teeth, and were slow-witted and peaceful'.[1] For long periods the history of Ecuador has been a dichotomy of mountain and coast: in the past the bustling tropical port of Guayaquil opposed the highly conservative Catholic governments that ruled from highland Quito; in more recent times the *costeños* (coastal people) – who, because of the prosperity of their port and the valuable produce of their fertile lowland fields, feel that they are the mainstay of the national economy – have been resentful that Quito should control the nation's finances; often revolutions against the authorities at Quito have begun in Guayaquil.

In Latin America mountains have cut off the main centres of population from one another. Nor have South America's huge river systems served, in any significant degree, to join the peoples together. The Magdalena, Orinoco, and Amazon may be busy with river boats, but these rivers are separated even from other parts of the very countries through which they flow by mountains and by jungles. So great are the distances that the Paraguay-Paraná-Plata system has not rescued the landlocked republic of Paraguay (1,000 miles upstream) from its isolation. From early times, expanses of sparsely populated land (arid *cordilleras*, unhealthy jungles) lay between the main inhabited regions. Spanish settlement perpetuated that pattern; and when, in the first quarter of the nineteenth century, the movement for emancipation spread through Spain's dependencies, each of the major population clusters had its own revolutionary leaders. In most cases those leaders secured self-government for their own region, and therefore the boundaries of the modern republics generally pass through the traditionally under-populated zones. History may not repeat itself, but geography constantly does.

1. Preston E. James, *Latin America*, New York, Odyssey Press, third edition, 1959, p. 65.

Railways and roads run from each country's interior productive districts to its own ports, but even today land communication between the individual republics is little developed. Travel by railway between the Atlantic and Pacific coasts is slow, and services are infrequent. The train journey from Buenos Aires to Antofagasta on the far side of the Andes takes five days. The exchange of goods within Latin America, such as that of Argentine grain for Chilean copper, or for Brazilian coffee and tropical fruits, is still effected chiefly by sea.

In many parts of Latin America the building of a railway did not cause any profound change in the life of the communities that it reached. This was particularly true of the towns and villages in the desert that stretches for nearly 2,000 miles along the western flank of the Andean *cordillera*. In Chile, mining towns such as Calama and Copiapó had railway connexions at a relatively early date, but the people's isolation was almost unaffected. They still remained pioneering communities, each dependent on snow falling in the heights of the Andes for the supply of water to a small river which alone made the rainless valley habitable.

H. T. Buckle declared that nowhere else in the world were natural obstacles so formidable as in Brazil. Even today his remarks apply to many parts of Latin America. 'The mountains are too high to scale, the rivers are too wide to bridge [he wrote]. The progress of agriculture is stopped by impassable forests, and the harvests are destroyed by innumerable insects.'[1]

When the aeroplane came to Latin America it was received gladly, as a delayed but deserved compensation for the obstacles presented by Nature. But the economic benefits of air travel are as yet very limited.

A CIVILIZATION IN THE MAKING

The Latin American republics differ among themselves in many ways. Each has its own national traditions and heroes, its own personality. (For example, the traveller who crosses the Río de la Plata from Buenos Aires to Montevideo feels that he has come

1. H. T. Buckle, *History of Civilization in England*, London, Longmans, Green, 1868, Vol. I, p. 106.

from a rather arrogant city to one of less tension and less pretension, although nothing but an estuary divides them.) Nevertheless, the Latin Americans in general have much in common.

They still have a powerful Iberian heritage, they occupy together one vast area – prolific in natural wealth, prolific in deserts – which is far distant from the regions to the north, where the course of modern history has been decided. The whole of Latin America until recently has been on the margin of world history. But the gap is narrowing; and most Latin Americans who have thought about it believe that when they are ready – or are compelled – to play a really active part in world affairs, their intervention will somehow be distinctively Latin American.

The Latin Americans are not merely transplanted Europeans. The Indians of the plateaux and the highland valleys taught the Spanish invaders to adapt themselves to strange surroundings: to sleep in hammocks and to paddle canoes; to smoke tobacco; to use the local medicinal herbs; to eat maize and potatoes. Thus the Spaniards entered into close relationship with the new land. By concubinage and marriage with the Indian women, a new mixture of races was produced. The new man – the *mestizo* – was neither Indian nor Spanish; and this was to be one of the causes of political friction in later years.

In Brazil, the Portuguese at first did not discover any precious metals; and the local Indian population was much too small to supply sufficient labour for profitable agriculture. Therefore Negro slaves were imported from Africa, and Negro women nursed the children of the Portuguese landowners, lulling them to sleep with old melodies from their African forests. The Portuguese were already familiar with tropical conditions in Africa and India, and the Negroes, by mingling with them, helped the process of adjustment. An impetuous, easy-going people grew from this association.

The Europeans of course made their own contribution to Latin America and to the embryo Latin American outlook. They brought their own animals (horses, cattle, sheep), their plants, science, and industry. They added their own culture, the Catholic religion, and their laws. They introduced a spirit of optimism.

Long before the birth of Columbus, Europeans had imagined that an earthly paradise – a land of plenty, with a perfect climate – lay to the west, across the Atlantic Ocean. In the early fourteenth century its features had been defined in an English poem:

> Out to sea, far west of Spain,
> Lies the land men call Cockaygne.
> No land that under heaven is
> For wealth and beauty comes near this.

Nearly 200 years later, Columbus wrote of the Caribbean landscape and described the abundance and fertility. From the other side of the ocean he sent home his heartening message:

The island and all the others are very fertile, to an extraordinary degree ... There are many rivers, good and large. ... Trees of a thousand kinds; and I am told that they never lose their foliage. ... Some of them were in flower, and some with fruit. ... It is a land to be desired, and, once seen, never to be left.

Among its other attractions, the mythical land of Cockaygne had offered precious metals and priceless stones:

> ... the bank about those streams
> With gold and with rich jewels gleams.

Columbus was able to reassure his promoters at home even in that respect. From the West Indies he wrote:

Many of these people, all men, came from the shore ... and I was anxious to learn whether they had gold. I saw that some of them wore little pieces of gold in their perforated noses. I learned by signs that there was a king in the south, or south of the island, who owned many vessels filled with gold.

The New World was rich indeed – but it was also formidable. The *conquistadores* who survived the tropical diseases, endured the rigours of the Andes, and subdued the local tribes who greatly outnumbered them, had a self-confidence that is still a trait of the Spanish American character today. Men who had taken part in the conquest now behaved almost as though they were of aristocratic standing, although usually they came from quite humble families. When Saint Teresa's brother returned to Spain from Quito, with great wealth, after thirty-four years of absence in the New World,

17

A History of Latin America

he let himself be called *Don*, as he was wont to do in America. . . . This act was a matter of much gossip in the provincial society of Ávila, and the Saint herself was grieved by such vanity and presumption.[1]

In general, Latin American affairs become more understandable if we remember that this is the continent of El Dorado – the gilded man. The legend of El Dorado lured thousands to their death. Originally it was thought that untold treasure would be found in the altitudes of the country that is now Colombia, where at a height of 10,000 feet is situated the desolate, grey, sacred lake of Guatavita, completely encircled by mountains. Unnumbered years before the Spaniards' coming, the beautiful and proud wife of an Indian chief, to whom she had been unfaithful, climbed from the high tableland of Bogotá to this lonely spot and drowned herself in the cold waters of Guatavita. Every year thereafter the unhappy chief came to the lake with offerings of gold. For the ceremony priests first covered his naked body with resinous gums and then spread fine gold dust over him from head to foot, so that he had (as a later chronicler recorded) 'a second skin of gold'. While thousands of his tribe stood around the rim of the lake, the chief appeared, golden and splendid in the morning sun. The spectators chanted and thumped their drums as the gilded man climbed upon a raft that was piled with gold and emeralds. This *balsa* was then paddled out into the middle of the lake, and there El Dorado threw his offerings of gold and jewels into the water and himself dived in to wash off his golden skin. The throng around the shore shouted and tossed their own gifts of carved gold – idols and ornaments – into the depths.

The story of this ceremony – it is undoubtedly founded on fact – fired the imagination of the Spaniards. They reached the lake, but never discovered the gold and jewels. Then, as Humboldt explained, the Indians, to get rid of the invaders, continually described the gold as being located elsewhere, a short distance ahead perhaps, across the mountains, or down the valley. The *conquistadores* heard of a tribe of warlike women in the south who were said to have quantities of gold, so El Dorado became associated with the Amazon. Later, El Dorado became identified

1. Pedro Henríquez Ureña, *Literary Currents in Hispanic America*, Harvard University Press, 1949, p. 35.

18

with a legendary city named Manoa on an imaginary lake, Parima, in the Guianas.

Besides the Spaniards, men of other nationalities embarked on the search. Sir Walter Raleigh was convinced that Manoa existed – a conviction which a contemporary poet, George Chapman, shared:

> Guiana, whose rich feet are mines of gold,
> Whose forehead knocks against the roof of stars,
> Stands on her tip-toes at fair England looking,
> Kissing her hand, bowing her mighty breast.

El Dorado developed into a golden mirage that moved over the whole continent, leading adventurous men forward to new exploits, new discoveries. In the highlands of Peru the Spaniards ransacked the Incas' stores of gold, and the rich silver mines. Moreover, El Dorado became symbolical of an attitude to life. The land where the *conquistadores* suffered almost incredible hardships was, nevertheless, a land where the European could get rich quick, without tilling the soil, without himself working in the mines, without himself having to make anything whatever.

Later generations of immigrants have inherited – or acquired – the El Dorado outlook; and the scenery encourages optimism. The Spanish philosopher, José Ortega y Gasset, wrote of Argentina:

Everyone arriving on these shores sees, first of all, the 'afterwards': wealth, if he be *homo oeconomicus*; successful love, if he be sentimental; social advancement, if he be ambitious. The *pampa* promises, promises, promises. The horizon is for ever making gestures of abundance and concession. Here everyone lives on distances. Scarcely anyone is where he is, but in advance of himself. And from *there* he governs and executes his life *here*, his real, present life. Everyone lives as though his dreams of the future were already reality.[1]

Of course the optimism of the white and *mestizo* populations is not shared by the Indians, still isolated in the mountains and the jungles. For them, Latin America is not a New World: indeed, the part of it with which they are acquainted is an immensely old world, where their ancestors for centuries worshipped their own gods and never coveted gold for personal enrichment.

1. *El Espectador VII*, Madrid, Revista de Occidente, 1930.

Thus two of the main Latin American characteristics are: first the optimistic, confident El Dorado urge – people tear the jungle apart, searching for wealth – and second, a reluctance to concede that man should dedicate himself to the labour of organizing material progress; and, among the Indians, an inability even to comprehend such a goal.

Naturally, these two tendencies clash. It is not surprising, therefore, that Latin American development should have been erratic. But both tendencies are helping to shape the civilization that is in the process of formation.

2

The Human Background

THE INDIANS

COLUMBUS, when he landed on one of the Caribbean islands in October 1492, imagined that he had reached Asia. For this reason the islands and mainland subsequently conquered by the Spaniards became known as the Spanish Indies. The people whom the Spaniards found living there were referred to as Indians. The name has stuck. And in English the arc of Caribbean islands still is the West Indies.

Although originating in an error, the name 'Indian' was not so misplaced as it might seem to be. It is now generally agreed that the American Indian is in fact the descendant of immigrants from Asia. According to the usual theory, when the last glacial era was ending, ice-sheets retreated northwards over the Asian continent; animals accustomed to cool climates went in the same direction, and they were followed by tribes of hunters who depended on them for food. Some hunters, moving up through Siberia, reached the shores of the Bering Strait and then followed the animals across the ice which in that age filled the strait in winter.[1] In this sense America was discovered many thousands of years before the arrival of Columbus.[2]

The groups of human beings crossing from Asia must have been small; and they lost contact with one another as they progressed southwards down the American continent. With the years, differences of dialect developed among the groups; and a multiplicity of cultures. But the people's general physical appearance did not greatly change. Wherever they went and settled, their descendants were men and women with dark eyes, straight black

---

1. cf. G. C. Vaillant, *The Aztecs of Mexico*, London, Penguin Books, 1950 (and later editions), Chapter I.

2. ibid., p. 271, Postscript by C. A. Burland: 'There is little doubt that men were living a hunting life in this area [the Mexican plateau] about 15,000 years ago.'

hair, and brownish-yellowish skin. Those characteristics are the same in the Indian of Latin America today, and their traces are apparent in the *mestizo*.

When Asian hunters settled in the Americas and learned to be farmers, their communities were able to support a larger population, including specialists who could dedicate themselves to public works such as irrigation and the designing of temples. Indeed, the two centres of most intense agricultural achievement (the Mexican area, and the Andes) produced the most highly developed civilizations. Endeavouring to simplify the very complex pre-Columbian scene, G. C. Vaillant indicated a fundamental difference between the civilizations of the two chief regions:

The Andean peoples, to generalize broadly, concentrated on the material technique of supporting life; the Middle American on spiritual or, more accurately, supernatural methods. In the Andes, especially in the coastal valleys of Peru, enormous cities were built and vast irrigation systems watered the fields. ... This civilization culminated in the Inca Empire, the original benevolent, monolithic state, unique in American annals as the only governmental system which combined territorial expansion with the amalgamation of conquered peoples into a social whole.

The Middle Americans, on the contrary, lived in independent tribal or civic groups, and created a religious art and architecture without rival in the Americas. The ceremonial aspect of life dominated the civil structure, and the remains of temples, not cities, gauge the splendour of the past.

Vaillant suggested that the nature of the land explained the difference. The Andean Indians could cultivate their highland valleys and terraces year after year, without changing their ground. The Middle Americans, by contrast, were engaged in forest agriculture: the soil of their farm clearings was quickly exhausted, so they had to abandon their villages for months in the year and work farther afield. Tribal rites, held at central ceremonial temples, served the purpose of periodically reuniting the people in social solidarity.

In Middle America, the Mayas occupied a large part of Honduras, Guatemala, and the Yucatán peninsula; the Aztecs dominated the central Mexican plateau.

The cultures of the most advanced tribes had much in common – the sculptures of gods and goddesses; the stone pyramids upon which the divinities were honoured; systems of writing, for the keeping of religious and tribal records; and calendars and an astronomy, for ritualistic purposes.

In arts, crafts, and mathematics, the Mayas were pre-eminent. Their sculpture was sophisticated, their hieroglyphs and calendar elaborate. The ruins of Maya buildings at such places as Copán (Honduras) and Chichen Itzá (Yucatán) are evidence that a majestic civilization existed. Its most flourishing period was probably between the fourth and tenth centuries A.D. Then – perhaps because the soil of their lowland forest clearings had been exhausted – there was an exodus. The old temples were abandoned, to be overgrown by the tropical vegetation. The people moved to the plains of northern Yucatán, where a new phase developed; but by about A.D. 1200 this also had ended. The reason for the decline is unknown. Certainly civil wars, epidemics, and immigration by other tribes contributed. But the Mayas of Yucatán and the southern jungles still speak their own language today, and the basis of their life is much the same as it was.

Everything the [pre-Columbian] Maya did, everything he believed was related to the cornfields [i.e. maizefields]. His temples and sacrifices were designed to assure a profitable crop. His elaborate theology was an instrument for propitiating the powers and winning abundant harvests. His calendar was devised as a working schedule for the recurring cycle of the cornfield. That cycle has changed very little in two thousand years. We can understand the ancient corn farmer by observing his modern descendant. ... There is the same ceremonial locating of the field, the assurance of water, the laying out of the fields into the traditional units about sixty-five feet square, the marking of the corners with stones, the cutting and burning of trees and brush, the planting of the seed, the weeding from May to September, the bending of the cornstalks after the ears have matured so that the ears point towards the ground, the harvesting from November to March or April, the storing of the corn, the marketing – each of these operations takes on a ceremonial significance today as it did a thousand or two thousand years ago. And in the Maya village, as in most of the villages of Mexico, the cadenced tapping of the *tortilla* makers is still the familiar music of the countryside.[1]

Unlike the Mayas, the Aztecs had not passed their zenith when the Spanish invaders arrived. The Aztecs – warriors from the arid north – probably reached the lake district of the central plateau (the so-called Valley of Anáhuac, where Mexico City now stands) during the thirteenth century A.D. They built a stronghold upon islands on one of the lakes, and from there they conquered a vast surrounding area. The people whom they subdued were not treated as citizens of the Aztec state: they became serfs – unless they were sacrificed on the pyramids, where priests tore their hearts from their living bodies.

The purpose of Aztec religion – as of Maya religion – was to encourage the gods to watch over the crops and provide protection. The offerings most appreciated by the Aztec gods were the hearts of men; and the most valuable of human hearts were those of prisoners captured in war, since they were the most difficult to acquire. Therefore a constant supply of prisoners was needed. So sacrifice led to war, and war back to sacrifice.

Aztec civilization never attained the refinement and splendour of the Maya, but the Aztecs surpassed the Mayas in social organization.

The economic basis of Aztec society was agriculture, with communal ownership of the land. Land was granted to men when they married, but it remained tribal property and only its produce belonged to the individual. Men were honoured according to the degree in which they served the community. For example, as the capture of prisoners for sacrifice was the chief glory of war, a warrior who showed particular prowess in securing victims might be rewarded with additional grants of land. In this way a social and economic stratification developed. The civil élite collaborated closely with the priesthood. The priests directed the intellectual life of the tribe and instilled in the minds of the people the realization of the power and proximity of the gods. The gods ruled; the priests interpreted and interposed, and the people

1. Hubert Herring, *A History of Latin America*, New York, Knopf, 1955, pp. 37–8.

obeyed, not the priests, but the rhythm of action whereby the gods lived[1] – for the gods were the personalization of the forces of Nature. Religion was a group activity, holding the tribe together and necessary for its well-being. Freedom of thought and personal riches alike did not exist. But the system worked.

Present-day Mexican Indians have inherited their ancestors' physical appearance; the ancient languages and the unpronounceable place-names; the knowledge that the land and the gods are theirs; a fatalism which the non-Indian looks upon as apathy; a courtesy which is derived perhaps from their long experience of submission; and a 'cold persistence – fire below, snow above, like the volcanoes of the country'.[2]

In the northern Andes, the Chibcha Indians settled as farmers cultivating maize and potatoes in the high basins of Colombia. They devised a relatively efficient political system, but their culture was never so advanced as that of the Incas of Peru.

The ruling caste of Incas may have entered the highlands of southern Peru in the twelfth century A.D. The basin of Cuzco, 11,500 feet above sea level, became the centre of their operations. After the year 1438, in spite of the mountains and deserts which cut western South America into unrelated segments, the Incas managed to extend their authority throughout the full length of Peru, southwards across Bolivia to the borders of modern Argentina, far into Chile, and northwards over Ecuador, where they established a secondary capital at Quito. They built a system of roads to link the various parts of the empire to Cuzco. As they had no animals that a man could ride, communication was maintained by relays of couriers who ran along the roads, crossing the ravines by suspension bridges made of fibre ropes (the arch was unknown). Relief runners waited at post-houses at regular intervals to take on the messages. The Incas had no form of writing, so their messages would be transmitted verbally or by means of a bundle of coloured strings – the *quipu*. This was a mnemonic device for keeping accurate records by varying the colours and the position of the strings and tying knots in them. The Incas were ignorant of the principle of the wheel, and therefore had no wheeled vehicles. Their beast of burden was the llama; but this

1. ibid., p. 186.   2. Henríquez Ureña, p. 70.

member of the camel tribe can only travel about ten miles a day, and the heaviest load that it will carry is 100 pounds. Litters were used for transporting heavy objects, and the nobility were carried in ornate litters decorated with gold and precious stones.

It was by highly efficient organization that the Incas controlled their huge domain, whose natural features today still render it particularly unsuited to political unification. They adopted the traditional *ayllu* – a small group of families, usually related to one another – as the basic social unit. There was no permanent private ownership of land. All land was held by the emperor in trust for the people. In each district the land was divided into three portions. The produce of one portion was allotted to the *ayllu*, for its own use. The crops of a second portion were reserved for the worship of the sun (i.e. to provide for the priesthood and religious ceremonies). The third share went to the emperor and the government. From the religious and government fields the harvests (maize, the *quinoa* grain, potatoes) were gathered into special storehouses. The government's store was drawn on for the support of the nobility and all state officials, artisan craftsmen, the army, and all other non-religious non-producers. In the latter category were the aged, infirm, and widows. The state storehouses also served as insurance against unforeseen calamities – earthquake, storms, and other causes of crop failure.[1] The religious and government lands were cultivated by the people *en masse*. A hierarchy of officials supervised these – and all other – activities. As the empire expanded, the inhabitants of newly conquered regions were transferred nearer to the centre, their former homelands being re-settled with people who were already 'conditioned' to the Inca way of life.

What now remains of Inca civilization? Pottery, textiles, fine gold and silver work; agricultural terraces and irrigation canals, built into the mountain sides; great mountain fortresses, or refuges; and at Cuzco the gigantic granite masonry upon which the Spaniards grafted a less forbidding architecture.

The most notable survival, of course, is the Peruvian Indian himself – short of stature, with a massive torso (adapted to the

1. J. Alden Mason, *The Ancient Civilizations of Peru*, London, Penguin Books, 1957, p. 178.

oxygen deficiency of the altitudes); still speaking the ancient Quechua language; in general still unadapted to a society – originally introduced by the Spanish invaders – wherein natural resources are exploited for personal profit.

THE IBERIANS

The conquest of Middle and South America was an Iberian – and primarily a Spanish – enterprise. Spain had been overrun again and again by invaders from beyond the Pyrenees; and then in A.D. 711 Moslems came across the straits from near-by Morocco. So the Spanish *conquistadores* who eventually sailed for the Americas were of mixed race and had been greatly influenced by Moslem culture.

The Moslems' rule of Spain was tolerant and useful. They taught the Spaniards how to irrigate their arid land, and to apply fertilizers to worn-out soils. They introduced new crops from the East, such as rice, sugar-cane, and cotton. They collaborated with the Spaniards in scholarship. Many present-day Spanish words are of Arabic origin, often indicating the activities in which the Moslems were particularly concerned. For instance, the Moslems were traders, and the Spaniards acquired from them the word *almacén* for 'warehouse'. Today in the villages of the Argentine *pampa* the *almacén*, on a corner of the central *plaza*, is the meeting-place for horsemen who ride in from the country to buy their ironmongery, their groceries, and to chat over a glass (or more than one glass) of wine or *caña* rum. The language of the Spanish-speaking republics of Latin America contains many such reminders of the Moslems' long stay in Spain. And the influence was transmitted in other ways. The Moslems' study and teaching of the medical properties of plants stimulated the Spaniards' interest in the herbs and drugs that they discovered in the New World. The Spaniards learned from the Moslems to hide their women behind walls and shutters, and this habit continued overseas. The Moslems left a permanent mark on the folk arts of southern Spain, whose music and dances later were taken across the Atlantic to become a part of the Latin American cultural tradition.

The Moslem occupation of the Iberian peninsula was never

complete. Christian Spain retained a stronghold in the northern mountains, and little by little the infidels were pushed southwards. The Spaniards recaptured Toledo in 1085. Córdoba (the Moslem capital) fell in 1236, Seville in 1248. But it was not until after the unification of 'free' Spain by the marriage of Isabella of Castile and Ferdinand of Aragon in 1469 that the drive to purge the rest of the country (i.e. Andalusia) reached its climax. In 1492 the Christians captured the last Moslem fortress, Granada. But it would be misleading to imply that those were 700 years of constant religious war. The true picture was rather one of intermittent spasms of crusading or merely martial fervour alternating with long periods of acceptance of the situation, with a coming and going between the Christian and Moslem areas and, frequently, inter-marriage. One writer believes that it was from the Moslems that the Spaniards learned 'to keep time in its place, and the conception that life is worth living for its own sake'. He even ascribes to Moslem influence the Spaniards' 'sense of personal dignity that finds itself ill at ease with impersonal authority, and their rejection of rational criteria and especially the cult of progress'.[1] Certainly those characteristics – whatever their origin may have been – existed in the Spaniards who went to live in the New World, and in their descendants.

The fighting against the infidels in Spain was not continuous, but the Spaniards always desired and required the expulsion of the Moslems from their country; and the war had a profound effect on Spain's internal development. As the 'frontier' was pushed southwards, successive Spanish kings granted privileges to nobles and groups of persons who, recovering land from the Moslems, settled and took charge of the conquered regions. Then the kings, the nobility, the privileged communities, and the Catholic Church (which had likewise been rewarded for its share in the crusade) were struggling among themselves for power. At last, during the reign of the 'Catholic monarchs' Isabella and Ferdinand the refractory and squabbling nobles were brought more closely under royal authority; agents of the crown, who had

1. William C. Atkinson, *A History of Spain and Portugal*, London, Penguin Books, 1960, pp. 60–1.

been sent to cooperate with municipal governments, managed to undermine local autonomy; by diplomacy the monarchs secured papal approval of the crown's right to control appointments to church offices and over church finances. Not only did this centralization of power ensure the success of the final campaign against the Moslems: subsequently it enabled Spain's rulers to keep a firm hold on the *conquistadores*, the colonial administration, and the colonial church in faraway America. The extraordinary coincidence of the discovery of America by Columbus with the surrender of the Moors at Granada in 1492 opened the way for the continuation of frontier conquests and colonization in the New World.

The influence of Spain can be seen in countless towns and villages from northern Mexico to the Chilean lakes, but it was the Portuguese who created the largest of Latin America's modern states, Brazil. Their racial origins were the same as the Spaniards' – primitive 'Iberian', Celt, Phoenician, Greek, Roman, Visigoth, Moslem. Like the Spaniards, the Portuguese were 'attracted less by the prospects of earning a living by persistent toil than by the opportunities for speculative profit'.[1] But in spite of these and other similarities, they had developed on their own lines.

The struggle to expel the Moslems from Portugal was much shorter than the reconquest of Spain: the Moslems had yielded the southern Algarve in the middle of the thirteenth century, and by 1267 the national territory was virtually complete. Two hundred years before the Spaniards, therefore, the Portuguese were able and ready to look beyond the peninsula where they dwelt; and as their country faced the Atlantic Ocean, a class of adventurous mariners arose, eager to explore faraway lands. While the Moslems were still in occupation of southern Spain, Portugal's Prince Henry the Navigator (1394–1490) was dispatching ships down the African coast to seek a passage to the wealth of the Orient. The zeal for exploration continued after Henry's death. Doubtless it was as a consequence of these maritime adventures that 'the Portuguese economy became possessed of the furious

1. Preston E. James, p. 399.

and parasitic passion for exploiting and transporting in place of producing wealth'.[1]

For such a small nation, the effort of expansion was tremendous, robbing the fields of Portugal of productive menfolk; but already during the reconquest of their homeland the Portuguese had used Moslem captives as slave labour, to supplement their own population – and to relieve them of some of the manual work which they disliked. Indeed, they had replaced the verb *trabalhar* (to work) by *mourejar* (to work like a Moor). When they reached Guinea, they began to import Negro slaves – the forerunners of those who were to play such a vital role in the evolution of Brazil. The Portuguese had the tradition of large private estates – a tradition which they, like the Spaniards, later carried on in Latin America – and while the riches acquired from trade with the Orient bred extravagance, the possession of slaves encouraged indolence. The Portuguese adventurers were ruthless slave-dealers, but they are said to have treated their slaves less cruelly than did other Europeans, although there certainly was cruelty on the sugar plantations.[2] The Brazilian writer Gilberto Freyre believes that 'the singular predisposition of the Portuguese to the hybrid, slave-exploiting colonization of the tropics is to be explained in large part by the past of a people existing indeterminately between Europe and Africa and belonging uncompromisingly to neither one nor the other of the two continents'. (The Spaniards of course did not have that experience.) Freyre sees Africa 'mitigating the Germanic harshness of institutions and cultural forms, corrupting the doctrinal and moral rigidity of the medieval Church, drawing the bones from Christianity, feudalism, Gothic architecture, canonic discipline, Visigoth law, the Latin tongue, and the very character of the people'.[3]

The crucial time for the future history of both Spanish and Portuguese colonization in South America was at the end of the

1. Gilberto Freyre, *The Masters and the Slaves*, New York, Knopf, 1946, p. 247.
2. See C. R. Boxer, *The Golden Age of Brazil*, University of California Press, 1962, pp. 7–9.
3. *The Masters and the Slaves*, pp. 4–5.

fifteenth century. In 1492 the Spaniards, having only just completed the reconquest of their country from the Moslems, were still organized for the pushing forward of the frontiers of Christendom. In that same year the Portuguese, although they had in the meantime sailed to the ends of the known world, were still inquisitive, still capable of performing extraordinary feats of exploration and endurance; but they would be more disposed than the Spaniards to settle down and enjoy the fruits of the South American tropics, which were now about to be discovered.

3

Discovery and Conquest

THE EXPLORERS

CHRISTOPHER COLUMBUS and his shipmates were not the first Europeans to set foot on American soil – Scandinavian mariners, for example, had already touched the northern shores. But it was only at the end of the fifteenth century that a European nation was ready to penetrate inland, conquering, exploiting, and settling.

At that time, moreover, general conditions in Europe were favourable for the transatlantic venture. The Middle Ages were past. The Renaissance, still in full progress, had created a restless spirit, which stimulated inquiry, invention, and the extension of commerce. Europe's wealthy class now considered almost as necessities the luxuries that Arab caravans brought overland from oriental countries to the eastern Mediterranean – spices, carpets, silks, muslins. Spices had a variety of uses.

Before the modern rotation of crops and the cultivation of turnips provided feeding for cattle during the winter, all the beef for consumption in Northern Europe during many months was killed in November and salted: in order to add flavour to this hard diet, there was an immense and hungry demand for spices, particularly pepper and cloves. Spices were used to give pungency to thin beer; to add supposed medicinal virtues to the druggist's wares; and as perfumes, to counteract the odours of the insanitary streets.[1]

But the Mediterranean had become more and more a Turkish lake, so that the Christians' trade routes were threatened; and the high price that the mercantile intermediaries demanded was draining Europe of its gold and silver. Therefore the impulse to discover an alternative route to the Orient – and new sources of precious metals – was constantly stronger. The Portuguese were seeking a passage south of Africa into the Indian Ocean. (It was

1. F. A. Kirkpatrick, *The Spanish Conquistadores*, London, A. & C. Black, second edition, 1946, p. 349.

not until 1498 that Vasco da Gama finally succeeded, by doubling the Cape of Good Hope.) Only one other possible way of reaching the East remained: that was to sail westwards, across the Atlantic.

Nobody knows for certain where Christopher Columbus was born, and his early years are obscure. Apparently he was a seaman of humble – and probably Genoese – origin. On one of his voyages he was thrown up on the coast of Portugal, which country became his base for some years. There he must have benefited from the knowledge of navigation that had accumulated since the pioneering days of Henry the Navigator. And it was there, on the very extremity of Europe, that he grew obsessed with the idea of sailing west. The Portuguese king – preoccupied with the opening of a sea route in the opposite direction – rejected his proposals. Columbus moved to Spain, where in 1492 he eventually persuaded Queen Isabella to sponsor a transatlantic voyage granting to him and his heirs 'the title and office of Admiral in all the islands and continents of the ocean that he or they might discover'.

On 3 August 1492 Columbus set sail with a fleet of three tiny ships from the Spanish port of Palos. The largest vessel, the *Santa María*, was only about ninety feet in length. There is no need to describe in these pages the well-known voyage – the discontent of the inexperienced crew, who imagined that the northeasterly wind that was wafting them across the uncharted ocean would never change, to blow them home again; the unshaken confidence of Columbus himself; on 11 October, the joy of seeing 'a little branch full of dog roses' floating by; and, during that night, the expectation aroused by the look-out man's report that he could see a moonlit shore a short distance ahead. At dawn on 12 October 1492 Columbus landed on a fertile, wooded island of the Bahamas group. He named it San Salvador (today it is known as Watling Island), formally took possession of it for the King and Queen of Spain, and said a prayer.

Columbus described the naked inhabitants of San Salvador as handsome and pleasant people; but (he wrote in his diary) 'I did not wish to stop, in order to discover and search many islands to find gold.' A fortnight afterwards the expedition was cruising along the northern coast of Cuba and decided that this was Japan, or the mainland of China; but they looked in vain for the splendid cities with gold-roofed palaces which Marco Polo had described two centuries before. Then they arrived at another island of promise, which they named La Isla Española – or Hispaniola, – today shared by Haiti and the Dominican Republic. There, on Christmas morning, the *Santa María* was wrecked on a reef. In January 1493 Columbus with the two remaining ships set forth on a stormy return voyage to Spain. His arrival was greeted with enthusiasm. The merchants of Seville and Cádiz, excluded from the Mediterranean by the Turks and from the African coast by the Portuguese, now believed that a way of their own to the Orient had been opened. The Spanish monarchs imagined that the East Indies were within their grasp.

Ferdinand and Isabella, aware of the jealousy of the King of Portugal, hastened to obtain recognition of Spain's ownership of the lands that Columbus had discovered. They at once appealed to the Pope, whose authority to allocate territory not possessed by a Christian prince was still acknowledged. The moment was propitious, as a Spaniard happened to be occupying the pontifical throne, and it was to the Spanish monarchs themselves that he owed his office. In May 1493 Pope Alexander VI issued a Bull which divided the uncharted world between the two rival powers by drawing a line of demarcation down the globe. The line passed 100 leagues to the west of the Cape Verde Islands and stretched from pole to pole. All new land that might be discovered to the west of the line was to belong to Spain; land to the east would go to Portugal. After some bargaining between the Spanish monarchs and the Portuguese king the Treaty of Tordesillas was signed in June 1494 whereby the line was fixed at 370 leagues to the west of Cape Verde. By chance, this re-adjustment placed the undiscovered coast of the country that is now Brazil within the Portuguese sphere. The treaty had other unforeseen consequences:

> The monstrous pretension of the two pioneers of discovery to monopolize all its fruits to themselves provoked before long the vigorous resistance of northern countries which were equally fitted by geography

34

for oceanic trade. ... And it was this, even more than differences of religion, which led to those prolonged wars with the English and Dutch in which the power of Spain was shattered.[1]

Columbus returned three times to the Caribbean. On his second voyage (1493–6) he took with him men, animals, and supplies – horses, tools, seeds, and shoots of sugar cane – to establish on the island of Hispaniola Spain's first permanent settlement in the Americas. He traced the rectangular plan for a city, inaugurated a municipal system on the traditional Spanish model, and assigned a group of Indians to every settler. It was a social pattern destined to be repeated thereafter throughout the Spanish Indies.

The settlement on Hispaniola proved to be a miserable, mutinous community. The local Indians – provoked by the severity of the forced labour and the seizure of their women – rose up in revolt, and were slaughtered. On his third voyage (1498–1500) Columbus sailed along the shores of Venezuela, and, seeing the huge volume of water flowing from the estuary of the Orinoco, rightly judged that he had reached a great continent. During the final voyage (1502–4) he explored the coast of the Central American mainland. In all those years he had little to show for his labours. He brought home a negligible quantity of gold. Hispaniola was in anarchy. He died in Spain in 1506 at the age of about fifty-five, discredited, and without even the satisfaction of having had his name bestowed upon the lands that he had given to Spain. This honour fell to a well-to-do scholarly Italian, Amerigo Vespucci, who sailed as a privileged passenger with several reconnoitring expeditions in the Caribbean area. Vespucci was no highly skilled navigator, but he had intelligence and insight. After one of the voyages in which he took part, he wrote: 'I have found, in these southern lands, a continent. ... One can, with good reason, name it the New World.' Amerigo's words were circulated in Europe long before the publication of Columbus's journals. In 1507 a German cartographer published a map whereon the word 'America' appeared. Columbus discovered; but he did not know what he had found. 'Discovery must be given

1. Sir R. Lodge, *The Close of the Middle Ages*, London, Rivingtons, fifth edition, 1922, p. 493.

a meaning. . . . Columbus remains the Discoverer of America and Vespucci its Explainer.'[1]

Even before the death of Columbus, other explorers had set out from Spain and were ranging up and down the Atlantic coasts of Middle and South America. Spanish settlement spread from Hispaniola to other Caribbean islands. In Cuba, and elsewhere, the invaders were ruthless in their treatment of the Indians, whose numbers were reduced also by the ravages of European epidemics.

In theory all the new territories were the property of the Spanish Crown, and it was only by royal favour that the settlers could acquire the right to exploit them. Soon the need arose for the establishment of a body to supervise the transatlantic traffic on the Crown's behalf. For this purpose the Casa de Contratación (an organization having approximately the functions of a Board of Trade) was set up in 1503 at Seville.

Gradually the Spaniards recognized that Vespucci had not been mistaken when he described the American continent as a New World. As such, it was of course an obstacle on the much desired western route to the Orient, and the principal aim now was to find a passage through or round it. In 1513, searching, probing the mainland, Nuñez de Balboa and a few companions crossed the isthmus of Panama and reached the Pacific Ocean, where this gay adventurer waded into the surf, raised the flag of Castilla, and took possession of the ocean and all lands surrounding it for his sovereign. In 1516 Juan Díaz de Solís, groping for a way to the East, explored the estuary of the Río de la Plata, where he was killed by Indians. Five years later, the Portuguese navigator Magellan, in the service of Spain, sailed through the strait which bears his name.

With the achievements of Balboa and Magellan, the purely exploratory era ended.[2] From the Indians whom they had met on the islands and the coasts, the Spaniards had heard of fabulous treasure – gold and precious gems – stored in the highlands of Mexico, Colombia, Peru. In consequence, the New World ceased

1. Jean Descola, *The Conquistadors* (trans. by Malcolm Barnes), London, Allen & Unwin, 1957, p. 103.

2. '. . . *l'ère des tâtonnements est close*' (Pierre Chaunu, *Histoire de l'Amérique Latine*, Paris, Presses Universitaires de France, 1949, p. 15).

to be an obstruction: it became, instead, a world to be plundered. After the year 1520, explorers were also *conquistadores*.

THE CONQUISTADORES

When the Spanish *conquistadores* set sail from Europe, they had only the vaguest notion of where they were going or what awaited them. They suffered appalling losses by shipwreck, disease, and in battle with the Indians. On the mainland of the New World they advanced – usually in small groups – through the tropical jungles and into the breathtaking altitudes. By the year 1550 these extra-ordinary men had practically completed the conquest of an area which included the southern part of the present-day United States and extended as far south as central Chile. (Brazil was out-side their control.) Moreover, by 1550 the *conquistadores* – true Spaniards that they were – had founded many of the cities which still today are major centres of population. For 'the civilization of Spain is an urban thing'. At home, 'the Spaniards had lived in cities and shunned the open countryside. ... When they came to the New World, they brought their urban instincts and leanings with them. Since they could not conceive of a civilization that was not built around cities, they literally founded cities as soon as they landed.'[1] Also, of course, it was by the setting up of a 'city' – even if it consisted of only a few huts – that a *conquistador* staked his claim to jurisdiction over the surrounding country.

A few examples will indicate how quickly and decisively the *conquistadores* fixed the urban pattern of Spanish America. They began to build Mexico City (on the ruins of the former Aztec capital) in 1521. Quito (Ecuador) was founded in 1534 and Lima (Peru) in 1535. A first attempt was made to establish Buenos Aires in 1536 – this was abandoned, because of Indian attacks, but the site was reoccupied later and is the same today. One thousand miles upstream from Buenos Aires, in the heart of the continent, Asunción (Paraguay) was founded in 1537. Bogotá (Colombia) was established in 1538, and Santiago de Chile in 1541. In the remote Andean fastnesses of Bolivia, Sucre (which

1. William Lytle Schurz, *This New World*, London, Allen & Unwin, 1956, pp. 339–40.

still is the country's legal capital) was founded in 1538, the silver-mining town of Potosí in 1545, and La Paz in 1548.

The men who accomplished the almost incredible feats of conquest and settlement were greedy for gold and fame. They were animated, too, by a sincere, if fanatical, desire to subdue infidels, to convert them to Christianity. They would not have succeeded in their enterprise had they not come from a land such as Spain, and had they not been sons of the Renaissance, a restless age when men sought new and wider scope for their activity.

The soil of Spain – except along the coasts – is poor and parched, accustoming the people to harsh standards of living, conditioning them for trial and endurance. Many of the outstanding *conquistadores* – notably Cortés, Pizarro, and Valdivia – came from Extremadura, Spain's most arid and bleak district. A large part of the ordinary troops were Andalusians, 'who distinguished themselves by their quick wit and resourcefulness and a certain swaggering gallantry, as well as by their irresponsible ways and their refusal to accept the official version of anything as the gospel truth'.[1] Few had had experience in the use of arms, before they crossed the South Atlantic. Some were ne'er-do-wells from the aristocracy. There was at least one fiddler, and one teacher of dancing. Obscure country squires went on the great adventure; nameless men, such as Almagro, who were known by the name of their native town; others, such as Valdivia, who did not even know their own birthplace; and some, like Nuño de Guzmán, who were little better than gangsters.

Catholic missionaries – Dominicans, Franciscans, or friars of other orders – accompanied every expedition. When a city was founded, it was usually given a religious name; a priest was always present to bless it; and invariably a church was one of the first buildings to be erected. Wherever the *conquistadores* ventured they were *adelantados* ('advance agents') not only of the Crown, but also of the Catholic Church, whose secular head – both in Spain and in Spanish America – was the King of Spain.

The story of the conquest of Mexico, Peru, and Chile need not be re-told in detail here. But the main features of the campaigns and occupation must be described, because it was in the impact

1. Schurz, p. 89.

between the Spaniard and the Indian that Spanish America was born.

Hernán Cortés – a far-sighted, courageous, well-educated, and charming Spanish gentleman of Extremadura – had spent some years in Cuba when, in 1519 at the age of thirty-four, he set sail from that island with about 550 men, sixteen horses, and a few cannon. His purpose was to conquer Mexico, rumoured to be a storehouse of gold and jewels. On the coast of Yucatán he was given an Indian girl, who – as she knew not only the Aztec and Maya languages, but also the local legends and superstitions – became a valuable interpreter and counsellor. Anchor was finally cast in a bay farther north. There the *conquistador* landed his men, horses, and firearms, to the bewilderment and terror of the natives, who had never before seen horses and knew of no weapons more effective than their own wooden clubs (edged with sharp blades of obsidian) and javelins. From the distant capital, Tenochtitlán, the Aztec emperor Moctezuma sent gifts of gold and silver, with the demand that the Spaniards should leave the country. To prevent any of his force from attempting to do so, Cortés destroyed his boats; and he calmly went through the formalities of establishing the 'city' of Veracruz, 'Villa Rica de la Vera Cruz', 'the rich city of the True Cross', because:

He would not have felt quite Spanish if he had left a municipal void behind him. The notary drew up the necessary proclamation and articles of incorporation, and read them aloud to the assembled soldiery. The names of the mayor and board of aldermen were announced, and Father Olmedo, the chaplain, blessed the unborn city and called down divine favour on its future. The site of the all-important central plaza was marked off and lots were distributed to the founding citizens. Only then could Cortés go about the business of conquering Mexico.[1]

Fighting and negotiating by turns – there was cruelty and trickery on both sides – Cortés led his men inland over the mountains, accompanied by members of Indian tribes whom he persuaded to rebel against their harsh Aztec rulers. Then one day, from the heights, the Spaniards looked down into the rich valley

1. ibid., p. 340.

of Anáhuac. A soldier-chronicler wrote: 'Never yet did man see, hear, or dream of anything equal to the spectacle which appeared before our eyes.'

Ahead of them was Lake Téxcoco, dotted with islands – and, upon the largest of the islands, the ramparts and temples of Tenochtitlán. Cortés and his followers crossed the causeway that led to the island city and were welcomed by Moctezuma, who must have been greatly perplexed by the appearance of the white men. For their part, they marvelled at the stone palaces, the luxurious furnishings, the spacious courtyards, and the exotic gardens. They saw the emperor's nephew being carried on a litter adorned with plumes, and precious gems set in pillars of solid gold.

Cortés soon seized Moctezuma and ordered him to collect and hand over a vast store of gold, silver, jewels. Next, the *conquistador* hastened back to Veracruz to deal with a Spanish force sent by the Governor of Cuba, who intended to supplant him before he became too powerful. Cortés captured the leader of this expedition and prevailed upon the troops to follow him and reinforce his own little army. Returning to Tenochtitlán, he found that during his absence the Spaniards whom he had left there had put to death some two hundred Aztec nobles, thus arousing the anger of the people. Surrounded by a hostile multitude, Cortés decided that he must withdraw from the city. The retreat took place one night in June 1520 – the so-called *noche triste*, the 'sad night'. It was a tragic affair. Many were slain as they fought along the causeway. Many were drowned by the weight of the gold and silver with which they were burdened as they tried to swim away over the lake to safety.

Cortés escaped, rallied his remaining forces, built ships for recrossing the lake to Tenochtitlán, and in May 1521 re-entered the city. Victory was not easy, and the invaders were unable to save their captured companions, whom they saw being forced up the steps of the pyramid and sacrificed on the altar at the top, according to Aztec custom. Isolated in the centre of Mexico, and with no prospect of persuading the Aztecs to surrender, Cortés determined that Tenochtitlán must be levelled to the ground. 'I knew not', he wrote, 'how to free ourselves without destroying their city – the most beautiful city in the world.' At last, in August, what remained of Tenochtitlán became the capital of Spain's first possession on the American mainland.

Superior military methods, firearms, and the collaboration of rebellious Indian tribes do not entirely account for the success of such a small force of Spaniards in breaking up the great Aztec empire. Aztec society at the beginning of the sixteenth century was probably in decline.[1] Certainly this society was in the grip of a fierce and terrible religion, obsessed with the possibility of total and imminent catastrophe. Without human blood, the sun could not rise, the crops could not grow, time could not continue. Every event on earth and in heaven was judged with fatalistic pessimism and increasing anxiety. But according to legend, a white-faced king named Quetzalcoatl would come one day from the waters of the East to release the people from their appalling need of human sacrifice. The arrival of Cortés at Tenochtitlán seemed to the Aztecs to correspond to the legend. When they discovered their mistake, it was too late.

When the fighting was over, Cortés did not rest. The Indians were driven to build a new city, in the rectangular Spanish form.[2] With local copper and tin, guns were forged. Sulphur, for making gunpowder, was obtained from the high volcanic crater of Popocatepetl. Ships were built on the Pacific coast, so that other unknown shores could be explored. Cortés wished to preserve the local pattern of government by confirming the authority of the Indian chieftains, whose tribes had been decimated by war and smallpox; but his men were so insistent in demanding the reward

1. For a contrary opinion see Jacques Soustelle, *The Daily Life of the Aztecs*, London, Weidenfeld and Nicolson, 1961.
2. Modern Mexico City is on this site. The Anáhuac basin is not naturally drained to the sea. In 1607–8, the basin was partly drained by the digging of a ditch and tunnel. In the present century, further drainage operations have completed the removal of Lake Téxcoco. (Cf. Preston James, op. cit., pp. 639–40.) But the spongy lake-bed provides no firm foundation for heavy buildings, and the continued drying of the silt has created problems for architects.

for their services that he was reluctantly obliged to assign *repartimientos* – i.e. groups of Indian serfs – to each settler, as Columbus had done in Hispaniola. Expeditions ranged far and wide, extending the dominions of the Spanish Crown.[1]

In 1522 Charles V[2] named Cortés Governor and Captain-General of the so-called 'New Spain'; but the nomination did not for long remain unqualified. During the long struggle against the Moors at home, the Spanish monarchs had learned to restrict the powers of the nobles who won their battles and pushed forward their frontiers. Royal authority now had to be imposed likewise in faraway America. Officials were sent out from Spain to Mexico to set up an *audiencia*, or high court of justice, a tribunal with administrative as well as judicial powers. The process was carried farther in 1535, when Cortés found himself superseded by a Viceroy. The appointment of the *audiencia* and Viceroy in Mexico marked the beginning of a system of government that was to operate throughout Spanish America until the wars of independence – a period of nearly three centuries.

The conquest of Mexico and of a vast surrounding area having been completed, it was to be Peru's turn next.

Francisco Pizarro was born in Extremadura in the early 1470s. An illegitimate child, he had the upbringing of a peasant. Unlike Cortés, he had no schooling, and he never learned to sign his name. Robust, brave, and stubborn, Pizarro was one of the most heartless of the *conquistadores*. He had been in Balboa's party that discovered the Pacific. He then settled in Panama, where he received a *repartimiento* of Indians and could have lived at ease for the rest of his days – but that was not the spirit of the *conquistadores*. Rumours of treasure in Peru attracted him southwards. On his preliminary expeditions he shared the leadership with another illiterate peasant, Diego de Almagro, a man of extraordinary vigour and endurance who was popular because of his generous and gay disposition. At that time Pizarro and Almagro were already over fifty years of age, 'elderly men by the

1. For the Spanish expeditions into North America, see Stephen Clissold, *The Seven Cities of Cíbola*, London, Eyre & Spottiswoode, 1961.
2. i.e. the Holy Roman Emperor, Charles I of Spain.

standard of those days'.[1] They suffered tremendous hardship in the rain-soaked tropical forests when they landed, and from hunger and the attacks of Indians – although at a first encounter, as in Mexico and elsewhere, the Indians were nonplussed when they saw the Spaniards' shining armour and met the fire of muskets and cannon, so noisy and lethal. On the Pacific coast the Indians still used only arrows and javelins; the mountain tribes hurled stones by means of slings and wielded wooden clubs or spears headed with a stone or tipped with copper or bronze.[2] Once, on the coast of Colombia, Pizarro and his men, being greatly out numbered, were saved by the dismay of the natives who, when the *conquistador* was thrown from his horse, imagined that some monstrous four-legged beast with a human body issuing from its back had broken in half. At this terrifying sign they withdrew, allowing the Spaniards to escape to their ships. Horses, indeed, gave the invaders an important advantage. A few horses were included in the equipment of every major expedition, and the utmost care was taken of them. 'After God, we owed victory to the horses' is a frequent phrase in the contemporary records.[3]

So disheartening were the sufferings of Pizarro's followers in Colombia that the men proposed to return to Panama. Pizarro accepted the challenge. He drew a line upon the sand, and declared that those who still wished to accompany him should cross the line. Thirteen men stepped across, and stood beside him. 'Seldom has a single gesture been so decisive in determining the course of history',[4] for it was these adventurers who were destined to provide the proof of the existence of the Inca Empire, which led to the later momentous campaign against it. Pizarro's tiny group, with Almagro and a few others, resumed their journey. They sailed as far south as the frontier of modern Ecuador and Peru. At Tumbes they went ashore and visited the Indian town. There, all Pizarro's most brilliant hopes were confirmed. He saw

1. Kirkpatrick, *The Spanish Conquistadores*, p. 145.
2. Mason, pp. 191–2.
3. R. B. Cunninghame Graham, *The Horses of the Conquest*, London, Heinemann, 1930, p. 1.
4. Kirkpatrick, *The Spanish Conquistadores*, p. 149.

solid buildings, and was convinced that the chieftain ruled over a vast, wealthy, and well-organized state. Gold and silver abounded. The people were skilled craftsmen, makers of fine textiles of vicuña wool.

Pizarro now required royal patronage, to enable him to undertake the conquest of this land. In 1528, therefore, he sailed for Spain, where he was received by Charles V. The king had only recently welcomed Cortés, who had brought gold, silver, and other rare gifts from Mexico, so he was in no mood to disbelieve Pizarro's stories of the riches of Peru. In 1528 Pizarro was appointed Governor and Captain-General of Peru, and *adelantado*, with a handsome salary that he was authorized to collect for himself on the spot. Before leaving Spain, he visited his native Extremadura, where he enlisted his four brothers ('as proud as they were poor') and other volunteers. He then returned to Panama where Almagro was indignant at having been granted nothing more than the governorship of Tumbes and a salary that was less than half Pizarro's.

At the end of 1530, and after the customary celebration of Mass and Communion, Pizarro embarked at Panama with about 180 men and twenty-seven horses. They landed on the coast of Ecuador and marched southwards, the tropical sun beating down upon their coats of mail and quilted jackets. Among other troubles they were afflicted with a deadly plague of ulcers. It was not until November 1532 that they at last scaled the western *cordillera* and entered the fertile upland valley of Cajamarca, where the Inca ruler Atahualpa was then living. The delay was probably fortunate for the Spaniards' purpose, because by then civil war had split the monolithic unity of the Inca Empire, and although Atahualpa had defeated his rival (whom he imprisoned in the remote southern fastness of Cuzco), the power of resistance had been seriously weakened.

Upon his arrival at Cajamarca, Pizarro sent emissaries to invite Atahualpa to call upon him. After a display of Spanish horsemanship, the invitation was accepted, for the following day. The *conquistador* prepared for the royal visit in typical fashion: the night was spent in prayer and in the polishing of swords. God would give the victory to His servants. At about noon the Inca, borne on a golden throne which appeared 'like a gleaming castle of gold' above the throng of attendants, came into view. The Spaniards were rather overawed by the spectacle, and by the number of Indians advancing upon them. A chaplain delivered to Atahualpa a discourse on the authority of the Pope and the supremacy of the Spanish King. Then, suddenly, at a prearranged signal, Pizarro's men fell upon the Indians, slaughtering thousands, and Atahualpa was taken prisoner. During his captivity he was treated as a reigning prince and was allowed to be attended by the women of his harem. He was taught to play chess. Soon, observing his captors' passion for gold, Atahualpa offered to have a large room filled with golden objects as ransom for his release. Pizarro agreed, and thereafter, day by day for two months, Indians came across the country in single file carrying gold vessels and ornaments, which they deposited in the room.

Early in 1533 Almagro arrived from Panama with reinforcements, and Pizarro then felt able to advance farther into Inca territory; but first he had to make the roomful of treasure transportable, so he commanded Indian goldsmiths to melt down the artistic handiwork of their ancestors into bars of gold. Of the total amount, one-fifth – the share of booty always exacted by the Spanish Crown – was duly dispatched to Spain. The rest was distributed among the invaders according to their rank. Then, before beginning the long march to Cuzco, Pizarro took the precaution of disposing of Atahualpa, who was accused of treason, condemned to death, baptized, and executed by strangulation. In November 1533 the invaders entered Cuzco unopposed, and straight away stripped the city of its gold. Schurz has written:

The economics of the conquerors was uncomplicated. ... Most of them were penniless and landless adventurers. If they appeared to place an extravagant value on the possession of gold, it was because the metal encompassed all their elemental concepts of wealth, and the riches of the Indies promised them release from the poverty they had always known. When gold fell into their hands as their share of the spoils of conquest ... they were prodigal with it, and when they had gambled away the loot of Cuzco before the next dawn, they then gambled away the golden images from the temple of the Sun, as if they were pitching *reales* in a roadside inn in Extremadura. Of the Spaniard's contempt for money, once they had it, Cieza [a soldier and chronicler of the conquest] said that 'if they required anything they thought nothing of it. They bought pigs in the sow's belly, before they were born.'[1]

Later comment, already quoted, confirms the survival of that attitude into modern times: 'Scarcely anyone is where he is but in advance of himself.'

At Cuzco, Pizarro set up a Spanish municipality, with its *cabildo* (town council) and *regidores* (councillors). Every Spanish settler was granted a *repartimiento* of Indian vassals. But Cuzco was too far distant to serve as a seat of government for the whole huge region that the Spaniards had won. Pizarro determined to create a capital that would be near a coastal anchorage. So he founded Lima, a truly Spanish city, the 'City of Kings'; and from that base he directed the exploration, 'pacification', and settlement of an area extending from Ecuador to Chile.

In 1537 the old warrior Almagro, after a terribly hard and quite fruitless march across the bleak *altiplano* of the Andes and the sun-scorched Chilean desert, arrived back in Peru to face Pizarro – whose ascendancy over the land that they had jointly conquered he bitterly resented. Both *conquistadores* were well over sixty years of age when their rival armies met in battle. Almagro was defeated, captured, sentenced to death, and strangled. But the feud did not die with him. In 1541 Pizarro, in his own city of Lima, was assassinated by a band of Almagro's men. The shrivelled remains of a corpse said to be Pizarro's can be seen today in a glass coffin in the splendid cathedral at Lima.

In their rivalries, *conquistadores* such as Pizarro and Almagro were the forerunners of the *caudillos* who, when the Spanish-American countries had attained independence, constantly fought among themselves, led revolutionary movements, and overthrew governments. The *caudillos* inherited the Spaniards' individualism, their pride and passion, their contempt for death. Still in modern times the Spanish-speaking American, like the Spaniard, is averse from compromise and concession. Sooner or later, political issues are reduced to personalities, thereby becoming

1. Schurz, pp. 122–3.

comprehensible. 'Personalism' is the general rule today, as it was during the conquest.

Before his death, Pizarro had ordered an expedition to cross the Andes from Ecuador into the Brazilian jungles (it was a disastrous journey, but Francisco de Orellana accomplished the remarkable feat of drifting more than 2,000 miles down the Amazon to the Atlantic Ocean) and Pedro de Valdivia was authorized to undertake the conquest of Chile.

Valdivia – one of the boldest, most intelligent, and most *simpático* of the *conquistadores* – was born in Extremadura in about 1500. His expedition set out from Cuzco in January 1540. He spent one year traversing the desert of northern Chile, and then, having reached the fertile Central Valley, founded the city of Santiago – for which (in the usual manner) he traced out the main *plaza* and streets, with sites for the church, town hall, and prison. During the next twelve years, constantly harassed by Indians, Valdivia explored and colonized. He distributed lands and Indians in *encomienda*, and thus laid the basis for the Chilean oligarchy, which after independence dominated Chilean history until the twentieth century.[1] In the damp forests beyond the Bío-Bío river, the Spaniards met the fierce resistance of the Araucanian Indians, whose leader Lautaro had learned to manage horses and devised tactics for engaging the Spanish cavalry in successive combats until they were exhausted. In 1554 Valdivia was captured by the Araucanians and executed.

The bravery of the Araucanians is the principal theme of an epic poem, *La Araucana*, written by a sixteenth-century Spanish officer, Alonso de Ercilla. The war commemorated by the poem was in fact a contest between Chile's two founding races. The struggle continued through the colonial period, with a steady intermingling of Spaniards and Indians brought about by the landowners' practice of using Araucanian captives as workers on their estates.

For several decades the wild, nomadic Indians on the *pampa*

1. *Encomienda* was a new name for the *repartimiento* of Cortés's day (see above, p. 42).

in what is now Argentina were almost undisturbed by Spanish invaders. Juan Díaz de Solís discovered the Plata estuary in 1516, but when he landed the Indians killed him. Ten years later Sebastian Cabot sailed into the estuary and built a fort. Cabot saw no signs of gold or silver (though it was he who optimistically named the brown, silt-laden river the River of Silver); the Indians destroyed his fort, and he returned to Spain. Charles V then suspected that the Portuguese had designs on the region, so in 1535 he dispatched Pedro de Mendoza to the Plata, with instructions to build forts, open a route across the continent to Peru, and colonize. Mendoza went ashore and established the riverside port of Santa María del Buen Aire, on the site of the modern Argentine capital. The town was isolated by hostile Indians. A German who was among the settlers wrote of their plight inside the stockade:

> So great was the suffering and disastrous the hunger that there were not enough rats or mice, nor snakes nor other reptiles [for food], and [therefore] boots and hides, everything, had to be eaten.[1]

Buenos Aires was evacuated in 1541. The horses and mares which had been brought from Spain were abandoned on the grassy *pampa*, where they multiplied, and the Indians learned to mount the animals, becoming the original *gauchos*, founders of a distinctive equestrian way of life.

Before the Spaniards' evacuation of the Plata shore, Mendoza had sent a reconnaissance force up-stream in search of a short cut to Peru. No such passage was discovered, but a more luxuriant country was entered, where the Guaraní Indians were amenable. There the Spaniards, after their dreary experiences on the estuary, were delighted to find an abundance of chickens, partridges, doves, and ducks; *mandioca*, sweet potatoes, peanuts, maize, beans, and pumpkins; deer, wild boar, river fish, and a wonderful variety of fruits.[2] In that neighbourhood – one thousand miles up

1. Ulrich Schmidl, *Derrotero y viaje a España y las Indias* (from the Spanish translation by Edmundo Wernicke), Buenos Aires, Espasa Calpe, 1944, p. 41.

2. Natalicio González, *Proceso y formación de la cultura paraguaya*, Asunción, Guarania, 1938, p. 97. The root of the *mandioca*, or cassava, plant is still the basic food of the rural population of Paraguay.

the river from the Atlantic Ocean – Martínez de Irala, needing to repair his little boats, took them into a small bay on the eastern bank of the Río Paraguay and erected a stockade on a riverside headland. The fort was baptized Nuestra Señora de la Asunción and was to become not only the capital of the land known as Paraguay but also, in spite of its remoteness, the headquarters of the whole area claimed by Spain in south-eastern South America.

The Spaniards mixed with the Guaraníes. The Guaraní women willingly bore children to the white men, and Governor Irala himself had several local concubines. It was only in the Jesuit missions that this racial mixture did not occur, for there the Indians were segregated, and the Jesuits themselves were celibates.[1]

Thus in fifty years the *conquistadores* had completed the 'pacification' of almost all of the territories – the Argentine *pampa* being one of the notable exceptions – that were to compose the Spanish Empire in the Americas.

THE PORTUGUESE PIONEERS

The empires created by Spain and Portugal were quite different. Both nations went overseas in search of India and trade. The Spaniards failed to reach India. Instead, they discovered 'the Indies'; and instead of trade, they found an opportunity to conquer a huge territory. The Portuguese, a race of seafarers, did reach the East, and developed the trade that they had sought. They concerned themselves with conquest only to the extent of securing sea routes and trading posts.[2]

Portugal's achievements in the East distracted her attention from the American lands to which, by the Treaty of Tordesillas, she could lay claim. It was perhaps merely by accident that, in 1500, Pedro Alvares Cabral, on his way to India, touched the coast of South America, where he raised the flag of Portugal for the first time. The land he discovered came to be known as Brazil, because of the reddish colour of the indigenous dye-wood resembling a live coal (*braza*), which for several decades was the country's principal export, used in Europe for the production of

1. See pp. 59–61.   2. Atkinson, p. 147.

dyes for the expanding textile industries. After a slight exploration of the Brazilian coast, Cabral rejoined the usual route around South Africa to India.

During the next thirty years, the French frequented the Brazilian coast almost as much as did the Portuguese, landing to cut 'brazil-wood' and raiding Portuguese shipping. At the same time, the Spaniards were spreading rapidly over the New World, and their expeditions to the Río de la Plata sailed close to the shores of Brazil.

By the year 1550, when the Portuguese were still only just holding on, without much conviction, to the edge of the southern continent, the Spaniards had virtually completed their conquests, and thenceforth the main concern of the Spanish crown was not the expansion but the organization of its American realm.

4

The Spanish Empire

GOVERNMENT AND ADMINISTRATION

THE special characteristics of the Spanish occupation of Middle and South America appear particularly marked when a comparison is made with the English colonization of North America. One important difference was in time. The Spaniards began much earlier than the English. Columbus had established a permanent settlement on the island of Hispaniola in 1493; the first permanent English settlement in North America was not made until 1607. Therefore, although both European countries 'reproduced themselves' in the New World,

the England so reproduced was the England of the Stuarts and the Commonwealth, whereas the Spain so reproduced was that of the Catholic Sovereigns and of Charles V. Spanish settlement coincideded with the period of adventure. ... Thus the two movements differed in the world which they brought with them; they differed still more in the world which they found: the English found no Mexico, no Peru.[1]

In the Americas the Spanish *conquistadores* straight away spread out over an area about twice the size of Europe and founded widely-separated centres of civilization. The English – who were colonists, not conquerors – made homes for themselves on the nearest fringe of the Atlantic coast, the land beyond the Allegheny mountains long remaining unknown to them. It was only gradually that the colonists in North America pushed the frontier 'from tide-water to up-country', until at last in the nineteenth century settlement was carried as far as the Pacific.[2]

There was a difference in the attitude to the Indians. Writing of the colonization of North America, Daniel Denton in 1670 remarked:

1. Kirkpatrick, *The Spanish Conquistadores*, pp. 345–6.
2. R. A. Humphreys, *The Evolution of Modern Latin America*, Oxford, Clarendon Press, 1946, p. 15.

It hath been generally observed that where the English come to settle, a divine hand makes way for them by removing or cutting off the Indians, either by wars one with another or by some raging mortal disease.[1]

Spain, by contrast, regretted the depopulation caused in Middle and South America. There, the invaders – rough men, in danger of being overcome by the several million Indians among whom they found themselves – were responsible for cruel massacres. The population was further reduced by the famine that often followed the fighting, the European diseases already mentioned, and ruthless slave-driving. But the Spaniards depended on the Indians to enable them to exploit the riches of the conquered lands, and they needed the Indian women, because the conquest was essentially a masculine undertaking. (Spanish America became *mestiza*; English America remained white.) In Spanish America the natives were regarded from the start as subjects of the Spanish Crown, and the authorities in Spain did their utmost to ensure that they should be protected, converted to Christianity, and instructed in useful crafts.

In Europe the King of Spain was the head of a number of kingdoms (Castilla, León, Aragón, etc.) all of which, following Roman precedent, had been incorporated into the realm on a basis of equality. This tradition was continued in the New World. The conquered territories and peoples were looked upon not as colonies of the English type, but as additional kingdoms, theoretically the equals of the kingdoms of the Peninsula, 'units of Spanish collective life linked up to the European ones by the person of the King'.[2] Madariaga explains that this organic conception of the State suited the varied conditions existing in the Americas and facilitated the emergence of an empire of great variety. The *conquistadores* went forward 'as if led by their love of a free and isolated life'. Differences of land and people had been the basis of the plurality and variety of Spain, and the same causes had similar consequences in the Americas, where the new kingdoms –

1. Quoted by E. G. Bourne in his *Spain in America*, New York, Harper, 1904, p. 214.
2. Salvador de Madariaga, *The Rise of the Spanish American Empire*, London, Hollis & Carter, 1947, p. 9.

esos reinos, as they were called – soon acquired personalities of their own.

Those several kingdoms resembled each other in that the grafted element was the same – Spanish. They differed from each other in that the soil and the [Indian] root and stem on which the graft was made were wide apart [Aztec, Maya, Inca, Araucanian, etc.]. ... These collective beings, these *nations* which Spain was nurturing overseas, were growing from the very beginning on individual biological lines of their own.[1]

From the separateness and individuality, the various movements for independence developed during the nineteenth century; and the distinctive, independent republics of modern Spanish-speaking America are the outcome.

Spanish and English practice differed in other ways. For example, Spain carried out a rigid control of immigrants into her American kingdom. The purpose was threefold: to exclude heretics; to maintain as far as possible the purity of the Spanish ruling stock; and to preserve for Spain the wealth and resources of the conquered territories. As late as the beginning of the nineteenth century, Humboldt declared that during five years' travel in Spanish America he had met only one German resident, and that the inhabitants of the remote provinces had difficulty in conceiving that there could be Europeans whose language was not Spanish. Non-admissible immigrants were defined as anyone not born in Spain, Mallorca, or Minorca. E. G. Bourne commented: 'These strict regulations stand out in sharp contrast to the later English indifference as to what sort of people went to the colonies.'[2]

So Spain's American kingdoms were almost exclusively Spanish and Indian. In the early days, the native tribes sometimes rebelled against their new masters. But many of them had been accustomed to submission to Aztec and Inca oligarchies, and in general they now accepted the domination of the King of Spain, whose captains replaced their previous rulers.

Only in the case of the wilder tribes, the 'unreduced' Indians [such as those of the far south of Chile and the Argentine pampa], do we have a situation more like that in English America.[3]

1. ibid., pp. 14–16.   2. Bourne, p. 247.   3. ibid., p. 254.

In theory – and to a remarkable degree in practice – the authority of the King of Spain was supreme in the Americas. His wishes were transmitted to his American kingdoms by the Council of the Indies – a powerful body whose functions included the issuing of laws, the supervision of the Church, justice and finance, and (through the agency of the Casa de Contratación)[1] the direction of trade and shipping. Instructions on almost every imaginable subject poured into the kingdoms, and although there was shortsightedness in the regulations regarding trade, the legislation in general revealed a humane consideration for the welfare of colonist and Indian alike. Even small details of everyday life received attention. For example, it was decreed that a member of the *audiencia*[2] must periodically inspect the apothecaries' shops and satisfy himself of the purity of the drugs; and Spaniards must not compel Indians to carry them in litters. Often the laws were ignored in the faraway lands: they were too numerous, and sometimes irreconcilable. Local officials argued that the King and his Council did not understand the conditions prevailing across the Atlantic. The formula for evasion was '*Obedezco, pero no cumplo*' ('I obey but do not fulfil').

The senior functionaries in the Americas were the viceroys. The Viceroy of New Spain held court in Mexico, with jurisdiction over the whole of Middle America. The Viceroy of Peru operated even more magnificently from Lima, nominally controlling almost the whole of Spanish South America, over the Andean *cordillera* as far as the Río de la Plata and Patagonia. The viceroy was a personal representative of the King. When he arrived from Spain, he was received with great ceremony. In the eighteenth century, in preparation for the viceroy's entry into Lima, the streets were cleaned and hung with tapestry, and magnificent triumphal arches were erected. The viceroy and his retinue approached on horses with trappings. The magistrates wore crimson velvet robes, lined with brocade of the same colour. Members of the town council, walking beside the viceroy, held a canopy over him. The procession, of considerable length, went its way to the great square and the cathedral, where the Te Deum was sung. Afterwards 'a splendid collation' was provided in the

1. See p. 36.   2. See p. 42.

viceregal palace. On the next day the viceroy returned to the cathedral in his coach, preceded by a troop of horseguards. All the riches and ornaments of the church were displayed, and the archbishop in his robes celebrated the Mass of thanksgiving. On that evening, and again on the following day, the collations were repeated, 'with plenty and delicacy', and 'to increase the festivity, all women of credit had free access to the halls, galleries, and gardens of the palace, where they are fond of showing the dispositions of their genius'. Then there were five days of 'bull-feasts', at the city's expense.[1]

As Spain's responsibilities in the Americas increased, it became necessary to provide additional centres of government. The Viceroyalty of New Granada – with jurisdiction over the northern part of South America – was created in 1717; but it was not until 1776 that the Río de la Plata was removed from the dominion of Peru. Lesser divisions (captaincies-general) were formed in Guatemala, Venezuela, Cuba, and Chile.

It would be unreasonable to blame the kings of Spain for having failed to concede self-government to the adventurers and the mixed communities in their American kingdoms. Nor was such a concession expected. The Spanish viceroy ruled on behalf of the king and in collaboration with the *audiencia*, or high court of justice, which consisted of *peninsulares*, persons born in Spain. There was a horde of lesser officials. The *criollos*, people of Spanish blood born in the Americas, were virtually excluded from the administration, but they did not question the King's authority. When complaints were uttered, these were against maladministration by the King's servants, and corruption. The cry ' *Viva el rey y muera el mal gobierno!*' (Long live the king and death to bad government!) was frequently heard.

It was only in the *cabildos* (town councils) that local citizens could exercise civic functions. Even then, their duties were very limited, and funds were always scarce. Nor did the *regidores* (town councillors) generally show much interest in the needs of the population. On the one hand 'it was no part of the policy of

1. Jorge Juan and Antonio de Ulloa, *A Voyage to South America*, London, fifth edition, 1807, Vol. II, pp. 47–9.

an absolute monarchy to nurture vigorous municipalities'[1]; on the other hand the *regidores* themselves were satisfied with the prestige that their office gave them, the wearing of fine uniforms at public *fiestas*.[2] They were flattered, and so until the eighteenth century – when measures for greater efficiency in the municipal system were introduced by the Crown, and the influx of liberal ideas began[3] – they did not seriously agitate for greater responsibility. The earliest *regidores* were nominated by the founders of the cities. Later, they would buy their seat, often with the right of bequeathing it to their heirs. Although in the modern sense the *cabildos* therefore were not representative institutions, the members did regard themselves as representing their cities. The *cabildos* are of importance in the history of Spanish American development, because they were destined to play a leading part in the movement for independence – particularly through their extension, the *cabildo abierto*, the 'open' *cabildo*. This was a general assembly to which prominent citizens were occasionally summoned to discuss urgent matters – for instance, defence against Indian attack. At the beginning of the nineteenth century such 'open' meetings were called to consider the situation created by Napoleon's invasion of Spain and his deposition of the king. In that emergency, in various places throughout the Empire the *cabildo* did give the impression of representing the populace.

THE CHURCH

The last Spanish flag has long since been hauled down, but the Cross is still silhouetted against the sky from Mexico to Argentina.[4]

The religious conquest of the New World was just as a great triumph as the military, and just as rapid. At the time of the discovery of America, Spanish Catholicism was still a belligerent faith. When Columbus visited Queen Isabella before embarking

1. John Lynch, *Spanish Colonial Administration* ... University of London, Athlone Press, 1958, p. 204.
2. Frederick B. Pike, 'The Cabildo and Colonial Loyalty' in *Journal of Inter-American Studies*, University of Florida, October 1960, pp. 405–20.
3. See pp. 66–8.
4. Herring, p. 169.

on his first voyage, their meeting took place at the armed camp outside Granada, which was the last Moslem stronghold in the Iberian peninsula and fell to the Spanish crusaders in that same year.[1] In the early period of colonial organization, friars and priests who went to the Americas were at least as numerous as the civilian officials sent out by the Crown. A hierarchy of arch-bishops, bishops, and lesser clergy was soon operating side by side with the secular administration. The Church of course was – by Papal concession – under the king's authority, and in carrying out its religious duties it served his purpose. It helped him to keep control of the Spanish population, by means of the Inquisition; and every advance into the interior of the continent amounted to an extension of his dominions, missionary outposts becoming Spanish villages.

Indians were baptized by the thousand, apparently accepting without much inconvenience the new priests who replaced their own. In the cities founded by the Spaniards, the church and its dependencies were usually the first buildings to be erected, with lodgings for the clergy and a temporary chapel. The congregations then were so great that they had to be accommodated in an unroofed courtyard, whence they could witness the services in the chapel, which opened on to it.[2]

The missionaries recognized that baptism and religious obser-vance did not necessarily signify true conversion, and they showed a wise tolerance. Christianity was grafted upon the ancient Indian religions, just as in Cuzco or Mexico City a Christian church was superimposed on the massive stone base of an Indian temple. Even today in Guatemala, and in other countries with large indigenous populations, the Indians may perform their ancestral dances and pagan rites on the steps of the church before entering to kneel in front of the altar. At one Guatemalan village the Indians will light candles in the church and then climb a nearby hill to offer candles, alcohol, and even crosses to the god of their forefathers. In 1960 villagers rioted when a

1. Schurz, p. 241.
2. George Kubler and Martin Soria, *Art and Architecture in Spain and Portugal and their American Dominions: 1500–1800*, London, Penguin Books, 1959, pp. 69–70.

priest arrived whom they suspected of intending to remove the shrine where they worshipped their Spanish-Indian *San Pascual*, Lord of Crops and Protector of Flocks.[1]

During early colonial times the clergy were always enjoined by both Crown and Church to protect the Indians from the rapacity of Spanish soldiers of fortune, who treated them as beasts of burden and drove them as slaves into the mines. In the defence of the Indians, the most dedicated and influential figure was Las Casas.

Bartolomé de Las Casas was born in Sevilla in 1474, may have studied law at Salamanca University, and went to Hispaniola to become a wealthy holder of *encomiendas*. He was ordained into the priesthood, without giving up his worldly privileges – until one day, at the age of forty, he surrendered everything, to devote the rest of his long life to the Indians, whose maltreatment by their Spanish masters suddenly aroused his compassion and anger. Las Casas travelled to Spain to argue his case. He was largely responsible for securing the promulgation of the New Laws of the Indies in 1542. Those benevolent laws could have corrected the abuses, but the practical difficulties of putting them into full effect on the far side of the Atlantic and the Andes, and against powerful vested interests, were never overcome.

Doubtless Las Casas in his writings exaggerated the brutality of the Spanish colonists – being an Andalusian *and* a propagandist, he would be doubly prone to exaggeration. Certainly his publications infuriated the colonists (who looked upon him as a meddlesome, trouble-making friar), delighted Spain's enemies, particularly the English, and were treated by generations of historians as the authentic account of Spanish colonial rule. In our own century, paintings by the Mexican artist Diego Rivera have helped to perpetuate the so-called 'Black Legend' of Spain, of which Las Casas was the most effective propagator.

The 'Black Legend' was not mere fiction. The treatment of the Andean Indians, for example, was appalling, even by the standards of that rough and ruthless age. The Indian miners in the high altitudes of Peru were subjected to a system of forced labour, the *mita*. According to the friar Vázquez de Espinosa, sometimes

1. *Time*, New York, 25 January 1960.

they would be compelled to stay inside the mine all the week, only being allowed out on Sunday to attend Mass. Their wives brought them food.[1] 'It would be a delusion to imagine that the Conquest was anything but a tragedy for the natives.'[2] Throughout Spanish America, in spite of the endeavours of the Crown and of high-minded churchmen to prevent it, the Indians were oppressed, in varying degrees. When the republics eventually attained independence from Spain, the exploitation of the Indians continued. In many regions even now it has not ended.

Understandably, zeal such as was displayed by the early missionaries was not a notable characteristic of the later clergy – who were inclined to laxity, particularly as the Church became enormously rich. But outstanding among those who preserved their integrity and discipline were the Jesuits: their greatest achievement was in 'Paraguay', a term used originally to designate an area that included not only the modern republic of Paraguay but also Uruguay, northern Argentina, and southern Brazil.

The first Jesuits arrived in Paraguay in 1588 with the purpose of converting and pacifying the Guaraní Indians. They gathered hundreds of Guaraní families into their mission towns, known as *reducciones*, or reductions, of which about thirty – with a total population of at least 100,000 – were in existence by the end of the seventeenth century. Each town was built round a large central square, which was covered with fine grass, kept short by pasturing sheep. One side of the square was formed by a towered church of stone or Paraguayan hardwood, and storehouses. The other three sides consisted of very long buildings, made of sun-dried bricks or wattled canes, in which the Indians lived. Each of these buildings accommodated a hundred or more families, in separate apartments but all under one roof and veranda. The Guaraníes were indolent by nature and unaccustomed to systematic work, so the Jesuits organized their communities in a semi-communal manner.

They marshalled their neophytes to the sound of music; and in procession to the fields, with a saint borne high aloft, the community each

1. Schurz, p. 76.   2. Henríquez Ureña, p. 37.

day at sunrise took its way. Along the paths, at stated intervals, were shrines of saints, and before each of them they prayed, and between each shrine sang hymns. As the procession advanced, it became gradually smaller as groups of Indians dropped off to work the various fields, and finally the priest and acolyte with the musicians returned alone. At midday, before eating, they all united and sang hymns, and then, after their meal and siesta, returned to work till sundown, when the procession again re-formed, and the labourers, singing, returned to their abodes.[1]

Other converts attended to the cattle which the Spaniards had introduced into the country and which had increased into many large herds. The Guaraníes were also taught to weave cotton, and they had tanneries, carpenters' shops, tailors, hat-makers, coopers, cordage-makers, boat-builders, cartwrights, and joiners. They made arms and powder and musical instruments, and produced beautiful manuscripts and printed books. All the lands and equipment were the property of the community, which worked under the direction of the two or three Jesuits who lived in each town. In exchange for their produce, the Indians received rations of food and clothing and of imported articles such as knives, scissors, and looking-glasses.[2] The main exports were *yerba mate*, cotton, tobacco, hides, and wood. The Jesuit 'reductions' also served as a defensive line: they protected the Spanish-owned territory against Portuguese raiders from Brazil.

Although Jesuit rule was in so many respects enlightened, it had its unfavourable aspect:

The Jesuit attitude towards their charges was indeed a paternal one, but it was the attitude of a father towards a backward boy who is never expected to grow up. Their neophytes were never trained to look after themselves, but to follow blindly in all things the orders and advice of their spiritual fathers. When they had become men, they had no chance of putting away childish things. They were thus inherently incapable of taking their place in the civilized society which was slowly developing around them.[3]

1. R. B. Cunninghame Graham, *A Vanished Arcadia*, London, Heinemann, 1901, pp. 178–9.
2. ibid., pp. 180–2.
3. C. R. Boxer, *Salvador de Sá and the Struggle for Brazil and Angola, 1602–68*, University of London, Athlone Press, 1952, p. 127.

The wealth and power of the Jesuits caused increasing concern in Madrid. In Paraguay their 'empire within an empire' aroused jealousy among the Spanish landowners, who were eager to share in the profitable trade in *yerba mate* and to obtain possession of the Jesuits' Indian labourers. When slave-raiders from Brazil attacked the 'reductions', the Spanish colonists made no serious efforts to help defend them.

Being very anxious to secure the Guaraní Indians for forced labour on their own *encomiendas*, they preferred to dispute their possession with the Paulistas [i.e. the raiders from São Paulo], after the Reductions had been destroyed, rather than to see their potential labour-supply guarded from them by the Jesuits.[1]

Finally in 1767 Charles III of Spain signed a decree banishing the Jesuits from Spain and all her dominions, and ordering the seizure of all their property. The clergy and civil administrators who were then sent from Buenos Aires to take charge of the missions in Paraguay were quite incompetent to manage them, and the Indians soon deserted the 'reductions' and either returned to their old way of life or became peons on the large estates. Within a few years the Jesuit buildings were in ruins and overgrown by tropical vegetation; the herds had been reduced to a fraction of their former dimensions; and the orchards and fields were again jungle. Some of the ruins have now been uncovered, and can be seen by visitors to the former mission territory around the upper Río Paraná.

The spreading of Spanish culture in the Americas was the churchmen's achievement. Having known the glories of Spain's golden age, they taught the Indians to imitate its cathedrals, carvings, and religious paintings. Soon there were churches in the Spanish style on the high tablelands and in the mountain valleys from Mexico to northern Argentina. High in the mountains at Quito the most sumptuous of churches was built, and so many monasteries and convents that these gradually occupied the greater part of the centre of the city, where they still stand today.

Architecture and sculpture were imitative of the Spanish, but the effect of local conditions is apparent also. The mid-sixteenth-

1. ibid., p. 72.

century churches in Mexico are massive structures, because at that time native labourers were not yet trained to produce finer work; furthermore, the friars and their villagers needed a refuge where they would be safe if attacked by the surrounding Indian tribes. In Central America, the colonists experienced their first earthquake; earthquakes recurred, so the buildings in that area became thicker and squatter 'as if growing a scar after each disaster'.[1] In sculpture the Indians' favourite figures were lacerated, blood-stained statues of Christ, to whom the sculptor often gave Indian features.

In 1551 Charles V granted his assent for the founding of the two great universities of Mexico and Lima, and other foundations followed from time to time. University education generally was dominated by the Church until the later decades of the eighteenth century, when the new ideas from Europe helped to undermine ecclesiastical authority, and prepared the way for political emancipation as well.

The indefatigable friars of the early sixteenth century studied the Indian languages, so as to be able to preach to the natives and instruct them in the Christian faith. But education in general was confined to the sons of the more prosperous Spaniards and *criollos* – though several schools for Indians were started in Mexico. The holders of *encomiendas* considered that to teach Indians would be to encourage subversion.

Henríquez Ureña presents the rather complicated cultural situation in these words:

In colonial times, strange as it may sound to unsuspecting ears, one of the guiding principles of that society, after religion, was intellectual and artistic culture. It was the crown of social life, just as sanctity was the crown of individual life. That culture was not progressive – it was based on authority, not on experiment – and it was not based on popular education, as the modern ideal requires; Charles Péguy remarks that the ideal of popular education did not emerge for the peoples who live within the Latin tradition until the French Revolution. But it was in no way aristocratic; learning was practically – though not nominally – within reach of all that might aspire to it, only it was not expected that all would aspire, and much less was it conceived that

1. Kubler and Soria, p. 83.

knowledge should be imposed upon all. Music, painting, and sculpture, especially, were often taught to people of very humble station.[1]

THE ECONOMY

It was not merely their exclusion from administration that placed the *criollos* in an inferior position : trade, too, was regulated in the interests primarily of the *peninsulares*. Spain designated 'monopoly ports' on either side of the Atlantic, so as to facilitate supervision by the Casa de Contratación and the collection of taxes. During most of the colonial period legitimate transatlantic trade was confined mainly to convoys which were supposed to sail annually between Seville and the American ports of Porto Bello (on the Caribbean shore of the Panamanian isthmus) and Veracruz (Mexico). The convoys had a naval escort, and the system 'was perhaps the inevitable solution of the problem how to handle a commerce of relatively high value in small bulk, with a region whose sea-approaches were in sickly tropical lowlands, at a time when corsairs and pirates swept the ocean'.[2] Nevertheless, it was a slow and costly procedure.

Porto Bello, although on the eastern coast of the continent, was the emporium of the Peruvian trade. In this strongly defended harbour the convoy from Spain would unload its cargo of European manufactures for the far-stretched Viceroyalty of Peru (silk gowns, woollen suits, iron hoes, etc.) and take on board the Peruvian gold and silver which had been transported by sea from Callao to Panama and carried thence on mule-back across the isthmus to the Caribbean. The more bulky goods for export (such as cacao, quinine, and vicuña wool) were brought down the Chagres river in boats. While the fleet was in harbour, the little town of Porto Bello was crowded with merchants, and a whole year's business was transacted in a few hectic weeks. In 1637 Thomas Gage, an English Dominican friar, happened to reach the town shortly before the arrival of the Spanish ships. Gage wrote in his journal:

When I came into the haven, I was sorry to see that as yet the galleons were not come from Spain, knowing that the longer I stayed in

1. Henríquez Ureña, p. 41.   2. Bourne, pp. 293–4.

that place, greater would be my charges. Yet I comforted myself that the time of the year was come, and that they could not long delay their coming.... What most I wondered at was to see the *requas* [droves] of mules which came thither from Panama, laden with wedges of silver; in one day I told two hundred mules laden with nothing else, which were unladen in the market-place, so that there were heaps of silver wedges like heaps of stones in the street.... Within ten days the fleet came [and] it was a wonder then to see the multitude of people in those streets which the week before had been empty. Then began the price of all things to rise.... It was worth seeing how merchants sold their commodities, not by the ell or yard, but by piece and weight, not paying in coined pieces of money, but in wedges of silver.[1]

The fair at Porto Bello was arranged to last as short a time as possible, because of the unhealthy climate,

which is very hot, and subject to breed fevers, nay death, if the feet be not preserved from wetting when it raineth; but especially when the fleet is there, it is an open grave ready to swallow in part of that numerous people which at that time resort unto it.[2]

The town, Gage said, should have been named not Porto Bello, but Porto Malo. Between fleets, it was deserted.

These restrictive regulations were increasingly a cause of discontent among the *criollos*. The most extreme case was the Río de la Plata. All legitimate trade between Spain and Buenos Aires had to go via Peru – the most circuitous route imaginable. Goods dispatched from Seville for Buenos Aires were landed at Porto Bello, taken overland to Panama, and shipped down the Pacific to Callao. They were then transported on mule-back over the Andes, to be conveyed across the southern continent on mules or in *carretas* – the ox-drawn covered waggons that became familiar on the *pampa* plains – finally reaching the Atlantic estuary town that was their destination. The quantities of manufactured goods so delivered were insufficient for local requirements, and their price was grossly inflated.

There is the significant example of the handkerchief:

The economic formula of the monopolists is epitomized in the sad tale of a fine handkerchief. A Spanish broker bought a pinch of good

1. Thomas Gage, *A New Survey of the West Indies*, London, fourth edition, 1711, pp. 444–6.
2. ibid., p. 450.

.[Peruvian] cotton at the fair in Porto Bello; a Spanish ship carried it to Seville; a broker sold it to the agent of a mill in Flemish Ghent; after another ocean voyage the cotton was carded, the thread spun, the fabric woven, the handkerchief fashioned; the delicate confection journeyed again, first to Seville, then to Porto Bello, then overland to Panama, then by sea to Callao and Lima; in due course it was sold to a fine lady in the viceregal court of Peru, or even in Tucumán or far-away Buenos Aires. The pennyworth of cotton had become a two dollar handkerchief, and the mercantilists' cycle had been completed.[1]

It is not surprising that contraband trade grew and flourished around the fringe of the 'legitimate' commerce – indeed, contraband in one form or another is still today a live Latin American tradition, and Latin Americans sometimes even now declare quite sincerely that they approve of it, because it 'humanizes the law'. English, French, Dutch, Portuguese – and many Spaniards, with their typical individualism and impatience of authority – devised means for bypassing the vexatious restrictions. Shipmasters and traders, under the pretence of having been driven off their course by storms, would put in at West Indian ports. Ships in the Canaries, ostensibly loaded for France or England, would cross the Atlantic westward. Ships, too, owned in the Canaries would load with wines, linens, or other contraband goods bought off foreigners, and then slip over to the West Indies.[2]

The Mexicans had a special opportunity to engage in illicit trade. In addition to the official connexion with the mother country through Veracruz, Mexico traded with the Spanish colony of the Philippine Islands, which, because of the Portuguese monopoly of the eastern seas and the danger of navigating the Strait of Magellan, were administered from Mexico. An authorized galleon sailed each year from the Mexican Pacific port of Acapulco (now the fashionable holiday resort) to Manila, carrying as its principal cargo priests for the Philippine missions and silver ('*plata y frailes*'), and returning with Chinese manufactures, notably silks and muslins, which were bought eagerly by the rich colonialists of the Spanish American west coast. Attempts were made to reduce, and then to prohibit, the importing of Chinese fabrics, as they competed with those of Spain in the Lima market;

1. Herring, p. 203.   2. Bourne, p. 286.

but the regulations could not be fully enforced, and a profitable coastal traffic was carried on by *contrabandistas*.[1]

While Spain's restrictive policies hampered the economic development of the American kingdoms, the stream of gold and silver from the New World had disastrous effects in Spain. The influx of so much easy money led to extravagance, stimulated inflation, and discouraged industry. The time arrived when Spain could no longer supply the manufactures that the colonists in the Americas demanded. The sailings of the convoys became more and more irregular, and when the last ships sailed in 1737 (shortly before the abolition of the convoy system) they were unable to dispose of their goods, because the markets were already overstocked.

The smuggler and the interloper had reaped the profits that should have gone to Spain. Cause and effect moved in a vicious circle. The more debilitated Spain became, the greater grew the contraband; the more the contraband, the greater Spain's debility.[2]

The enemies of Spain – eager to break into her El Dorado – weakened her by long years of plunder and commercial infiltration. They acquired bases in the West Indies and then on the American mainland itself.[3] Nevertheless, in spite of the pressure from outside and the unhappy results of Spain's own policies within, the Empire lasted for some 300 years. At the end of the eighteenth century, Spain still held sway from California to Cape Horn.

THE LAST PHASE

Spain was politically and economically bankrupt in 1700, when the last of the Habsburg kings died and the first of the Bourbons succeeded to the throne. Thereafter, in their work of reorganizing and reviving the country, the Bourbons applied principles of government which had been evolved by the more efficient monarchy in France.[4] It was particularly in the reign of the enlightened Charles III (1759–88) that the reforms were extended from Spain to the American territories. The purpose was to augment

1 Bourne, pp. 289–90.   2. Humphreys, *Evolution*, p. 34.
3. See pp. 77–80.   4. Lynch, p. 1.

revenue by means of better administration, to promote commercial prosperity, and to strengthen the defences of the colonies against penetration by England and Portugal.

Under the Habsburgs, local government in the Americas had grown increasingly ineffective and corrupt – royal funds were used as private capital, Indian labourers went without pay, exorbitant prices were charged for inadequate supplies of merchandise.[1] The Bourbons' chief remedy for the administrative abuses was the introduction of an 'intendant' system, on the French model. The Empire was divided into provinces, each of which was usually placed under the care of a peninsula-born *intendente*. The responsibilities of the *intendente* were immense. He was expected to maintain the peace within his province, watch over the conduct of government officials, ensure the proper collection of revenue, and assist economic development.[2] Some such tightening of authority was urgently necessary; but the 'intendant' system meant more officialdom, encroachment on ancient municipal rights, and supervision of matters hitherto conveniently neglected. The long-standing animosity between *criollos* and *peninsulares* was aggravated. The best of the *intendentes*, by arousing the *cabildos* from their lethargy and by giving them a new view of the economic opportunities, stimulated their desire to take over the management of their own affairs. The reforms therefore 'helped to precipitate the collapse of the imperial régime they were intended to prolong'.[3]

The Bourbons' realistic trading innovations had a similar, and likewise unexpected, effect. During the eighteenth century, the Crown gradually loosened the rigid controls on commerce, until finally all of the American lands were entitled to trade with one another, and directly with a number of approved ports in the mother country. Spanish merchantmen, instead of being obliged to discharge their cargo at Porto Bello, were allowed to sail by Cape Horn to Chile and Peru. Shipping multiplied, and in the decade 1778–88 Spain's trade with the Americas is said to have expanded by as much as 700 per cent.[4] This economic activity bred greater regional self-consciousness, facilitated the influx

1. ibid., p. 22. 2. ibid., pp. 48–9.
3. ibid., pp. 288–9. 4. ibid., p. 23.

of liberal ideas from Europe, and made yet more glaring the anomalies of the imperial structure.

The other main feature of Bourbon imperial reorganization resulted from the knowledge that the colonies on the eastern shores of South America were weak and vulnerable, and that British governments had lent a sympathetic ear to suggestions that, in the interests of British trade, they should be helped to attain independence. Spain began to pay more attention to the defence of her dangerously exposed possessions. The most important measure, put into force in 1776, was the separation of Buenos Aires from the unwieldy Viceroyalty of Peru. As an administrative centre, instead of a dependency of faraway Lima, Buenos Aires would be better able to protect the southern mainland – to which the Plata estuary provided the most convenient access – and the southern sea route into the Pacific.

The creation of the Viceroyalty of the Río de la Plata had an exhilarating influence on Buenos Aires. Already, in consequence of the greater freedom of shipping, the town had entered a period of unprecedented prosperity. Adequate supplies of manufactured goods were now received direct from Europe, and at prices about one third of those which had previously prevailed. The exportation of hides, skins, tallow, horns, and wool expanded. But the reforms came too late to save the Empire.

In 1796 Spain was again at war with England, whose control of the seas interrupted communication between the colonies and the mother country. There was a renewed scarcity of imported manufactures, and the value of exports from Buenos Aires, which had amounted to $5\frac{1}{2}$ million pesos in 1796, fell to 335,000 pesos in 1797. The discontent of the *criollos* in Buenos Aires and other parts of Spanish America was all the greater because of the improved economic conditions to which they had been accustomed in recent years. This was the end of the colonial era. The Spanish Americans had not yet declared their independence, but Spain's authority – weakened by the Bourbon reforms which had been intended to strengthen it, and then by the British blockade – would never be fully reimposed.

5

Portuguese Brazil

DURING the decisive period of the Spanish-American conquest, the Portuguese were preoccupied with the Orient and gave only casual attention to the vast region in South America which the Treaty of Tordesillas had allotted to them.

Their business was with Rajahs of Hindustan, Sinhalese potentates, Sultans of the Moluccas and of Malaya, and Chinese Mandarins. Their treasure fleets were laden not with gold and silver ... but with pepper and cloves, muslins and silks.[1]

For many years the Portuguese settlers on the Brazilian coast probably were no more numerous than the Frenchmen who landed there to take away cargoes of dyewood. Gradually Portugal realized that unless she exerted herself she would lose even the few bases that she had acquired. And although the Brazilian jungles lacked the attractions of the oriental lands, the prospects of profit from the dyewood trade were far from negligible.

In the 1530s, with the object of affirming his country's rights, King John III of Portugal divided into twelve *capitanias* the coast between the Amazon estuary and São Vicente (the latter being a settlement founded in 1532 by Martin Affonso de Sousa near the site of the modern port of Santos). Each *capitania*, enormous in extent, was granted to a nominee of the Crown named a *donatário*, who had wide powers and heavy responsibilities. He was expected to settle colonists, promote agriculture and commerce, and defend his territory – at his own cost – against marauders. There was a shortage of Indian labour, and in fighting the French the *donatário* got little help from Portugal. None of the *donatários* was rich enough to finance such costly undertakings, and some of the *capitanias* remained unsettled.[2] Most of the emigrants packed off from Portugal to South America were unruly exiles.

By 1549 John III, realizing that a central authority was

1. Kirkpatrick, *Latin America*, C.U.P., 1938, p. 34.
2. C. R. Boxer, *Salvador de Sá . . .*, p. 3.

necessary, sent out a Captain-General to establish a government at Bahia (the present-day Salvador). The Captain-General sailed for Brazil with a large company, including a small contingent of Jesuits. By their work of taming the native Indians and educating Portuguese Brazilian boys, the Jesuits were to make a valuable contribution to the unification of the colony, though one of the pioneer teachers suggested that the colonial students were rather unpromising material.

The students in this country [wrote José de Anchieta, s.j.], as well as being few, likewise know but little, owing to lack of ability and want of application. Nor does the nature of the country help of itself, for it is relaxing, slothful, and melancholic, so that all the time is spent in *festas*, in singing, and in making merry.[1]

In spite of Anchieta's suggestion of indolence among the Portuguese Brazilians, they did succeed in driving away the French intruders, and eventually they expelled the persistent Dutchmen, who between 1630 and 1654 had occupied an extensive region to the north of Bahia. Portuguese settlement for a long time was concentrated in the coastal area (indeed, more than three quarters of Brazil's population still live within a hundred miles of the Atlantic seaboard today). The majority of the colonists settled in the north-east, to plant sugar for exporting to Europe, where it was increasingly in demand. (By 1602, sugar – formerly a luxury which English ladies 'and some of the gentlemen' were accustomed to put in their wine – had become so usual a condiment that almost no kind of food was taken without it.[2]) The news of the growth in the colony's prosperity attracted wealthier people from Portugal, who had experience of managing large estates and could afford to build sugar refineries and acquire sufficient labour. Chronologically, sugar (which had been introduced into Brazil from Madeira) was the second (if dyewood – always a royal monopoly – be counted the first) of the export commodities which, in turn, have dominated the Brazilian economy. While sugar was supreme, other crops of the north-east – such as tobacco, cacao, and cotton – were of minor importance. As a result, Bahia, a prosperous town of well-built stone houses and fine churches, suffered from a lack of flour.

1. Boxer, p. 9.   2. ibid., pp. 177–8.

The characteristic pattern of colonial settlement was that of plantations grouped around sugar mills. Usually the mill (the *engenho*) was situated near a river and operated by water-power.[1] The main labour force consisted of Negro slaves, imported by the thousand from Portugal's West African colony, Angola. It was essentially a rural civilization, the plantation owners living on their estates and only visiting the towns to attend religious ceremonies or *festas*. During colonial times even the chief towns – Bahia, Olinda, and Rio de Janeiro – were very modest places by comparison with the great Spanish-American cities like Mexico, Lima, Potosí. Brazil had no university and no printing press until the nineteenth century.

The landowners' country mansions were of simple architecture, in a style that owed something to the Franciscan monasteries. They had thick walls, and a wide veranda in front and at the sides, with sloping roofs of tiles or straw as protection against the tropical sun and rain. Adjoining the main house were a chapel (beneath whose floors the family buried their dead) and the slaves' quarters, made of mud and thatch. In later years Maria Graham called at one such establishment, where 180 slaves were employed as labourers, besides those in the service of the family. She wrote with approval of the patriarchal atmosphere and the expansiveness of the people. All the food, except butter, was produced on the estate.

Everything was served up on English blue and white ware. The table-cloths were of cotton diaper, and there was a good deal of silver plate used. After the midday meal, some of the family retired to the siesta; others occupied themselves in embroidery, which is very beautiful, and the rest in the business of the house, and governing the female in-door slaves, who have been mostly born on the estate and brought up in their mistress's house. I saw children of all ages and colours running about, who seemed to be as tenderly treated as if they had been of the family.[2]

As the colony passed out of the experimental stage, laws to regulate its affairs were received from Lisbon in increasing

1. ibid., p. 12.
2. Maria Graham, *Journal of a Voyage to Brazil*, London, 1824, pp. 279–80.

quantity. Generally these were similar to those which applied – or were supposed to apply – in the Spanish territories. But the methods of the Portuguese were never so thorough as those of the Spaniards. Perhaps the Portuguese character was gentler. Certainly Portugal had been weakened by her efforts to preserve her Asian Empire. It was fortunate that the task which she undertook in the Americas – the occupation of an accessible and fertile coast – was much less difficult than that embarked on by Spain.

In Brazil the official powers of the King's captain-general (later given the title of viceroy) were strictly limited. They were further restricted in practice by the *câmaras* (town councils, locally elected in part and roughly equivalent to the Spanish *cabildos*) who were responsible for local administration. The town councillors were jealous of their privileges, and they resented the appointment of Peninsula-born Portuguese to the chief posts in State and Church, the regulations controlling commerce, and the prohibition of industry (only sugar-refining was allowed). Councillors interfered in political and ecclesiastical matters, laws were evaded, and the Brazilians revealed themselves as consummate smugglers (a talent which has survived to the present time). When, during the seventeenth century, Portugal granted them certain rights to trade with other countries, they took advantage of the new opportunities to a degree neither intended nor foreseen. So the dictates from Lisbon did not affect the life of the Brazilians to the same extent as those from Madrid affected the Spanish Americans. This lightness of touch in government partly explains the fact that the Brazilians never felt the need to launch a war of independence, such as those which caused so much suffering in the Spanish American lands.

The exploration of the vast interior of Brazil was begun in earnest by the Jesuits – who pressed forward, setting up mission outposts in the wilderness – and, more or less simultaneously, by colonists from São Vicente, who had emigrated from the poorer parts of Portugal and did not possess enough capital to enter Brazil's northern sugar region. When they climbed inland to the plateau, where the skyscraper city of São Paulo now stands, they had to content themselves with rearing cattle and cultivating crops of maize, rice, and cotton on the fertile red soil, for their own use. They enslaved Indians, whom the Jesuits (as elsewhere in Latin America) did their utmost to protect from this fate; and with the Indian women they bred a race of hardy and ruthless half-breeds known as *mamelucos*. Indian labour in the vicinity became scarce; the purchasing of Negro slaves on the coast would have been too expensive; so the *mamelucos* ranged inland, hunting more remote Indian tribes.

Armed slave-raiders from São Paulo penetrated ever further into the interior of Brazil in organized bands, marching barefoot, in single file. Such a company might number several hundred men, including already-enslaved Indians, and each party would have its own flag (*bandeira*), from which they probably got the name of *bandeirantes*. Sometimes the *bandeirantes* would be away for months and even years at a time. Generally they lived off the land (game, fish from the rivers, wild honey), although sometimes, when threatened with a shortage of food, they would stop for long enough to plant and harvest a crop of *mandioca* or maize. They travelled enormous distances, arriving within sight of the Andes and reaching the banks of the Río Paraná and the Plata. From the second decade of the seventeenth century their favourite hunting-ground was far away on the borders of Paraguay, where the Guaraní Indians (having been gathered into Jesuit 'reductions'[1]) were a double attraction: as the Jesuits had given them some domestic education, the Guaraníes would be particularly valuable as slaves; and as they were concentrated in small areas, their capture was relatively easy. So the *bandeirantes* descended again and again on those unlucky people, who were seized and driven away to work on the farms of São Paulo or to be sold in the slave markets on the coast. Countless Jesuit neophytes died during the appalling trek eastwards across the continent.

No one would deny that the *bandeirantes* were rapacious and cruel. But they are honoured today as the courageous pioneers who (while the Spaniards were preoccupied with the silver of Potosí) pushed the national frontier far to the west of the Tordesillas line, completing the creation of Brazil as it now appears on the map. The inhabitants of modern São Paulo, of many mixed

1. See pp. 59–61.

races, have a reputation for being the most energetic and enterprising section of the Brazilian community, and they take pride
in asserting that they inherited these qualities from the *bandeirantes*.

At the end of the seventeenth century the *bandeirantes* discovered alluvial gold in the uninhabited hills of Minas Gerais –
thus initiating a new cycle in Brazil's economic history, and the
development of another region. Diamonds were found a few
years later. These discoveries

came at a time when the prosperity of the sugar-cane planters of the
North-east had passed its zenith. Declining yields on soils which had
been cultivated for many years, and increasing competition from other
areas [i.e. the English, Spanish, French, and Dutch islands in the Carib-
bean] were decreasing profits in the Brazilian region. It is not in the
Brazilian tradition, under such circumstances, to aim at reducing the
costs of production through the use of better agricultural practices.
Income in the North-east was spent to raise the standard of living of
the aristocracy, not for investments which might lower the cost of production. Brazil suffered, moreover, from the curse of a great area;
virtually limitless area meant the ever-present possibility of moving on
to new lands and of exploiting new resources. ... When gold was
announced in Minas Gerais, the result was a gold rush, in which not
only *Paulistas* and Portuguese from the home country participated, but
also many sugar-cane planters of the North-east, who came bringing
their slaves.[1]

The gold period lasted until the end of the eighteenth century,
by which time the best deposits had been exhausted. Meanwhile
the wilderness of Minas Gerais had been populated and cultivated.
Towns were built – such as the beautiful Baroque town of Ouro
Preto, with its many churches – while Río de Janeiro was developed as a port for the shipment of gold and diamonds. Large
quantities of gold were sent to Portugal, to the great delight of
the king.

During and after the era of gold, cotton was a major export
commodity, and the European demand for cotton increased with
the invention of new spinning and weaving machines. Moreover
– at any rate to begin with, before buyers began to be insistent

1. Preston James, p. 402 (see also Boxer, *The Golden Age of Brazil*).

about length of staple and quality – cotton was an easy crop to grow; and the Brazilian planter liked an easy crop. Land in the north-east which for generations had produced nothing but sugar was turned over to cotton. Further to the south, a new form of speculative enterprise began: coffee was planted near Rio de Janeiro. In the nineteenth century, as the taste for coffee developed in Europe and North America, the plantations spread into the state of São Paulo, and people from the now decadent mining towns of Minas Gerais migrated to this new region of prosperity. Brazil's next economic cycle was dominated by coffee – with a rubber boom running concurrently, for a while.

In Portugal, as in Spain, the second half of the eighteenth century was notable for the emergence of a strong and enlightened ruler. The reforms of the Spanish monarch Charles III[1] were matched by those of the Portuguese minister, the Marquis of Pombal, who ruled as a virtual dictator from 1751 to 1777. In 1755 Pombal declared that the Indians in Brazil were free citizens of the colony, and therefore could not be enslaved. He made the Brazilian administration more efficient, reduced discontent by admitting locally-born citizens to public office, encouraged the expansion of agriculture, and promoted certain industries which did not conflict with those of Portugal. In 1763 he removed the capital from Bahia to Rio de Janeiro, thereby placing the central authority in a more central position. He gratified the Brazilian landowners by expelling the Jesuits from the colony.

Nevertheless, the days of Portugal's glory were past, and when Pombal fell, that nation was without a leader. Brazil, the only remaining colony of any importance, now had much more vigour than the mother country, and the Brazilians were becoming proud of being Brazilians. Like the *criollos* of Spanish America, at the end of the eighteenth century some Brazilians envisaged the possibility of national independence, but they were more given to compromise than were the Spanish Americans, and their movement towards independence was gradual and peaceful.

1. See pp. 66–8.

6

Other Europeans

THE French, English, and Dutch refused to accept as final the sharing out of the whole New World between the kings of Spain and Portugal. François I of France was provoked to demand that he be shown 'the clause in Adam's testament' which entitled them to it. Corsairs from Dieppe, Brest, and the Basque towns probably were the first to begin the harrying of Spanish ships and of the Spanish settlements in the Caribbean. As early as 1523, Frenchmen seized some of Cortés's vessels. But it was the English who were the greatest menace to Spain, whether they sailed in the service of their sovereign or merely with his (or her) connivance – a distinction which was never very clear. Legally, the difference depended on whether a state of war existed between England and Spain at any given moment, and whether the voyage had been sanctioned by the government or not. In practice, however, this was usually a matter of no more than academic importance.

Queen Elizabeth, while she publicly excused or disavowed to Philip II the outrages committed by Hawkins and Drake, blaming the turbulence of the times and promising to do her utmost to suppress the disorders, was secretly one of the principal shareholders in their enterprises.[1]

As a rising maritime and trading power, it was inevitable that England should challenge Spain. England was jealous and fearful of Spanish predominance in Europe and of the stream of gold and silver from the New World which enabled the Spanish Crown to pay its armies and man its fleets. The best way to weaken Spain seemed to be to seize her treasure ships as they passed through the bottleneck of the Caribbean, and English seamen were dazzled by the prospects of booty. Furthermore, Protestant Englishmen were bent on revenge, for they had heard of the horrible sufferings of their compatriots at the hands of the Spanish Inquisition.

1. C. H. Haring, *The Buccaneers in the West Indies in the XVII Century*, London, Methuen, 1910, p. 31.

Miles Philips, one of Hawkins's men taken by the Spaniards in 1568, had vividly described how he and his companions were treated by the Inquisition in Mexico. Over fifty of them were condemned to be scourged on horseback and then to serve in the galleys. Three 'had their judgement to be burnt to ashes, and so were presently sent away to the place of execution in the market place, where they were quickly burnt and consumed'.[1] Philips himself was imprisoned, but eventually escaped.

Closely related to the privateers and buccaneers were the smugglers, whose activities continued throughout the colonial period. Generally the smugglers were welcomed by the Spanish colonists, for they brought manufactured goods which, as mentioned in a previous chapter, Spain herself could not supply in sufficient quantities; and they brought Negro slaves. Spain had never secured a firm foothold on the slave coasts of Africa, so her colonists were always customers of foreign slave-traders, in spite of the existence of stringent laws against dealing with foreigners. But the inhabitants of the Spanish ports in the Indies lived in constant anxiety,

never knowing, when a strange sail appeared, whether it was to be welcomed officially as a Spaniard, received discreetly as a foreign trader, or fired upon as a raider. ... They both feared and resented the constant outbreaks of war [between Spain and other European powers] which loosed fleets of privateers upon the West Indies. They deplored Spain's naval policy, which was largely ineffective against raiders, but which treated peaceful smugglers as if they were raiders, and so encouraged them to go around and take to raiding. [Thus there was] a conflict of commercial interests between settlers and home government which was to remain characteristic of the West Indies throughout their history as European colonies.[2]

It was the Dutch who, by their example, finally convinced the French and English that Europeans could live in the Caribbean by other means than plunder and contraband. When the Dutch were expelled from Brazil in 1654 they went to Guiana and to some of the smaller islands, taking with them the knowledge of

1. Richard Hakluyt, *The Principal Navigations Voyages Traffiques and Discoveries of the English Nation*, Glasgow, Maclehouse, 1904, Vol. IX, p. 428.

2. J. H. Parry and P. M. Sherlock, *A Short History of the West Indies*, London, Macmillan, 1956, pp. 27–8.

the planting and refining of sugar – with Negro labour – which they had learned from the Portuguese. They passed on the sugar technology to the little groups of French and English settlers who already had come to the West Indies to try their luck. This amounted to an economic revolution, which had political consequences. Local planters began to prosper, and it was realized that after all the islands were worth possessing.

The present book is not the place to tell the long and very complicated story of the European alliances and wars which one after another affected the course of West Indian development. Gradually the foreign maritime guerrillas wore down Spain's resistance. In 1655 an English force seized Jamaica from the Spaniards – a capture which differed from all previous English acquisitions, for it was carried out not by private adventurers but by a naval and military expedition paid for by the government. In 1670 a treaty was signed whereby Spain recognized the English title to Jamaica and to all England's other *de facto* possessions in the Americas. The English government maintained that those possessions included a colony of buccaneers or ex-buccaneers who had settled on the Central American coast, beside the Belize River, to cut and export dyewood; but Spain denied that Belize was covered by the treaty, with the result that today the republic of Guatemala (as the heir to Spain's territory in a part of that region) still refuses to acknowledge the legitimacy of Great Britain's sovereignty over British Honduras.[1]

By the treaty of 1670 England, for her part, undertook to stop the depredations of privateers and buccaneers. The undertaking – even if sincere – was more easily made than fulfilled. Buccaneering had long been a way of life in the Caribbean. The privateers and buccaneers had performed a national service. In the absence of a regular naval force, they had aided and protected the establishment of English outposts, and their loot had helped to enrich the island colonies. On the other hand, the communities of increasingly prosperous English planters and traders saw that the advantages of peaceful commerce would now be greater than those which the lawless seamen could offer. It was an awkward problem.

1. See R. A. Humphreys, *The Diplomatic History of British Honduras 1638–1901*, O.U.P. for R.I.I.A., 1961.

The antagonism between piracy and trading was obvious and insurmountable. [This] is seen very clearly in the politics of Jamaica; two factions grew up there in the 1670s, the buccaneering party of Morgan and the party led by Lynch, which preferred to promote the trade with the Spaniards. They represented two conflicting tendencies in the policy of the English Government, which hesitated at that time between bringing Spain to heel by means of the buccaneers, and trying to procure, with the consent of the Spanish Court if possible, a greater freedom of trade with the Spanish colonies. ... The tradition of plunder died hard.[1]

In the long run the governors of the English islands adopted drastic measures to put down the buccaneers, many of whom left the West Indies and went a-roving in the Pacific Ocean. Others, however, remained here and there in the Caribbean. British naval commanders found them useful, because of their local knowledge.[2]

In the Pacific the more hardened pirates ranged up and down the coast pillaging the Spanish ports. Lionel Wafer, the buccaneer-surgeon, recorded how in 1687 he landed at Arica (today Chile's most northern town):

We ransack'd the Place, meeting with little or no Resistance: we got a few Hogs and Poultry, Sugar and Wine.[3]

Until well into the eighteenth century the English were dreaded along those shores. As late as 1835 Charles Darwin, visiting Chile, noted in his diary:

To this day they hand down the atrocious actions of the Buccaneers. I heard Mr Caldcleugh [a British businessman] say, that sitting by an old lady at dinner in Coquimbo, she remarked how wonderfully strange it was that she should live to dine in the same room with an Englishman. Twice as a girl, at the cry of 'Los Ingleses' every soul, carrying what valuables they could, had taken to the mountains.[4]

For three centuries Spain's enemies preyed upon her shipping and her colonies; but the empire survived. At the end of the

1. Richard Pares, *War and Trade in the West Indies*, Oxford, Clarendon Press, 1936, pp. 6–7.
2. P. K. Kemp and Christopher Lloyd, *The Brethren of the Coast*, London, Heinemann, 1960, p. 75.
3. Lionel Wafer, *A New Voyage & Description of the Isthmus of America*, Hakluyt Society, 1934, p. 121.
4. Nora Barlow, *Charles Darwin's Diary*, Cambridge, 1934, p. 311.

eighteenth century the acquisitions of the other European powers were still confined to a few settlements on the Guiana coast (an isolated and insalubrious region which never had been of interest to the Spaniards), the English log-wood encampment at Belize, and a scattering of Caribbean islands. Nevertheless, the relentless pressure of the enemy had of course made breaches in the Spanish monopoly, and the local people had become increasingly aware of the commercial and other disadvantages of their subservience to Madrid. The discontent was not ignored in London. The British Government wrote to the Governor of Trinidad in 1797 (the year of its capture by Britain) directing him

to promote the measures most suitable to liberate the Spanish colonies, and to place them in a position to resist the oppressive authority of their government, in the certainty that they could count upon all the resources to be expected from H.B. Majesty, be it with forces, or with arms and ammunition to any extent, with the assurance that the view of H.B. Majesty goes no further than to secure to them their independence, without pretending to any sovereignty over their country or even to interfere in the privileges of the people, either in their political, civil, or religious rights.[1]

Nevertheless, the British in the Caribbean did not play a prominent part in the subsequent wars of liberation. The islands served as little more than temporary places of refuge where Spanish American rebels plotted their return to the mainland, or as rallying-points for foreign volunteers on the way to join the liberating forces under Simón Bolívar in Venezuela.

The Dutchmen's most ambitious venture was their attempt to create a Dutch El Dorado in Brazil. But they did nibble also at Spanish territory – where (strange though it may seem) their chief aim was to obtain salt. Europe's appetite for raw materials – spices, dyewood, sugar, etc. – had always been a powerful motive for overseas enterprises; and at the end of the sixteenth century, when war with Spain cut off the Netherlands from their main source of salt, the Dutch had to go elsewhere in search of supplies. Salt was

1. Quoted in Ricardo Levene, *A History of Argentina*, University of North Carolina, 1937, p. 193.

a vital commodity required in great quantities by the Dutch themselves for their fishing industry, and all over Europe for the preservation of meat. Most of the salt used in northern Europe in the late sixteenth century came from the south coast of Portugal, and was carried in Dutch ships. Their normal supply reduced because of the war, the Dutch salt merchants turned first to the Cape Verde Islands and then to the Caribbean, where they discovered and began to exploit the great salt deposits of Araya, near Cumaná in Venezuela. ... The Dutch skippers anchored there for weeks at a time, and employed their own crews in the work of breaking out and loading great lumps of the rock-hard salt.[1]

Of course the Dutch ships did not come out in ballast, but with cargoes of European goods, and so Araya – situated on one of the most desolate of South American coasts – was soon a centre for contraband trade. Then the Spanish governors of Venezuela took such stern action against the intruders that Araya became too uncomfortable, and the Dutchmen turned instead to the Caribbean, where they seized several islands between 1630 and 1640. Their most important capture was the island of Curaçao. In addition to being a convenient base for smugglers, Curaçao had valuable salt-pans. In modern times the island (still a Netherlands possession) has prospered by refining Venezuelan oil.

It was the Dutch, not the English, who most seriously threatened the Portuguese settlements in Brazil. England and Portugal had been allied since the fourteenth century; occasional violent raids along the coast by English buccaneers caused no lasting breach in the amicable relationship. There had been Englishmen among the first colonists at São Vicente, where, for example, William Whithall became a person of substance. 'I give my living Lord thanks,' Whithall wrote to a friend in England in 1578, 'for placing me in such honour and plentifulness in all things,' adding, 'Now I am a free denizen of this country.' Whithall arranged for a shipload of merchandise to be sent out to him from England. He asked for Manchester cottons, wool, silk, and velvet; nails, scissors, knives, and 6,000 fish-hooks; locks, tin dishes, axes, and hatchets; guitar strings, 'white soap', and wine; shirts, doublets, and hats; and two dozen reams of writing

1. Kemp and Lloyd, *The Brethren of the Coast*, p. 46.

paper. When the ship arrived, after a voyage of three months from Harwich, there was much rejoicing and satisfaction among the local population. As a present for Whithall's Brazilian wife the captain brought a fine walnut bedstead, 'with a canopy, valances, curtains, and gilt knobs'.[1] The friendly relations between Great Britain and Portugal continued into the nineteenth century.

The Dutch invasion of north-eastern Brazil in the first half of the seventeenth century was a direct consequence of happenings in Europe. The annexation of Portugal by Philip II of Spain in 1580 had exposed Portugal's colonies to attack by Spain's rivals, among whom the Dutch at that time were particularly formidable. Their principal reason for choosing to embark on the conquest of Brazil was that 'Brazil, being colonized by the Portuguese, who were either indifferent or hostile to their Spanish king, would be easier to conquer than any *Spanish* colony'.[2] And the earnings of the thriving sugar industry would pay for the campaign.

After taking Bahia but failing to hold it, the Dutch captured the town of Olinda and its port, Recife, in Pernambuco, which remained in their hands from 1630 to 1654. At that date the district of Pernambuco was said to be the most delightful, prosperous, and fertile of all Portugal's overseas possessions. Although life there was provincial by comparison with the great Spanish-American centres, in Pernambuco

both gold and silver were beyond count, and almost disregarded. There was so much sugar that there were not sufficient ships to load it all. ... The luxury and display in the houses was excessive, for anybody whose table-service was not of solid silver was regarded as poor and wretched. The women were so elegantly and richly dressed that they were not content with taffetas, camlets, velvets, and other silks, but bedecked themselves out in fine tissues and rich brocades. So many jewels adorned them that it seemed as if it rained pearls, rubies, emeralds and diamonds on their heads and necks. ... This region resembled nothing so much as the portrait of an earthly paradise.[3]

1. Schurz, pp. 208–9.
2. C. R. Boxer, *The Dutch in Brazil*, Oxford, 1957, p. 14.
3. ibid., p. 35.

Of course, there was another side to the picture: if this was an earthly paradise for the wealthy sugar-planters, it was an earthly hell for the Negro slaves.

During the twenty-four years that the Dutch were in north-eastern Brazil, they extended their control over an area that stretched from the Amazon delta to the São Francisco. Their rule was tolerant and economically beneficial. Life was orderly, streets were clean. Today pleasant examples of Dutch architecture can still be seen in the town of Olinda.

In 1640 a Portuguese king regained the Portuguese throne. Meanwhile, naturally, it had been impossible for most Brazilians (sons of Portugal) to consider the Dutchmen, no matter how admirable personally, as other than invaders. The Dutch took away from the country the profits of the plantations. And they were Protestants. After 1640, guerrilla warfare against them was in earnest. Recife, their last stronghold, was reconquered in 1654. This was the end of the dream of a Dutch El Dorado in South America.

The expulsion of the Dutch was mainly a local affair of the north-east but, like the exploits of the *bandeirantes* in the faraway West, it contributed powerfully to the increasing awareness that Brazil was becoming a nation – a nation composed of wide-spread and very different regions, each having its own geographical and racial characteristics and its own local interests and loyalties, but a unity none the less.

As with the Spanish Americans, so with the Brazilians: Napoleon's invasion of the Iberian Peninsula precipitated a change in the relationship with the mother country. A change was in any case ultimately inevitable, but the form that it took in Brazil was unexpected and unusual.[1]

1. See pp. 120–4.

7

The Emancipation of Spanish America

FOR three hundred years Spain gave her empire substantial peace. With the years, protests against Spanish policy became more common; but until early in the nineteenth century Spain's rule was never seriously threatened. In the towns, the vigorous *criollo* minority might resent the *peninsulares'* privileged position and complain about restrictions on trade that hampered their own economic advancement, but they scarcely questioned the authority of the Crown – partly, perhaps, because they knew that the overthrow of that authority would leave the colonies without any force to maintain order.

In 1808–10, for reasons to be discussed hereafter, the situation abruptly changed. Revolutionary movements started in Mexico and elsewhere, and wars of independence developed which, after the Spanish fashion, were much more ferocious than the North American war of 1775–82. Each of the uprisings was spontaneous and local, and, although all were the product of the same or very similar circumstances, they were unconnected with one another. From Venezuela a revolutionary army heroically fought its way to the Pacific side of the mountains and then (following the direction of the *conquistadores*) moved down towards Peru. Far away in the south, another such army set forth from Argentina, marched over the Andes into Chile, and later – considerably reinforced by Chileans and by British naval volunteers – sailed northwards up the Pacific coast, finally entering the Peruvian capital. This huge pincer movement against the Spaniards – whereby revolutionaries from Venezuela and Colombia (or 'patriots', as they now were) met others from Argentina and Chile – was not carried out according to some master plan. No unified command, however, could have arranged it more symmetrically or effectively. The fall of Lima – the City of the Kings,

84

and Spain's greatest South American centre – was an event whose dramatic quality must have impressed Spaniards in the Old and the New World alike.

By 1825 – that is to say, within the space of fifteen years – nothing of the vast empire that had lasted for so long remained in Spanish hands except the islands of Cuba and Puerto Rico. Politically, Spain was now back – so to say – at her fifteenth-century starting-point in the Caribbean.

As explained in previous chapters, the process of Spanish settlement in Middle and South America differed fundamentally from that of English colonization in the North.[1] There was a remarkable difference, too, in the consequences of independence. Whereas out of the North American struggle against the English, thirteen colonies became one United States, the Spanish American insurrections and wars prepared the way not for unity but for the emergence of seventeen separate republics.[2] It has been argued that if Spanish American emancipation had been delayed for just fifty years, until railways could be built, such national fragmentation might have been avoided.[3] But the Spanish settlements were not so contiguous as the English colonies in North America, where the steam-boat and the railway – when they came – contributed to unification. Even today, in spite of modern facilities for extending transport and communication, the geographical obstacles in the Spanish-speaking area have proved to be quite formidable. At the end of the colonial period, moreover, Spanish America contained a much greater variety of widely contrasting social elements than English America. It was already an old and complex society, composed of locally-born *criollos*, who had inherited the pride of their Spanish ancestors but had acquired something of an American spirit; *mestizos*, who were partly Spanish, partly Indian, and really belonged to neither race; and Indians, who either laboured as serfs for the *criollos* and

1. See pp. 51–2.
2. The other two of the nineteen present-day Spanish-speaking republics, Cuba and Panama, do not owe their independence to the wars of this period.
3. Bourne, p. 316.

mestizos or lived in isolation among the highest mountains, whither their forefathers had retreated from the foreign invaders. No wonder the overthrow of Spanish rule failed to produce a United States of Spanish America!

Many years of disorder lay ahead. In the English colonies, the people from the first had been educated to self-government; the founders of independence in Spanish America had little such experience to guide them.

When the wars of independence ended, no real *social* revolution had occurred. The structure of colonial society, inherited from Spain, remained essentially unaltered. The urban *criollos* (the principal leaders of the revolutions) quarrelled among themselves for the places of the deposed *peninsulares*. Rural *caudillos* – the 'strong men' on horseback – fought against the new authorities. To the mass of the population the change of masters was of no great consequence.

Yet the emancipation of Spanish America – together with the typically non-violent attainment of independence by Brazil – was, as the discovery had been, one of the formative events in the history of the world. It not only marked a further stage in the shift from a Mediterranean to an Atlantic civilization: it opened an enormous region to trade and immigration, and it brought into existence a number of new states which thereafter would have to be taken into account by statesmen of other parts of the world in the conduct of diplomacy and strategy.

EXTERNAL INFLUENCES

The demonstrations which occurred in widely separated cities of the empire between 1808 and 1810 in favour of some degree at least of self-government, and the movements for independence which followed, were not the result simply of the traditional *criollo* grievances mentioned in previous chapters. Events in other parts of the world and the influence of actions and ideas that were neither Spanish nor Spanish American in origin had prepared the way. The North American Revolution had set an example of how people in the New World could attain independence, and the French Revolution had encouraged men to think of liberty and to discuss it in their *tertulias*. News of the defeat of British invaders in the Río de la Plata in 1806-7 had roused *criollo* pride everywhere. By 1810, Napoleon's seizure of Spain had weakened irreparably the link between the colonies and the Crown. Meanwhile Spanish America had not been immune from the doctrines of the eighteenth-century European Enlightenment[1] – that mankind should be guided by reason; that superstition and intolerance must be destroyed; that religious and intellectual liberty must be assured; that, as the origin of society was a contract between all members of the community, every citizen must be allowed to participate in the making of laws; that man – and this of course would include the American Indian – was born free. (It has been justly remarked that the adoption of Rousseau by Spanish American idealists did not usually cause them to treat the 'noble savage' in their own lands any more humanely than before.)[2]

As we have already seen, in spite of Spain's restrictions on trade Spanish America was not entirely deprived of merchandise from non-Spanish sources; and among the contraband, the smugglers brought books that were proscribed by the Inquisition. A French visitor to a house in Venezuela was shown a hollow beam in the roof, where the owner kept his Rousseau. In Bogotá in 1794 Antonio Nariño – one of the intellectual *precursores* of the Emancipation – secretly printed a Spanish translation of the *Déclaration des droits de l'homme*. Editions of the *Contrat social* were printed in Buenos Aires and elsewhere. Younger members of well-to-do *criollo* families – who had sometimes been educated at home in literature and the arts by private tutors acquainted with the writings of the forbidden authors – travelled to Europe, where they were deeply affected by the spirit of the times. The most remarkable of the early travellers was Francisco de Miranda, the *precursor* of Venezuelan independence.[3]

1. On this subject generally, see *Latin America and the Enlightenment*, edited by Arthur P. Whitaker, New York, Appleton-Century, 1942.

2. Herring, p. 246.

3. For a masterly biography of Miranda see W. S. Robertson, *The Life of Miranda*, 2 vols., University of North Carolina, 1929.

Miranda, born of *criollo* parents in Caracas in 1750, went to Spain, and then to the United States, where he studied the political institutions and social customs of democracy, always collecting information that would be useful to him later on. He liked Yale College – its debating exercises seemed to him a good preparation for public life – but he was not uncritical: for example, he remarked that the Constitution of Massachusetts gave 'all the dignity and powers to Property, which is the blight of such a democracy'. Miranda made many friends in the United States, and according to John Adams admiration of him became 'quite fashionable'. (In Europe, many years afterwards, Napoleon called him 'a Don Quixote – with this difference, that he is not mad'. And Napoleon is said to have added: 'That man has a sacred fire in his soul.') While in the United States, Miranda formed his plans for the liberation of Spanish America – 'Colombia', as he called it, was to be one great nation extending from the Mississippi to Cape Horn. Then he travelled all through continental Europe, from Turkey to Sweden, became a friend of Catherine the Great in Russia, and served briefly as a general in the armies of the French Republic. He lived for years in London, where his home was a centre for conspirators against Spain. Miranda led an unsuccessful expedition to Venezuela in 1806 (a premature opening to the wars of independence); returned to London; and at last in 1810 was welcomed back to Venezuela as a national hero, though his popularity was of short duration.

The greatest of the liberators, Simón Bolívar – another Venezuelan *criollo* – was educated according to the principles of Rousseau's *Émile* and read and assimilated Hobbes, Locke, and Spinoza. At the turn of the century he, too, travelled to Europe, and it was in Rome that he took the oath to free his country from Spanish rule.

In the early years of the conspiracy, Miranda sought ceaselessly to enlist the aid of Great Britain against the Spaniards in South America. The British expedition which eventually set out did owe something to Miranda – its leader, Commodore Sir Home Popham, had been impressed by his persuasive arguments in London – but instead of going to Venezuela, it went to the

Río de la Plata, and it was quite unauthorized by H.M. Government.

Popham had long been attracted by the commercial possibilities of the Spanish colonies, and in 1806, having recently taken part in the capture of Cape Town from the Dutch and now being without any immediate work to be done, on his own responsibility he set sail from South Africa with his whole squadron, crossed the South Atlantic, and entered the Plata estuary. He took with him General Beresford, a Highland Regiment, and some artillery. Buenos Aires was quickly captured, and the Spanish Viceroy fled to the interior. Popham and Beresford immediately dispatched to London glowing reports of the wealth and other attractions of the 'New Arcadia', and they sent home nearly $1,100,000 of prize money as evidence that their enthusiasm was not unfounded. This booty was paraded through the streets of the West End and City of London in eight wagons, each drawn by six horses, adorned with ribbons and flags whereon the word 'TREASURE' was inscribed in letters of gold. Visions of El Dorado caught the imagination of British businessmen and adventurers, who hastened to ship large cargoes of manufactures to the Plata. The Government, deeply committed by Popham's unauthorized action, had to send out reinforcements to consolidate the position. Meanwhile, however, the people of Buenos Aires had risen against Beresford and his troops and compelled them to surrender. (The captured British regimental colours are still displayed today in the church of Santo Domingo in Buenos Aires.) The British officers were interned in the interior of the country, where they marvelled at the 'fertile wastes' of the *pampa*, the abundance of wild life and cattle, and the laziness of the inhabitants. The officers occupied their time in fishing, hunting, and playing cricket.

The news of Beresford's defeat caused consternation in London. Popham was recalled to be court-martialled, and further reinforcements were hurriedly dispatched. General Whitelocke was placed in command of all the forces.

While these measures were being taken the earlier reinforcements had arrived off the coast of the Banda Oriental (present-day Uruguay), and as they were too few to undertake the recapture

A History of Latin America

of Buenos Aires they had to content themselves with occupying the smaller town of Montevideo, on the opposite side of the river. In that harbour all the British warships and transports and a large fleet of merchantmen, with goods for the Buenos Aires market, lay at anchor awaiting Whitelocke's arrival. Stranded at Montevideo were 'about six thousand English subjects, of whom four thousand were military, two thousand merchants, traders, adventurers, and a dubious crew which could scarcely pass muster even under the latter designation'.[1]

The people of Buenos Aires, naturally, had gained a new feeling of confidence by their success against Beresford, and they were determined to resist the second onslaught, which they knew must be imminent. The viceroy, having abandoned the *criollos* to their fate, was in disgrace, and after the fall of Montevideo they deposed him, nominating one of their military leaders – Santiago Liniers, a Frenchman – in his place. It was evident that Spain could not defend the colony, so the local citizens proceeded to enlist and train their own militia. Whitelocke arrived at Montevideo in May 1807 and was joined by yet more reinforcements in the following month, by which time the total force under his command amounted to more than 10,000 men.

Whitelocke was a weak and vacillating commander; and the British Government, in ignorance of local conditions, had addressed to him instructions which even a capable general would have found to be quite unrealistic:

He was to reduce the province of Buenos Ayres by force of arms, and exile the authors of the insurrection which had overthrown Beresford; and yet he was to consider that his main object was not to distress or annoy the enemy, but only to occupy a portion of his territory. Again, he was to attach the inhabitants to British rule, but was forbidden to give them assurance of protection against the vengeance of Old Spain after the conclusion of peace.[2]

H.M. Government failed to understand that Beresford had

1. J. and W. Parish Robertson, *Letters on Paraguay*, London, 1838, Vol. I, pp. 96–102.
2. J. W. Fortescue, *History of the British Army*, London, 1910, Vol. V, p. 435.

90

been defeated, not by the machinations of a few pro-Spanish conspirators, but by an uprising of the mass of the population; and when Whitelocke's red-coated columns entered the narrow streets of Buenos Aires on 5 July 1807 it was the citizens crowding on the flat house-tops who destroyed them 'with musketry, hand grenades, stink pots, brick bats, and all sorts of combustibles'.[1] During this one day the British Army lost over 400 killed, 650 wounded, and 1,925 taken prisoner. Faced with a calamity of such dimensions, Whitelocke gave up the fight and agreed to evacuate the Río de la Plata, taking with him not only his troops and warships but even the merchantmen from Montevideo. In London he was court-martialled and cashiered.

The achievement of the native citizens of Buenos Aires in twice defeating the British Army resounded throughout Spanish America, and although it did not precipitate the overthrow of Spanish rule it planted the seeds of revolution and fertilized the soil. In the Plata itself, the *invasiones inglesas* showed up the weakness of Spain and enabled the so-called *porteños* (the 'people of the port') to gauge their own strength. Moreover, during his brief administration at Buenos Aires General Beresford had demonstrated the advantages that might come from liberal government – for example, he pleased local businessmen by lowering the Customs duties and abolishing the State monopolies of certain basic commodities. The British commander in charge of Montevideo likewise was an enlightened governor, and his occupation of the town was a revelation. The British merchants who had been stranded in that harbour unloaded and offered for sale a great quantity and variety of manufactured goods, which had originally been intended for the much larger but now inaccessible Buenos Aires market. Never had Montevideo enjoyed such activity and prosperity as in those seven months. After White-locke's evacuation, the Uruguayans were increasingly reluctant to revert to their status as the poor dependants of the Viceroyalty of La Plata, dominated by Buenos Aires. The political separation of the eastern from the western bank of the Río de la Plata, which

1. W. B. Gurney, *The Trial of Lieutenant-General Whitelocke*, London, 1808, Vol. II, pp. 509–10.

was to produce at last the independent republic of Uruguay, was thus foreshadowed in 1807.[1]

In spite of *criollo* restlessness, everything was not wrong with the empire.

The Spanish colonies possessed vastly greater wealth than English America, and had achieved all the outward signs of opulence: imposing public buildings, universities, churches, hospitals, and populous cities which were centres of luxury, learning, and refinement. Mexico and Lima were larger cities in 1790 than Philadelphia and New York. When the North American revolution began, the population of the thirteen [English] colonies was still almost wholly rural, and almost entirely devoted to agriculture.[2]

Moreover, during the eighteenth century the quality of the Spanish officials had improved. All things considered, the widely-felt – though not uncritical – faith in the Crown might have held the empire together for many years more, if Napoleon had not in 1808 invaded Spain and placed his brother Joseph Bonaparte on the throne.

THE WARS OF INDEPENDENCE

Napoleon's invasion of Spain and occupation of Madrid shook the whole foundation of the empire. In 1808 meetings of the *cabildos* indignantly repudiated the French usurpation of the Spanish throne. Just as juntas loyal to the legitimate king were formed in the chief provincial centres of metropolitan Spain to organize defence against the invaders, so, in 1810, *criollo* juntas were nominated in many of the principal South American cities – Caracas, Buenos Aires, Bogotá, Cartagena, Santiago – to take over the government of their surrounding regions.

In each case the local citizens proclaimed their loyalty to the deposed King Ferdinand VII and declared that their purpose was merely to act on his behalf during his captivity. But temporary self-government of course encouraged the desire for permanent

1. R. A. Humphreys, *Liberation in South America 1806–27*, University of London, Athlone Press, 1952, pp. 13–14.
2. C. H. Haring, *The Spanish Empire in America*, New York, O.U.P., 1947, p. 344.

independence, and *criollos* became revolutionaries even before they were aware of it.[1] What had begun as resistance to France developed into war against Spain.

Mexico was the one country where the war originated not in the chief city but in a rural village, by name Dolores. There, in 1810, the parish priest, Father Miguel Hidalgo y Costilla, roused the Indian peasants with the appeal: 'My children, will you be free? Will you make the effort to recover from the hated Spaniards the lands stolen from your forefathers three hundred years ago?' In later Mexican history the recurrent revolutionary cry was to be the same: a demand for the restitution to the Indians of the lands that they had lost.

It may seem strange that an uprising of such a kind should have been led by a Catholic priest; but since the days of Las Casas[2] there had always been churchmen who cared for their Indian flock. Hidalgo was in that tradition. Furthermore, he himself was the son of a poor farmer. Having won distinction as a scholar, he had then earned the disapproval of the ecclesiastical authorities by his advanced ideas – he read Rousseau and other French philosophers. After the so-called *grito de Dolores* – the battle-cry uttered in the church of that village – Hidalgo led his Indians across country. An unruly and predatory mob, growing to number many thousands, they plundered the land and overwhelmed and killed all Spaniards whom they encountered on their way. Hidalgo was unable to control the force that he had let loose. Perhaps he became disillusioned. Certainly he lost confidence.

The decisive factor against him was that few of the *criollos* joined him. As early as 1808 the *cabildo* of Mexico City, on hearing of Napoleon's assumption of power in Madrid, had made an abortive attempt to set up a provisional government of their own. But Hidalgo's movement was of a different sort. 'The *criollos* beheld with alarm their fate depending on an ignorant and infuriated body of Indians, and were compelled to rally

1. C. K. Webster, *Britain and the Independence of Latin America*, O.U.P., 1938, Vol. I, p. 8.
2. See p. 58.

round the existing authorities as the only means of personal safety.'[1] Hidalgo was captured by the royalists and executed. His campaign – which lasted no more than ten months – was a gruesome failure; but he remains the first hero of Mexico's struggle for independence, the first leader of a Latin American revolution which might have become a real social revolution, and the forerunner of the social-agrarian revolution which in fact did begin in Mexico one hundred years later.

The revolt that Hidalgo had started did not end with his death. He was succeeded by other leaders, who managed to hold their ground in some of the provinces. Outstanding among his lieutenants and successors was José María Morelos, a *mestizo* who had worked as a farm labourer until he was twenty-five, became a priest, and then proved himself a soldier and administrator of remarkable ability. He was captured and executed in 1815. After his execution there was no longer any serious danger of general anarchy, and so the *criollos* who had helped to break the revolt now resumed their discussions on the desirability of independence.

Then, once again, Mexico – like the rest of Spanish America – felt the impact of events in the mother country. In 1814 Ferdinand VII, newly restored to the throne, imposed a reactionary and despotic régime upon the Spanish nation. The most contemptible of Spain's monarchs, Ferdinand persecuted the liberals who had fought for him against Napoleon, and, in conjunction with a *camarilla* of his own stamp, governed the country with a total disregard for every national interest.

One member of the camarilla was the Russian minister; through him, and without the knowledge of his own Minister of Marine, Ferdinand purchased in 1817 eight warships as transport for an expedition against the rebellious American colonists, at a price and in a condition so outrageous that the Czar, to help quieten the scandal, threw in another three frigates.[2]

The response of the Mexican patriots to Ferdinand's policies was to demand independence with increasing vigour. In Spain

1. The comment of a contemporary North American observer quoted in Kirkpatrick, *Latin America*, p. 78.

2. Atkinson, pp. 268–9.

itself the liberals rose against their King, and at last in 1820 a military movement at Cádiz compelled Ferdinand to capitulate.

The consequences of the events of 1820 were profound. Wealthy Mexican conservatives and some of the higher clergy were so alarmed by the liberal measures now being introduced in Spain (and soon, no doubt, to be applied to the colonies) that they adopted the cause of independence, thus finding themselves surprisingly in alliance with liberal *criollos* and freemasons 'in order to save traditional New Spain from radical Spain'.[1] Out of the conflict of interests and the confusion of counsels a *criollo* adventurer, Agustín de Iturbide, emerged as leader of the army of independence. In September 1821 Iturbide entered Mexico City in triumph, and independent Mexico began its chaotic and violent career.

Meanwhile the wars of independence in Spanish *South* America had taken a separate course. In the southern countries the royalists – reinforced from Spain after the end of the Peninsular War – succeeded in crushing, one after another, the revolutionary movements that had developed since 1810 (except in Buenos Aires, where Spanish rule was never reimposed). The repression, of course, was only temporary. In Venezuela the young Bolívar profited by the repeated experience of short-lived victory and bitter defeat to improve his understanding of his countrymen and of the enemy, to adapt his political ideals to South American realities, and to become acquainted with the terrain of future campaigns. In Argentina San Martín methodically prepared his crossing of the Andes to liberate Chile, which had been reconquered by royalists from Peru.

Simón Bolívar was born in Caracas in 1783. He came from a line of wealthy *criollo* ancestors – landowners who performed such public services as Spain allowed to local citizens. His tutors included Andrés Bello – the outstanding Spanish American man of letters and educator of the time – and Simón Rodríguez, who used *Émile* as his textbook. In 1799 and again in 1803 Bolívar went to Europe, where he observed the weaknesses of the Spain

1. Kirkpatrick, *Latin America*, p. 80.

of Charles IV and was caught up in the excitement of revolutionary Paris. In 1804 he was distressed to see his hero, Napoleon, betray the revolution by adopting the trappings of Emperor. On his return to South America in 1807, Bolívar was struck by the contrast between his ideals of justice and liberty – acquired in Europe and from European books – and the apathy and lack of ideals prevailing in his native land. He decided that if liberation from Spain was ever to be achieved, the movement would have to be inspired and led by the educated *criollo* minority. The trouble was that they were so few.

Bolívar was at once romantic and practical, a seer and a soldier. He became a brilliant example of the romantic man of action. (Lord Byron owned a boat that he named *Bolívar*, and he considered going to settle in Venezuela.) When we watch Bolívar at close range – in his writings and the memoirs of his contemporaries – it is obvious that we are in the presence of a man of extraordinary gifts, of talents that amount to genius.[1] He was short in stature, thin and wiry, with a lean face, animated black eyes, and crisp black hair. He was a man of amazing vitality and endurance, a fine horseman and swimmer, always in movement, avid for fame. His soldiers were devoted to him; his enemies heaped abuse and calumny upon him. Women found his charm irresistible (as he did theirs).

In the time of his military campaigns, when his headquarters were in a city, town or village, dances were arranged nearly every night, and his pleasure was to dance and valse, then vanish from the room to dictate some orders and dispatches, and again dance, and work again. In this way his ideas became clearer and stronger, and his style more eloquent. In a word, dancing inspired him and excited his imagination. . . . When the bad weather prevents our going out, H.E. gets his own back by lying on the hammock and rocking fast, or walking along corridors of the house sometimes singing, sometimes reciting verse, or conversing with others who walk with him.[2]

Bolívar was in Venezuela in 1808 when the news of Napoleon's invasion of Spain was received. He was among the conspirators

1. R. A. Humphreys, *Listener*, 12 February 1959.
2. Quoted in Salvador de Madariaga, *Bolívar*, London, Hollis & Carter, 1952, p. 70.

who now advocated the creation of a Venezuelan junta, on the analogy of those that had been set up in Spain. The first junta of Caracas was in fact created in 1810. This government dispatched a diplomatic mission to London – Bolívar being one of the members – to ask the British Government for naval protection against France and to offer commercial advantages in return. Bolívar was back in Caracas in 1811, when Venezuela's independence was formally declared and a republican Constitution promulgated. He was an officer in the republican forces which fought against the royalist reaction. When Caracas was destroyed by an earthquake in 1812, he made one of his many memorable pronouncements.

If Nature opposes our designs, we shall fight against her, and make her obey.

But Miranda, the republican *generalísimo*, lost heart and capitulated to the royalists. Bolívar and other young officers, deeming Miranda a traitor, handed him over to the royalist commander, who sent him to Spain, where the unfortunate *precursor* died in a dungeon at Cádiz. By the end of 1812 Venezuela was once more a Spanish colony. Bolívar was allowed to leave the country.

Finding refuge at the port of Cartagena in New Granada (modern Colombia) – which also had declared its independence – Bolívar set about the writing of the first of his great manifestoes. He did not accept the overthrow of the Venezuelan republic as final – far from it. But he had learned a lesson in practical politics, and he wished to explain this to the people of New Granada so that the same errors should not be repeated. It was not the Spaniards alone who had broken the republic. The junta of Caracas had made the fatal mistake of trying to do in South America what was being done in Europe and North America, without regard for local conditions. Instead of dealing with practical problems of administration, they imagined that they could bring a perfect State into being simply by humanitarianism and tolerance.

The codes consulted by our magistrates [Bolívar declared] were not those which could teach them the practical science of government but were those devised by certain benevolent visionaries, who, creating fantastic republics in their imaginations, have sought to attain political perfection, assuming the perfectibility of the human race. Thus we were given philosophers for leaders, philanthropy for legislation, dialectics for tactics, and sophists for soldiers. ... The militia went to meet the enemy not knowing how to handle arms and unaccustomed to discipline and obedience.

The dissipation of public taxes for the payment of salaries to 'an infinite number' of office-holders had obliged the junta to seek recourse 'in the dangerous expedient of issuing paper money'. In the eyes of most people this was a direct violation of property rights, because they felt that they were being deprived of objects of intrinsic value in exchange for others of uncertain and even problematical worth. The paper money roused discontent among the otherwise indifferent people of the interior; hence they called upon the commandant of the Spanish troops to come and 'free them from a currency that they regarded with a horror greater than slavery'.

The Venezuelan republican Constitution of 1811 had been modelled on the Constitution of the United States and the French Declaration of the Rights of Man. The chief defect was in the adoption of a federal form of government. Each province had set about governing itself independently, on the theory that all men and all peoples were entitled to establish arbitrarily the form of government that pleased them.

The federal system [Bolívar declared] although the most perfect and the most capable of providing for human happiness in society, is, nevertheless, the most contrary to the interests of our infant states. Generally speaking, our fellow citizens are not yet able to exercise their rights themselves in the fullest measure, because they lack the political virtues that characterize true republicans.[1]

What a new-born South American republic needed first of all was strong, centralized government and a well-trained army.

Having delivered himself of the Manifesto of Cartagena, Bolívar went to war again. He saw that the only way to safeguard the precarious independence of New Granada was by destroying

1. *Selected Writings of Bolívar*, compiled by Vicente Lecuna, NewYork, Colonial Press, 1951, Vol. I, pp. 18–21.

the nearest centre of Spanish reaction – and that was in his own country, at Caracas. So at the head of a few hundred men he crossed the frontier into Venezuela. He caught the royalists in small isolated forces, which he defeated one by one. In August 1813 he re-entered Caracas, where he set up the strong government he had previously advocated. A *cabildo abierto* conferred upon him the title of 'Liberator'. But in the following year the Spaniards, reinforced from the Peninsula and aided by wild *mestizo* horsemen from the Venezuelan plains, gradually overwhelmed the republicans. Once again Venezuela was lost, and Bolívar in exile.

After spending six months in Jamaica, Bolívar went to the Negro republic of Haiti, which had been independent of France since 1804.[1] The President of Haiti had already befriended a number of Spanish American patriot refugees from the mainland, and he now helped Bolívar to equip an expeditionary force. In return, Bolívar undertook to declare the freedom of all slaves in Venezuela, and he fulfilled his promise when he reached those shores. In December 1816 he sailed for the southern continent for the last time. It is one of the great coincidences of Latin American history that at this very moment San Martín was about to lead his army into Chile.

Bolívar's new plan of campaign was brilliantly conceived. Instead of launching yet another frontal attack on the Spaniards at Caracas, he would seize the estuary of the Orinoco and from there operate in the rear of the enemy, advancing in a wide outflanking movement by boat up the rivers, and on horseback or on foot through the flooded tropical valleys and the jungles, then climbing the heights of the Andes to capture the mountain city of Bogotá. Bolívar, unlike San Martín, was an 'intellectual', and he was much more impulsive than the Argentine general, but by sheer force of character he made himself a military strategist and commander of the first rank. His letters and papers contain his instructions on such details as the pattern of horseshoes and the particular quality of soft iron to be used in their manufacture; the quantities and the transporting of ammunition; and the number and destination of *damajuanas* of black powder.

1. For the emancipation of Haiti, see p. 117.

Towards the success of the final campaign, two of Bolívar's achievements – as he travelled tirelessly back and forth in the Orinoco basin – were to be of special importance: his establishment of a 'capital' city, and his winning over of the wild native horsemen to his cause. As soon as he had compelled the Spaniards to evacuate the tropical town of Angostura (now named, in his honour, Ciudad Bolívar) the Liberator declared it to be the capital of an independent republic. At that time sleepy Angostura consisted of little more than 'one line of houses extending for nearly a mile' along the bank of the Orinoco, some of the houses having balconies to the first-floor windows, the lower floor being devoted to the storing of merchandise. The designation of this remote settlement as capital of a virtually non-existent republic was not a mere quixotic gesture. Angostura was a strategic point, the trading centre (as it still is) of all the eastern half of Venezuela, commanding a vast river system and a land where cattle and horses for the army were plentiful. Moreover, by setting up a government and summoning a Congress – no matter how few the provinces that it represented – Bolívar staked a claim for international recognition. From that date his luck turned, and his star began to rise.

The Liberator knew very well what he was about. When it became known abroad that Angostura and the Orinoco provinces had fallen, the cause of independence recovered its good name. ... In London, López Méndez, the Venezuelan agent, was now able to organize volunteers, float loans, and send arms and equipment.[1]

The years after Waterloo were a propitious time for seeking aid in Britain. A great part of the British army and navy had been demobilized; thousands of officers and men who had been thrown out of work were looking around for suitable occupation; and British merchants gladly shipped their surplus war material to the West Indies for sale to the mainland. The military adventurers who sailed for South America were a motley crowd; but the best of them fought courageously and helped Bolívar to win decisive battles in his long marches across the continent. By the year 1819 about 5,000 English, Scots, and Irish had joined his army:

1. J. B. Trend, *Bolívar and the Independence of Spanish America*, London, Hodder & Stoughton, 1946, p. 127.

hundreds lost their lives in the fighting or from tropical diseases; relatively few of them ever got back to their own country.[1]

The other body of men who greatly contributed to Bolívar's victories were the cowboys of the grassy river-plains, the fearless *llaneros*, with their deadly lances. Led by José Antonio Páez, they had been incorporated in Bolívar's forces by 1818.[2]

There is no space or need to describe in this book the ordeals of Bolívar and his ragged troops as they crossed the swamps and scaled the mountains, the quarrels among the officers, the intrigues and betrayals.[3] Bolívar rode triumphantly into Bogotá in August 1819, but he did not remain for long in that town. The comment of an unfriendly critic in this instance is quite just:

> He had not the patience to live like a civil servant, and even the president of a republic is a civil servant. His life followed regularly the same pattern: he secured all powers, either on the battlefield or in a congress, or by a combination of both; he had one of his nominees appointed vice-president to do the donkey work; and he himself moved on.[4]

Soon Bolívar was announcing a grandiose scheme for combining Venezuela, New Granada, and the still unconquered Ecuador in a state to be called Gran Colombia. A new capital was named, a new constitution dictated. Meanwhile Bolívar was already turning his attention to Ecuador and Peru. He knew that San Martín, having liberated Chile, had sailed up the coast beyond Lima and had sent some troops even further, to the Ecuadorian port of Guayaquil. The two movements, from north and south, were meeting. In May 1822 Bolívar's ablest general, Sucre, captured Quito from the royalists. Bolívar, after entering the old Spanish city amidst the pageantry that always pleased him, then hastened down from the mountains to Guayaquil, determined to incorporate the port into Gran Colombia before San Martín – who

1. cf. George Pendle, 'British Adventurers in the South American Wars of Independence' in *History Today*, April 1960.

2. For a biography of Páez, see R. B. Cunninghame Graham, *José Antonio Páez*, London, Heinemann, 1929.

3. The most reliable, though not the most entertaining, biography of Bolívar is Gerhard Masur's *Simón Bolívar*, University of New Mexico Press, 1948.

4. Madariaga, *Bolívar*, p. 357.

now was coming northwards from Callao – could claim it for Peru.

From that moment self-determination, so far as the people of Guayaquil was concerned, was an academic question. When San Martín, who believed that Bolívar was still in Quito, arrived at Guayaquil, Bolívar was already there to welcome him to 'Colombian soil'.[1]

San Martín, like Bolívar, had been more than five years on the way, performing extraordinary military feats, and had been plagued by political dissension in his homeland and the territories that he liberated.

After the *cabildo abierto* at Buenos Aires in May 1810, Argentina, unlike Venezuela and New Granada, had not experienced a reimposition of Spanish rule; but Argentine independence could never be secure so long as there were Spanish armies in existence on the other side of the Andes, in Chile and Peru. San Martín – a soldier by profession – had taken upon himself the responsibility of destroying those forces. Appointed a provincial governor with his capital at Mendoza, he went to that town in 1814 and spent the next two and a half years patiently preparing his campaign. In full view of the town, and stretching across the entire western horizon, was the formidable barrier of arid, snow-topped mountains that separated him from the enemy.

José de San Martín was born in northern Argentina in 1778, the son of a Spanish officer. While still a boy, he was taken to Spain, where he trained for a military career and fought in the Spanish army. After hearing of the South American movements for independence, he returned to the land of his birth, where in 1812 he offered his services to the Buenos Aires authorities.

The Argentine liberator was more restrained than Bolívar, much less inclined to the dramatic, and had much less desire for personal glory. John Miers, the London botanist, described him:

He was tall, well-made, very broad across the shoulders, and upright in his carriage; his complexion was sallow, and he possessed a remarkably sharp and penetrating eye; his hair was dark, and he had large whiskers. His address was quick and lively; his manners affable and polite. . . . What more particularly excited my attention [in his private study] was a large miniature likeness of himself, hung up between

1. Humphreys, *Liberation*, p. 113.

prints of Napoleon Buonaparte and Lord Wellington, all three being framed in a corresponding manner.[1]

At Mendoza San Martín set about the task of recruiting, disciplining, and equipping the 'Army of the Andes' with all the thoroughness of a European commander. The result would have met even Wellington's standards.[2] He increased his forces by enlisting Chilean refugees who, after the victory of the Spanish reaction at Santiago, had escaped over the Andean passes to Argentina; and from among them he wisely set up as their leader Bernardo O'Higgins, son of an Irishman who had risen to be Viceroy of Peru. Patriots and soldiers of fortune, arriving from the east, helped to swell the numbers. San Martín imposed special taxes on the town and province to maintain his army. To equip it he built an arsenal, a powder-factory, and a textile mill, and he put the male and female population to work making cannon, shot, horseshoes, bayonets, knapsacks, boots, and uniforms. The ladies of Mendoza contributed their jewels. The Buenos Aires government, in response to insistent demands, added to the military supplies. San Martín dispatched agents across the mountains to Chile with instructions to spread false rumours about his intentions. Nothing was left to chance.

At last, in January 1817, the Army of the Andes – numbering 4,000 soldiers with an auxiliary militia of 1,400 more – went forth to scale the *cordillera*. The crossing was made by four principal passes on a front of some 500 miles. The artillery was dragged nearly 200 miles by mountain trails over altitudes of 12,000 feet. Of more than 9,000 mules which left Mendoza with the expedition, less than half reached Chile; and less than a third of the 1,600 horses survived the journey. But the whole operation was carried out with mathematical precision. Having crossed the passes unopposed, the several columns descended the well-watered western slopes of the Andes, where waterfalls cascade from the mountainsides into pleasant green valleys.

The main columns joined forces on the far side of the *cordillera* exactly at the appointed place and time. They took the

1. John Miers, *Travels in Chile and La Plata*, London, 1826, Vol. I, pp. 158–60.

2. Masur, op. cit., p. 471.

Spaniards by surprise and routed them at the battle of Chacabuco.
Two days later San Martín entered Santiago. In the following
year the remnants of the Spanish forces were decisively defeated
at Maipú. San Martín had freed Chile, but he asked nothing for
himself. He merely said: 'We have won the action completely.'
O'Higgins became head of the new republic. San Martín was
already busy planning the final stage of his campaign: the invasion
of Spain's greatest stronghold in South America – Pizarro's City
of Kings, Lima, the capital of Peru.

There had been relatively little fighting in the territory which
now constitutes the republic of Argentina. The lands of the
Plata still were of only minor economic interest to Spain – the
precious metals of Peru had not ceased to be the vital element of
the Spanish economy. Bolívar and San Martín both foresaw that
Peru would not easily be taken, but they knew that the wars
would not end until the Spaniards in that country were defeated.
It was not merely by chance that the two liberators met on the
Pacific coast.

It would have been impossible to march an army, with all its
equipment, northwards from Santiago across the Atacama desert
as far as Lima. A fleet had to be created to carry the troops.
Although short of money, O'Higgins somehow managed to buy
ships from British and North American owners, and he seized a
number of Spanish vessels at sea. Gradually the navy grew.
British and North American merchants, recognizing that the
removal of Spain's control would enable them to set up their own
businesses in the ports, financed the purchase of arms and ammunition. In 1819 the distinguished British naval officer Lord
Cochrane reached Chile. He was given command of the navy and
at once began a series of daring and brilliantly successful operations against the Spaniards.

With the progressive liberation of the coast, foreigners –
especially British – arrived and set up shop. After inspecting the
little port of Valparaíso, Maria Graham wrote:

English tailors, shoemakers, saddlers, and inn-keepers hang out
their signs in every street; and the preponderance of the English
language would make one fancy Valparaíso a coast town in Britain.
The North Americans greatly assist in this, their goods consisting of

common furniture, flour, biscuit, and naval stores. ... The number of pianofortes brought from England is astonishing. There is scarcely a house without one.[1]

In 1820 the liberating expedition was ready to sail for Peru. Cochrane now commanded a navy of seven ships of war and eighteen transports. These were gathered in Valparaíso harbour, where the troops embarked. 'It was' (remarked the most estimable of British military volunteers, General William Miller) 'an imposing and exciting spectacle to behold that bay crowded with shipping.' The men marched down to the shore 'with music playing, through cheering multitudes. The population of Santiago and of the country had poured into Valparaíso, and every avenue was crowded with spectators.'[2] After a sea voyage of more than 1,000 miles the army landed on the Peruvian coast; but San Martín hesitated for months before he advanced upon Lima. His caution has been well explained:

No area of Spanish America was more unready for revolt. Peru was dominated by wealthy families, *criollos*, and *peninsulares*, who had been granted privileges by the Crown. These ruling Peruvians had suffered the insidious corruption of easy money, and their vigour had been sapped by the abundance of slave labour. To none of her American domains had Spain more effectively transferred her rigid class system. Peru had fewer men of independent mind than had Argentina and Chile.[3]

San Martín, while delaying, replied to his critics with the dignity that was typical of him:

The people are asking why I do not march on Lima immediately. I could do it and would do it right now if it were convenient to my plans; but it is not convenient. I do not seek military glory, nor am I ambitious for the title of conqueror of Peru: I only wish to free it from oppression. What good would Lima do me if its inhabitants were hostile politically?[4]

While during the first half of 1821 San Martín (to the annoyance

1. Maria Graham, *Journal of a Residence in Chile*, London, Longman, 1824, p. 131.
2. John Miller, *Memoirs of General Miller*, London, Longman, 1829, Vol. I, p. 278.
3. Herring, p. 279.
4. ibid.

of, among others, the restless Cochrane) was awaiting a favourable moment to advance upon the city, it became apparent that the liberal uprising in Spain in the preceding year[1] had undermined the authority not only of the Spanish king but also, naturally, of the local Viceroy. Moreover, the large army which had been assembled at Cádiz under orders to sail for America to reimpose Spanish rule was now disbanded, and no further military action from the mother country was to be expected. As the spirit of rebellion spread among the people of Lima, the Viceroy moved his troops into the interior of the country. Thus the capital was delivered up. San Martín made his entry on 9 July 1821.

He assumed the title of 'Protector of Peruvian Freedom', a title which was characteristic of his temperament.[2]

San Martín's rule was precarious and unhappy. The royal army in the mountains was still undefeated, but his own force was too weak to face it in battle. To the inhabitants of Lima the Argentine general was a foreigner. When, convinced that South Americans were not yet ready for republican government, San Martín recommended that a European prince should be invited to set up a monarchy in Peru, he was accused of having designs on the crown for himself. Ill and disillusioned, he sailed for Guayaquil, hoping to obtain military aid from Bolívar for the completion of Peru's liberation and support for his idea that monarchy alone could save the country from disintegration.

The two great men met in secret conference at Guayaquil on 26 and 27 July 1822. The meeting was doomed to failure. Bolívar and San Martín were rivals. They were poles apart in character. Bolívar had forestalled San Martín by annexing Guayaquil to Colombia (an unpleasant surprise), and he had no sympathy for San Martín's monarchical proposals. San Martín, the older man, was in trouble, needing help, but the military aid that Bolívar offered was insufficient. Nothing could be gained by prolonging the discussions.

On the night of 27 July a ball was given for San Martín. Bolívar, as usual at affairs of this kind, thoroughly enjoyed himself. San Martín remained cool and aloof and seemed depressed. At one o'clock in the

1. See pp. 94–5.   2. Masur, p. 475.

morning he called his aides, and told them he wanted to leave because he could not stand the noise. His luggage was already on board, and, unobserved, he left the hall, went to his ship, and set sail from the port.[1]

When he arrived back in Lima, San Martín found that a revolution had occurred during his absence. Feeling that he was no longer needed, he resigned, left Peru, and took no further part in South American politics. He died in France, a lonely exile, in 1850.

With San Martín's departure, the way to Peru was open to Bolívar.

Bolívar, too, had begun to feel the effects of twelve years of war. He had grown grey. But he gave little importance to his own condition. He was prepared to exhaust his energies.[2]

He was still only thirty-nine years of age.

San Martín and Cochrane had obtained control of the sea – always a vital matter for the countries of the Pacific coast – but the Peruvian *sierras* were still dominated by a well-organized Spanish army. Bolívar reached the *sierras* in August 1824. There, at Cerro de Pasco, he reviewed his troops – who now in fact were an international force. General Miller, that loyal and able British officer, commented on the event:

Nothing could exceed the excitement felt upon this occasion. Every circumstance combined to impart a most romantic interest to the scene. The view from the table-land, which is at an elevation of more than twelve thousand feet above the level of the sea, is one of the most magnificent in the world. On the west arose the Andes, which had just been surmounted with so much toil. On the east were enormous ramifications of the Cordillera, stretching towards the Brazils. North and south the view was bounded by mountains whose tops were hidden in the clouds. On that plain, surrounded by such sublime scenery, were now assembled men from Caracas, Panama, Quito, Lima, Chile, and Buenos Aires; men who had fought at Maipú in Chile; at San Lorenzo on the banks of the Paraná; at Carabobo in Venezuela; and at Pichincha at the foot of Chimborazo. Amidst those devoted Americans were a few foreigners, still firm and faithful to the cause, in support of which

1. ibid., p. 482.   2. ibid., p. 489.

so many of their countrymen had fallen. Amongst those few survivors
were men who had fought on the banks of the Guadiana, and of the
Rhine; who had witnessed the conflagration of Moscow, and the
capitulation of Paris.[1]

The ensuing battle – the battle of Junín – took place in the
fantastic setting of high mountains. The combatants were almost
entirely cavalry.

No firearms were used by either side; and except for the sound of
hoofs on the plain, and the hoarse shouts of the men engaged, the
battle was fought in silence – in a landscape more like the mountains of
the moon than an earthly battlefield.[2]

The Spaniards were dispersed, but not destroyed. In December
1824 the rival armies met again. This battle was fought at
Ayacucho, more than 9,000 feet above sea level, on the road
between Lima and Cuzco. The republicans were led by General
Sucre, and this time they won a decisive victory. It was the end of
Spanish power in Peru, and in South America.

Yet Bolívar still continued his travels. He rode all the way to
Arequipa and Cuzco, the former Inca capital, issuing as he went
short, precise orders for the improvement of the living conditions
of the people, the betterment of their education, the expansion of
their agriculture and commerce. He crossed Lake Titicaca in one
of the Indian boats made, as they are today, of tightly packed
reeds. Then he rode into La Paz, and to Potosí – the town beside
the fabulous mountain of silver – and to the pleasant university
town which today bears the name of Sucre.

Before his visit, those remote regions of Upper Peru had already
become an independent republic, named, in honour of the
Liberator, Bolivia; but Bolivia was a state little more than in
name. A vast territory of arid mountains and Amazonian jungles,
it had no political, social, or geographical cohesion; the Indians
in the high Andes lived in misery; the jungles in the eastern foot-
hills were almost uninhabited; the old Spanish trade route from
Lima to Buenos Aires, which had passed through La Paz, was
now abandoned; and the mining industry was in ruins. The
criollos (a small minority) and the *mestizos* were incompetent to

1. Miller, Vol. II, pp. 159–60.   2. Trend, pp. 183–4.

rule, and Bolivia was doomed to suffer many decades of anarchy and tyranny.[1]

From the Andean altitudes Bolívar rode back to Lima, where he dictated an unworkable Constitution for Bolivia. He then returned to Colombia to try to deal with the disorder which had developed during his long absence. But it was a hopeless task. Gran Colombia was already breaking up into its component parts – Venezuela, Columbia, Ecuador. Bolívar himself was exhausted, ill, and disillusioned. An attempt was made on his life. Slowly he moved away towards exile, following the Colombian coast until he reached Santa Marta. He never went any farther. He died on the edge of his continent, in 1830, at the age of forty-seven. In the previous year he had written:

There is no good faith in America, nor among the nations of America. Treaties are scraps of paper; constitutions, printed matter; elections, battles; freedom, anarchy; and life a torment.

Shortly before his death he added:

America is ungovernable. He who serves a revolution ploughs the sea.

Bolívar had liberated South America from the Spaniards, but his work was in ruins. The reasons for his failure provide the explanation of much of the later history of Spanish America.

Bolívar destroyed Spanish authority. To replace it, he was eventually compelled to resort to despotism. Faced with the disorder in Colombia, he assumed the dictatorial powers allowed by the Colombian Constitution in times of emergency. He was thus the forerunner of the many Latin American *caudillos* who were to suspend Constitutions and depose elected authorities. Democratic aspirations – in the tradition of the early days of revolution – survived, but were not fulfilled, and it became customary to employ the army to impose order and to suppress liberalism, 'the fountainhead of anarchy'.

Likewise, the financial characteristics of the later Spanish American régimes had already appeared in Bolívar's day. When

1. See R. A. Humphreys in *New Cambridge Modern History*, 1960, Vol. X, p. 667.

the government of Gran Colombia first issued loans, they were eagerly taken up in London; but the Colombians, burdened with the expense of maintaining a large army, were never able to make regular payments of the interest. Confidence naturally declined, and in 1827 Andrés Bello wrote to Bolívar from London: 'One thing deserves your attention above all others, and that is the public credit of Colombia. It is impossible to raise another loan in London.'[1] The succession of defaults and funding loans, so familiar in subsequent years, had begun.

Republican administration was already inefficient and corrupt. When Bolívar visited Venezuela in 1827, he found that education had deteriorated. Teachers' wages were paid irregularly, if at all. Agriculture and cattle-raising were neglected. A foreign firm had a monopoly of the tobacco market, paying a minimum price for the crop. The owners of the plantations were at the mercy of unscrupulous money-lenders.[2]

Before Bolívar's death, the fragmentation of the former Spanish Empire into its present-day nations was almost complete. Bolívar had hoped to hold the liberated territories together in some form of federation,[3] but the sense of separatism – typical of people of Spanish origin – was too strong, and the geographical obstacles to unity too great. The *cabildos* were always on their guard against any attempt to usurp their powers. Local *caudillos* were not at all interested in Bolívar's idea that disputes should be settled by arbitration; they and their followers were veterans of the revolutionary wars, long accustomed to attaining their ends by means of the lance and the musket. Now that the struggle against Spain was over, there was little trade and little sympathy between the new republics. They each had their own loyalties, and already regarded the others as foreign countries. It remained for the rest of the world to recognize them as such.

RECOGNITION

From the earliest days of the revolution, the patriots sought to develop their connexions with countries outside the Latin Ameri-

1. Trend, p. 194.   2. ibid., pp. 238–9.
3. See p. 114 (Congress of Panama).

can area. One of the first acts of the revolutionary juntas was to open the ports to the ships of all nations. The new authorities needed money and goods. Great Britain in particular was able and eager to supply them. During the wars, the British Foreign Secretaries, Castlereagh and Canning, maintained an attitude which was officially neutral, but they made it quite clear that they had no intention of allowing Spanish America to be closed again to British commerce.

Already there was rivalry between Britain and the United States. Each feared the territorial expansion of the other. In this the British fears were not unfounded, for by a treaty ratified in 1821 the United States acquired the Floridas from Spain, and later in the century the frontier was pushed southwards into Mexico as far as the Río Grande. At one time it seemed possible that the United States might permanently annex Cuba. Furthermore, Britain and the United States disagreed on systems of government. Castlereagh and Canning would have preferred to see monarchies established in Spanish America, as in Europe, while the United States were firmly opposed to such an un-American proposal. Also, in the former Spanish colonies – unlike Brazil[1] – the monarchical tradition had been violently broken and could never have been revived. Finally there was commercial rivalry, although

in part such commercial rivalry was unreal. Not till the end of the nineteenth century did United States capital accumulate in sufficient quantities to look abroad to any considerable extent. Nor, at the beginning of the century, was there any very serious conflict between the trade of the United States and that of Great Britain. The United States exported in the main the products of the farm, Great Britain of the factory. ... For the moment British trade, British capital, and the British fleet were of more importance to Latin America than were those of the United States.[2]

In the competition for prestige and advantage, the United States gained a point by being the first to accord recognition,

1. See pp. 120–4.
2. R. A. Humphreys, *British Consular Reports*, London, Royal Historical Society, 1940, p. xii.

in 1822, to some of the republics. Almost at the same time the Colombian envoy in Paris issued a public manifesto in which he threatened that the ports of Colombia would be closed to the commerce of countries which refused to recognize her. British merchants were perturbed by the news of the United States action and alarmed by the Colombian threat. Baring Brothers, Barclay's, and many others of the most respected houses in the City of London signed a petition urging that some kind of recognition was necessary. Castlereagh therefore decided to recognize the flags of vessels belonging to the republics.[1] The process was carried further in 1823, when Canning appointed consuls to Buenos Aires and Montevideo and to Chile, Peru, Colombia, and Mexico.

The chaplain on board one of the ships carrying the British representatives was not very favourably impressed by the state of civilization in the countries that he visited. For example, although there were good shops in Montevideo, 'well furnished with French silks and Birmingham hardware', there was 'not a book-seller's shop in the place'. When a book was handed to a lady, 'she took it and, after holding it some time upside down, returned it, saying she had never seen it before. Another lady, being asked where her daughter was, said "With her master, learning something called geography", but she did not know what it was.'[2] Everywhere, of course, the people and the countryside were suffering from the effects of the wars and of the political chaos that followed. At Concepción, in Chile, 'you may see both men and women in rags, standing with their arms folded, against the corner of the house; and yet the lands about the town appear entirely uncultivated, producing nothing but grass.'[3]

In 1823 France invaded Spain to restore Ferdinand and despotism. Did Canning fear that intervention in Spain foreshadowed intervention in Spanish America? At any rate, he now turned to the United States with a proposal that Britain and the U.S. should go hand in hand in announcing a common Latin

1. Webster, I, p. 16.
2. [Rev. Hugh Salvin,] *Journal written on Board of His Majesty's Ship 'Cambridge'*, Newcastle, 1829, pp. 18–19.
3. ibid., p. 117.

American policy. The United States' Secretary of State, John Quincy Adams, was thus given just the opportunity he needed for a display of United States leadership. Adams knew that the United States had not the means to defend the Spanish Americans in the event of attack; but also he knew that, as the greatest naval Power of the day was opposed to European intervention, the United States would be taking no risk in publicly assuming the role of arbiter of the New World. The opportunity was turned to brilliant advantage in the message to Congress read by President Monroe in December 1823. Meanwhile, however, Canning had obtained an assurance from France that she had no designs on Latin America, and he then made public Britain's earlier determination to protect the republics from foreign intervention.

The Monroe Doctrine propounded four principles: the United States (1) would not intervene in European affairs; (2) would respect 'the *existing* colonies or dependencies of any European Power'; (3) could not admit that the recognized republics be considered 'as subjects for future colonization by any European Power'; (4) could not view 'any interposition [in those republics] for the purpose of oppressing them or controlling their destiny by any European Power in any other light than as a manifestation of an unfriendly disposition towards the United States'. Adams had so worded the Doctrine that it drew a distinction between America and Europe, including Britain. 'The difference, moreover, was made to depend not on geography, but on a difference in political systems.'[1] The intention was to erect an American system as opposed to a European one.

The Monroe Doctrine had little effect on the course of events. It was no more than a unilateral statement, and the suggestion (often made) that it was the first step towards the development of Pan-American collaboration in the defence of the hemisphere is incorrect, for the Latin Americans themselves had no share in it. (Indeed, in later years the Doctrine became anathema to Latin American statesmen, who regarded it as a cover for intervention by the United States in their countries' affairs.)

The Doctrine's most noteworthy immediate consequence was

1. Webster, I, p. 48.

that it increased Canning's determination to demonstrate that Britain, not the United States, was the Power which could contribute most to Latin American security and prosperity. In this he had little difficulty and was completely successful. In 1825, by negotiating commercial treaties with Buenos Aires, Colombia, and Mexico, the British Government began the granting of *de jure* recognition to the republics, while, in 1826 Canning made his famous boast that he had 'called the New World into being to redress the balance of the Old'.

While Great Britain and the United States were manoeuvring to promote their rival interests in Latin America, Simón Bolívar returned again and again to his idea that the American – or, at least, the Spanish American – republics should join together in a league of nations. He had been thinking on those lines for many years, and although the continental congress which he convened at Panama in June 1826 achieved nothing, it did – unlike the Monroe Doctrine – give expression to the ideals of cooperation and conciliation that were to be the inspiration of the Pan-American movement which has evolved in recent decades. Bolívar's hope was that the Congress of Panama would 'act as a Council in great conflicts, to be appealed to in case of common danger, and be a faithful interpreter of public treaties, when difficulties should arise, and conciliate, in short, all our differences'. If his plan were to succeed, 'What, then,' Bolívar said, 'shall be the Isthmus of Corinth, compared with that of Panama?'[1]

The dream did not come true. Only four national plenipotentiaries – those of Peru, Colombia, Mexico, and Central America – attended the Congress. The times were not propitious. The republics distrusted one another; they were rent by internal strife; and neither Britain nor the United States had any desire to encourage the creation of a Spanish American bloc.

If Bolívar's proposals for consultation and arbitration could have been put into practice, the subsequent inter-American wars might have been avoided. Latin Americans often say that they have set an example to the world by their peaceful settlement of

1. Charles G. Fenwick, *The Inter-American Regional System*, New York, McMullen, 1949, p. 16.

frontier and other disputes. This is an exaggerated claim. In addition to numerous lesser conflicts in the area, the South American republics have been involved in five major wars among themselves: Argentina against Brazil, 1825–8; Argentina against Uruguay and then Brazil, 1842–52; Paraguay against Argentina, Uruguay, and Brazil, 1864–70; Chile against Peru and Bolivia, 1879–83; Bolivia against Paraguay (the Chaco War), 1932–5. In all of those wars the purpose of one side was to obtain control over a neighbouring country or else to seize some part of a neighbour's territory.

More recently, however, the Organization of American States, by its success in effecting the peaceful settlement of more than one dispute between countries in Central America, has shown that although Bolívar's continental project was premature, it was not impracticable.[1]

1. For further reference to this organization, see p. 220.

8

Emancipation and the Caribbean Islands

WITH the landing of Cortés in Mexico (1519), the Caribbean islands acquired strategic importance for Spain and also for Spain's rivals. For Spain, the islands became outposts in the defence of her mainland colonies, while for British and French buccaneers they provided bases from which to sally forth against Spanish treasure fleets, which would be contending with the north-east trade wind at the start of the homeward voyage. In our own time the islands have had a vital place in Britain's strategy for the protection of South Atlantic shipping routes, and in the United States' defence system covering the Panama Canal.

The Caribbean has always been a region of traffic and transit, with generally rather makeshift communities. It is not surprising therefore that the historical development of the Latin American colonies on the islands should have differed in important respects from that of the mainland territories. In Western Hispaniola, for example, a community of French buccaneers who had established themselves and had grown in numbers was during the seventeenth century officially recognized by Spain as a French colony, by name Saint-Domingue, although Spaniards still occupied the eastern two thirds of the island. In the next ninety years or so, the French colonists prospered by hard work, slave-trading, and slave-driving, and supplied half Europe with sugar. But Saint-Domingue was a bitterly divided society.

There were nearly half a million slaves, more than half of them African-born (for it was cheaper to import than to breed), kept down by fear and themselves a constant fear to their masters. There were about 30,000 free coloured people, many of them slaveowners and landowners, but kept apart by a rigid colour line, debarred by law from the liberal professions and liable to insult and outrage from the lower class of whites. There were about 35,000 whites: French European officials, arrogant and aloof; some European planters and merchants; Creole landowners and bourgeoisie, unfriendly to the Europeans, resenting

116

their own exclusion from office. .... The French system, more despotic than the Spanish, had nothing corresponding to the *cabildo*.[1]

Suddenly in 1789 the news of the French Revolution broke upon this disunited French colony. The landowning, slave-owning aristocracy raised the cry of 'liberty', in the sense of liberty to run their country in their own way, which meant proceeding even more drastically than before against the coloured people. The mulattoes, for their part, interpreted the declaration that 'all men are born free and equal' as giving them a right to vote. And finally

in answer to signals conveyed by drum-beats or through nocturnal ritual gatherings the slave population rose in revolt, systematically setting fire to the cane fields and houses and murdering the white inhabitants.[2]

From 1791 to 1804 Saint-Domingue suffered the most horrible of civil wars. In the course of the fighting there emerged the first of a series of remarkable Negro leaders. He was Toussaint L'Ouverture, a former slave. By 1800 this able and (in spite of his ruthlessness) widely respected man had obtained control of the colony. He was then captured by an expeditionary force which Napoleon had sent out from France, and he died in prison. The French troops, in turn, were overcome by tropical diseases and a new rising of the Negroes. In 1804 Toussaint's brutal Negro successor, Dessalines, proclaimed the independence of the country, to which he gave the local name of Haiti ('place of mountains'), the first area in all Latin America to cut its ties with the Old World. From 1808 to 1818 southern Haiti was ruled by Pétion, a mulatto who had been educated in France, where he acquired a liberal outlook. It was he who, when Bolívar sought refuge on the island, helped to equip the Liberator's final expedition to South America.[3]

The later history of Haiti is a record of tyranny, incompetence, and poverty. Even now, French continues to be the official language, though a French Creole patois is more generally spoken. Haiti is a member of the Latin American family of

1. Kirkpatrick, *Latin America*, p. 394.
2. Parry and Sherlock, pp. 161–3.   3. See p. 99.

nations, but its society remains basically African, and its culture is scarcely more 'Latin' than that of the Indians in the Andes.

Not only did the Negroes of Saint-Domingue massacre many thousands of whites and mulattoes in their own part of the island, they also swarmed into the Spanish colony of Santo Domingo, in eastern Hispaniola.

Santo Domingo, whose city of the same name was once the capital of the Indies, had become in the course of the centuries a somnolent backwater. Spain had soon lost interest in the island, having found richer regions to exploit in Mexico and Peru, so that when the Haitian Negroes invaded the neglected colony, it was an easy prey. The Haitians ruled Santo Domingo oppressively from 1822 to 1844, hostile to everything Spanish and everything white. Many Spanish inhabitants emigrated to other lands. In 1844, when the invaders were at last expelled and the independence of the Dominican Republic proclaimed, the population consisted largely of Spanish-speaking mulattoes, as it does today. After the declaration of independence, the Dominican Republic resembled Haiti in its poverty, its disorganization, and the violence of its public life. Mutual hatred between the two nations has continued into modern times.

For geographical, racial, and international reasons Cuba, too, developed on different lines from the mainland countries. For several decades the island was almost unaffected by the independence movement which overthrew Spanish authority in Mexico, Central America, and South America. Cuba, with its fine natural harbours, was Spain's chief base for naval and military operations against the patriots on the mainland, and the Spaniards clung stubbornly to it. The presence of a powerful military garrison ensured that such attempts at revolt as did occur on the island had no chance of success. Moreover, with the expansion of the sugar industry, the number of Negro slaves had increased, and the wealthy *criollos* – much as they resented being ruled by peninsular Spaniards – feared that agitation for independence would provoke a Negro uprising. The example of the massacres in Haiti was fresh in their minds, and they considered a Spanish colony preferable to a black republic.

During most of the nineteenth century, indeed, the Cuban independence movement consisted mainly of conspiratorial discussions by committees of Cuban exiles in the United States, and a few ineffectual armed expeditions from near-by points on the American continent. The Cuban idealists and American adventurers who took part in those forays believed that by landing on the island they would provoke a general uprising against the government, but like the invaders of Castro's Cuba in April 1961, they were too optimistic.

So Cuba (and Puerto Rico) experienced Spanish rule for many more years than did any of the other colonies, and during most of the nineteenth century that rule was appallingly corrupt. It was a time when the majority of Spanish officials sought only to enrich themselves, yet when the Spanish forces were eventually defeated, 'this evil pattern of government was the idea which all too many Cubans clasped to their political bosoms',[1] and Cuba's own ruling class repeated the old abuses.

The Caribbean islands did not play an important role in the wars of independence, or in the early years of independence. Indeed, they remained on the margin of Latin American history until, at the end of the nineteenth century, the United States became involved in the Cuban movement against Spain.[2]

1. Lowry Nelson, *Rural Cuba*, University of Minnesota Press, 1950, p. 6.
2. See pp. 172–4.

9

The Emancipation of Brazil

WHILE the Spanish colonies on the American mainland were involved in the wars of independence, Brazil's emancipation in contrast took the form of a gentle transition. There are several outstanding reasons for this. Compromise was alien to the character of the Spaniards and the Spanish *criollos*, whereas the temperament of the Portuguese was more pliant; in addition, Portuguese rule in Brazil up to the year 1808 had been relatively light,[1] and also cohabitation with Negroes in a tropical climate had produced a people of easy-going disposition. Even so, the Brazilians would not have tolerated indefinitely the dictates of the now weak and bankrupt Lisbon régime,[2] and, indeed, as early as 1788 a Brazilian nicknamed *Tiradentes* ('the tooth-puller', for he was a dentist) organized a quite serious rising against Portuguese rule. In Portugal, as in Spain, it was Napoleon who suddenly brought matters to a head, forcing the ruling Prince to make a choice which had momentous consequences in the Americas. But whereas Napoleon in 1808 lured the King of Spain to captivity, thereby hastening the break in the link between Spain's colonies and the Spanish Crown, he failed in his attempt to seize the Regent of Portugal, Dom João, with the result that the connexion between Brazil and the Portuguese Crown, instead of being weakened, was reaffirmed. This happened in the following manner. When the French general Junot and his army arrived at Lisbon in November 1807, they discovered that, on British advice, the Portuguese royal family and court, numbering (with their hangers-on) some two thousand persons in all, had escaped to the fleet in the Tagus two days previously, taking with them the treasury's gold and jewels, and were sailing for Brazil escorted by British warships.

The consequences of the transference of the monarchical centre of gravity to the other side of the Atlantic were far-reaching.

1. See p. 72.   2. See p. 75.

Rio de Janeiro would now supplant Lisbon as the capital of Portugal; and the preservation of monarchical institutions ensured that Brazil – although she would not be entirely free from provincial rebellions – would be spared the unsettling succession of juntas and military dictatorships which plagued the Spanish American lands after the power of the Spanish Crown had been destroyed.

In January 1808, at the end of an extremely uncomfortable voyage, Portugal's royal refugees reached Brazil. The bay of Rio de Janeiro, where Dom João arrived in March, was wonderfully beautiful; but behind it was a neglected colony. John Parish Robertson, who went to Rio in that same year, remarked on the beauty and also on the squalor. The bay was 'a fairy-land', he wrote, 'a gorgeous succession of richly-wooded mountain scenery, and before us the large city of Rio de Janeiro with its houses all whitewashed and conspicuously contrasting with the deep shades of tropical vegetation around'. But a closer inspection revealed features that seemed less attractive. As he approached the shore and entered the city, the traveller noted 'filthy canoes; uncouth market-boats, covered with thatch so as to constitute sorts of floating houses, filled with blacks and mulattoes, male and female, in the most scanty and filthy habiliments, and much of the fruit stale, sending forth a very noxious smell; the beach covered with the offal of a huge city'. And as for the city, which had looked so fairy-like from afar –

We proceeded into the town; and what objects presented themselves to us there! First, there was the custom-house, which surpassed all the conceptions I had ever formed of Babel. Hundreds of people were crowding into it, and out of it, and every one of them obstructing the way of the other. . . . There were pipes of wine slung by thick cords to a long pole, which was laid on the shoulders of six nearly naked Negroes. These marched off with their swinging load, and sang, in marvellous dissonance, to the unequal but elastic motion of their burthen, as they carried it over streets in which every huge stone stood up and left a yawning gulf between it and its next neighbour. . . . Now and then low-wheeled hurdles were introduced upon which to bear off unwieldy bales. . . . The merchandise of Tyre could not have been more cumbrous and varied than that of Rio de Janeiro.

A History of Latin America

I now threaded my way through streets so narrow that it was with the greatest difficulty one carriage could pass another in them. The houses were from two to four storeys high. Not a pane of glass was to be seen in any one of them. Instead of this, the openings in the house for light and air were shrouded by balustrades of latticed wood-work.

The means of private transport and the costumes worn by Rio's lower classes in 1808 seemed archaic to the European visitor.

Every here and there two athletic blacks were to be observed carrying a large palanquin, the female inmate of which was scarcely guarded from public gaze by the close and richly-embroidered folds of a scarlet or blue cloth.... The few carriages I saw were drawn by two mules.... As I proceeded I saw two Negroes meet each other dressed in tattered and ragged coats, waistcoats, knee-breeches, and opera-hats, but without shoes or stockings! They stood bowing the one to the other, hat in hand, and in polite contention as to which should be covered first.[1]

With the coming of the royal court – who were received with great enthusiasm by the local population – Rio de Janeiro entered a period of improvement. The city, said the Regent, must be made fit for kings. When, in 1824, after earlier visits to Brazil on the way to and from Chile, Maria Graham[2] took up her post as governess in the royal palace at Rio, a theatre had been built; a printing-press had been installed, and a gazette was published regularly; new industries had been inaugurated, and woods and hills had been cleared for agriculture – 'the delicate table vegetables of Europe and Africa were now added to the native riches of the soil and climate'. Last, but not least (for the author of *Little Arthur's History of England*, like the Brazilians themselves, enjoyed parties), 'the numbers of the royal family furnished birthdays for frequent galas'.[3]

The British – whose government and navy had been godfathers to the new era in Portuguese-Brazilian affairs – eagerly took part in the commercial activity which accompanied Rio's transformation from a sleepy colonial town into a major Latin American

1. Parish Robertson, *Letters on Paraguay*, London, 1838, Vol. I, pp. 137–45.
2. See pp. 104–5.
3. Maria Graham, *Journal of a Voyage to Brazil*, London, 1824, pp. 49–51.

122

city. To the British merchants, plunged in gloom by the débâcle in the Río de la Plata,[1] Brazil was now the land of hope and promise. Rio's bay was crowded with British ships, and the city was abundantly supplied with British goods – ironmongery and nails, salted fish and cheese, cloth and hats, earthenware and glassware, cordage, bottled and barrelled porter, paints, gums, resin, tar. 'Stays and coffins (neither of which happened to be used in Brazil), saddles, even skates, glutted a market in which they could never be sold and to which they should never have been sent.'[2] Hardly more appropriate than skates were the warming-pans which British speculators shipped to those tropical regions. On Rio's ramshackle quays much of this merchandise rusted, rotted, and broke; many British trading houses had to close down; but when the wreckage of the initial speculation was cleared away, Britain was pre-eminent in the Brazilian market.[3]

In 1815 Dom João announced the elevation of Brazil to full equality with Portugal. In the following year he formally became king of the two countries. But a King of Portugal could not remain for ever in South America, and in 1821, when he seemed to be in danger of losing his Portuguese throne, Dom João returned to Lisbon, leaving his son Pedro at Rio de Janeiro as Regent. As it became increasingly apparent that the Lisbon government planned to reduce Brazil to its former colonial status, Dom Pedro, in September 1822, with the encouragement of Brazilian patriots, uttered the historic cry: 'Independence or death!' Before the end of the year he was proclaimed Pedro I, Emperor of independent Brazil.

The assumption of independence was an act of continuity rather than of revolution, and it was carried out almost without bloodshed. The few Portuguese troops in the country were soon forced to withdraw, being attacked by the Brazilians from the land and by a tiny squadron (under the command of the ubiquitous Lord Cochrane[4]) from the sea. This was the end of Cochrane's

1. See pp. 89–91.   2. Humphreys, *Liberation*, p. 17.
3. On this subject see A. K. Manchester, *British Pre-eminence in Brazil: its Rise and Decline*, University of North Carolina Press, 1933.
4. See pp. 104–7.

contribution to South American independence – Cochrane, '*ce grand seigneur aventurier, boucanier, et héros*'.[1]

So in Brazil there was no abrupt break with the colonial past and no long struggle for the control of the instruments of government. From the beginning of independence the country possessed trained administrators, and it was peculiarly happy in the character of its second emperor, Pedro II, who governed constitutionally and wisely, until in 1889 the monarchy withered away and the republican era began.[2]

1. Chaunu, p. 80.   2. See pp. 155–6.

10

The Age of the 'Caudillos'

' Many tyrants will arise upon my tomb' – Simón Bolívar

THE Spanish American wars of independence were not uprisings of the masses against alien domination. Usually, as we have seen, they were started by a relatively small group of *criollo* enthusiasts. It has even been argued that Bolívar liberated peoples against the wish of the majority.[1]

The wars had fostered the military not the political virtues, and they created economic havoc. Mines fell into disuse, lack of security discouraged farming, and when the fighting ended swarms of penniless men drifted into the towns to become the ragged beggars whom British travellers so often described in their journals.

Economic distress was accompanied by social and political chaos. The discipline previously maintained by practised Spanish administrators had gone. No middle class had yet emerged, to provide stability, and there was no organized public opinion. In the cities the *criollo* élite took the place of the deposed Spanish officials and drew up liberal constitutions and laws which they were unable to enforce, since the idealists' theories for the creation of a brave new world conflicted hopelessly with the real state of affairs to which they were to be applied. And so, as lawlessness increased, effective political power went into the hands of personal leaders – *caudillos*, who in many cases had led armies in the wars. Wealthy landowners (and the Catholic Church was the greatest of these) were satisfied that authoritarian rule should continue.

So the new republics did not develop naturally into parliamentary democracies. *Caudillismo* was inevitable, and even necessary. As Bolívar had learned, the people were not ready for representative government; in parts of Latin America they are not ready for

1. Kirkpatrick, *Latin America*, p. 108.

it today. The social structure of the majority of the Latin American republics is still profoundly undemocratic. The widespread illiteracy and poverty, the great cultural cleavages in the Indian and *mestizo* states, the concentration of land and political power in the hands of small minorities, these are factors inimical to the setting up of true democratic government – especially when they are combined with a tradition of authoritarianism and a highly personalist interpretation of politics.[1]

Parliamentary democracy is not necessarily the best form of government at all times and in all places; indeed, one of the principal causes of misunderstanding between the United States and Spanish America in recent years has been the North American assumption and insistence that it is.

By the time that the Spanish colonies attained independence from Spain, the European conception of liberalism itself had changed, and in so far as European ideas still influenced Spanish American political thought, it was now in the direction of strong executive rule, thus reinforcing local tradition. In Europe the liberalism of the Enlightenment had given way to a romantic and nationalist liberalism, with a cult of heroes and strong leaders.[2] It is not surprising that Carlyle should have written with admiration of Dr Francia, who ruled Paraguay dictatorially from 1814 to 1840.[3] Francia's government was stern and ruthless, but it was justified at least to the extent that it preserved internal order and saved Paraguay from the anarchy which during that period existed in most other parts of Spanish America; and in spite of its severity, the dictatorship did not affect the majority of the population. As has happened under most other dictatorial régimes in Spanish America, the mass of the people were left to continue their frugal lives, cultivating the landowners' estates and their own patch of maize and *mandioca*. The individual rights of the majority may not have been officially recognized, but they

1. R. A. Humphreys in *Soldiers and Governments*, edited by Michael Howard, London, Eyre & Spottiswoode, 1957, p. 161.

2. Miguel Jorrín, *Governments of Latin America*, New York, Van Nostrand, 1953, pp. 77–9.

3. George Pendle, *Paraguay: A Riverside Nation*, London, Royal Institute of International Affairs, second edition, 1956, pp. 15–17.

were not interfered with. And that doubtless is democracy of a kind.

At Bolívar's death in 1830 the territorial divisions of the Latin American map had more or less assumed their modern shape. (Until 1838 the five Central American states – Costa Rica, Guatemala, Nicaragua, Honduras, and El Salvador – were joined in a confederation, but this was merely nominal. The only new state still to be born, if that is the right word, was Panama.) In Spanish America, independence was a time of breaking up, '*une ère de morcellement*'.[1] Centres of population, separated by prairies, jungles, mountains, and deserts, became centres of rivalry, and each of the new states was profoundly divided within itself. The *cabildos* now contributed to the disunity: when the Spanish functionaries were deposed, every city, as though animated by Spanish individualism, 'felt itself to be the capital of its own district rather than a member in a community of cities'; and the struggle between town and country developed. The policy of the provincial *caudillos* was commonly styled federalism, 'the word being used in a sense almost opposite to its usual meaning, and implying an effort not at union but at separation'.[2] Opposed to the federalists were the centralists, who wanted all power to be lodged in a national government in the capital city. When a *caudillo* was strong enough to impose his authority on a whole nation, he was a centralist, residing in the capital, and perhaps wearing a frock-coat; but if he lacked such strength, he contented himself with dominating a province, a horseman still, with a *poncho* over his shoulders. In either case he treated his domain as his personal estate, and its treasury as his private property.

Finally, although the liberals who drew up the Spanish American constitutions followed the model of the Constitution of the United States, they almost invariably conferred powers on their presidents which virtually legalized dictatorship. Today in most of the Spanish American republics the president is still authorized to declare a 'state of siege' – i.e. to suspend the liberties that the constitution guarantees to the citizen – if in his

1. Chaunu, p. 87.
2. Kirkpatrick, *Latin America*, pp. 109–10.

opinion there should be any danger of public disturbance. In short, the constitutions of the Spanish American republics recognize the practical usefulness of the *caudillo*.

Independence from Spain did not produce political stability, but it brought liberal reforms and a widening of horizons. The Inquisition of course disappeared, and people now could freely discuss ideas which were formerly heresy. Restrictions were removed from foreign trade; the freedom of the press, though not always maintained, was at least proclaimed; and attempts were made to improve and extend education.

MEXICO

As parliamentary democracy could not be adapted to the conditions prevailing in most nineteenth-century Spanish American countries, the only way for one ruler to replace another was by force or the threat of force. It will be impossible here to follow in detail the long succession of *coups d'état* in each of the republics. Everywhere, from Mexico in the north to Argentina in the south, the Spanish Americans had to pass through the Age of the *Caudillos*. In most regions – Chile was a notable exception[1] – that age lasted for many decades; in some, it has hardly ended today.

Nowhere was the Age of the *Caudillos* more turbulent than in Mexico; in no other country were the people less ready for self-government. Indian peasants, scattered in small communities among the mountains, could not possibly understand that they were now supposed to be citizens of a constitutional republic, socially the equals of the urban *criollos*. What they did know was that on their semi-arid hillsides they still grew scarcely enough maize and beans to feed themselves. (Mexico is rich in minerals, but poor in watered agricultural land.) In the provincial centres the *mestizos* – closer to the Indians than to the *criollos* of Mexico City in their way of life and outlook – resented the power of the new *criollo* rulers. And so, for some fifty years, the political history of Mexico consisted of revolts and counter-revolts, *pronunciamientos* and barrack mutinies.

1. See pp. 144–5.

The Age of the 'Caudillos'

The first period of Mexico's independence was dominated by a group of men who, in the main, were *criollo*, conservative, and centralist. The outstanding personality – whether he was in the presidency, or in temporary retreat – was General Santa Anna, a professional soldier and one of Latin America's most spectacular *caudillos*, 'astute, watchful, persuasive, and plausible; singular in his power of winning and holding men; a masterly composer of specious manifestoes'.[1] Fanny Calderón de la Barca – the British wife of Spain's first Minister to the Mexican republic – who met Santa Anna in 1839 when he was having a spell at his country estate at Jalapa described him as

a gentlemanly, good-looking, quietly-dressed, rather melancholy-looking person, with one leg. He has a sallow complexion, fine dark eyes, soft and penetrating. Knowing nothing of his past history, one would have said a philosopher, living in dignified retirement. ... It is strange, how frequently this expression of philosophic resignation, of placid sadness, is to be remarked on the countenances of the deepest, most ambitious, and most designing men. ... It was only now and then that the expression of his eye was startling, especially when he spoke of his leg, which is cut off below the knee. He speaks of it frequently.[2]

From 1821 to 1855 Santa Anna was six times President of Mexico, retiring between times to the lovely, tropical country-side of Jalapa, enjoying his favourite sport of cock-fighting, waiting to see which way the political wind would blow, while his nominees remained in charge in Mexico City.

Besides their internal conflicts, the Mexicans suffered interference from foreign powers. In the 1820s a well-intentioned but imprudent United States Minister, J. R. Poinsett, was accused of trying to force North American political ideas upon the country and was declared *persona non grata*. (Poinsett has since been regarded as an early example of '*Yanqui*' imperialism.[3]) In 1829 a Spanish expedition was sent from Havana to regain control of the colony, but was defeated by Santa Anna. The effect of the

1. Kirkpatrick, *Latin America*, p. 319.
2. Madame Calderón de la Barca, *Life in Mexico*, London, Chapman & Hall, 1843, p. 27.
3. In Mexico '*Yanqui*' interference became known as *poinsettismo*; in the United States a flower he introduced from Mexico was named in his honour poinsettia.

westwards expansion of the United States was felt in 1826 when North Americans who had crossed the frontier from Louisiana routed Santa Anna's men, and the independence of Texas was declared. A French squadron landed troops at Veracruz in 1838, claiming indemnity for French residents in Mexico who had suffered losses and injuries during civil strife, including 60,000 dollars for a pastrycook whose shop and wares had been damaged. Santa Anna, after the Texan defeat, had made one of his periodical retirements to Jalapa, but he was 'always the first to scent the field of glory',[1] and on receiving news of the French landing he hastened to Veracruz. Seated on a white charger, he led a party to cut off some Frenchmen who were retreating to their boats, when a discharge of grapeshot killed his horse and wounded the general's leg, which had to be amputated. This encounter was the end of the so-called 'Pastry War', and it enabled Santa Anna to appear once again as a national hero. Moreover it gave him an emblem – the amputated leg was conveyed to a cemetery in Mexico City, where a funeral oration was delivered and it was solemnly buried beneath a monument specially erected for the purpose. Texas was formally annexed to the United States in 1845. War with the United States broke out in 1846 and resulted in the loss of the territory that is now California, New Mexico, Arizona, Nevada, Utah, and part of Colorado, reducing the original area of the Mexican republic by about half.

The disastrous war against the United States had been fought by a Mexico split by jealousies and hatreds, and weakened by poverty. Fanny Calderón (encouraged by W. H. Prescott) had already published an account of her own experiences of disorder in Mexico City:

15 July 1840. Revolution in Mexico! or *pronunciamiento*, as they call it. The firing has begun! People come running up the street. The Indians are hurrying back to their villages in double-quick trot. As we are not in the centre of the city, our position for the present is very safe, all the cannon being directed towards the palace. All along the street people are standing on the balconies, looking anxiously in the direction of the palace.

18 July. There is a great scarcity of provisions in the centre of the

1. Herring, p. 319.

city, as the Indians, who bring everything from the country, are stopped.

I had just written these words, when the Señora, who lives opposite, called out to me that a shell had just fallen in her garden. Both parties seem to be *fighting the city*, instead of each other. It seems also a novel plan to keep up a continual cannonading by night, and to rest during a great part of the day. One would think that were the guns brought nearer the palace, the affair would be sooner over.[1]

Later, when Santa Anna was back in command of the city, Fanny added:

Having stopped the carriage on the way home, at a shoemaker's, we saw *Santa Anna's wooden leg* lying on the counter, and observed it with due respect, as the prop of a hero. With this leg, which is fitted with a very handsome boot, he reviews the troops next Sunday, putting his *best foot foremost*. A gentleman had brought a message from the general, desiring some alteration to the boot.[2]

As the years passed, Santa Anna's rule grew increasingly despotic, extravagant, and corrupt. By 1855 he had become so discredited that he was obliged to go into exile, and he never returned to power. After his departure anarchy continued; but during the next twenty years the disturbances were something more than mere barrack revolts – they reflected a conflict of social interests and ideas. Fundamentally it was a struggle between established privilege and liberal reform. Moreover, the leaders of the new, liberal movement were not just another band of *criollo* army officers: the outstanding figure was a full-blooded Indian, Benito Juárez, and the others were *mestizo* civilians.

The liberals had two chief aims. First, they aimed at subordinating the army and the Church to civil authority, hoping thereby to unite the country, preventing its further dismemberment by the United States. Second, they would curb the power of the landed aristocracy by breaking up the great estates and restoring the land to the Indians from whom it had been taken during Spanish colonial times. (Since the days of Hidalgo's abortive uprising in 1810,[3] the redistribution of land has been the main item in every Mexican plan for social reform.)

1. Calderón de la Barca, pp. 183–7.   2. ibid., p. 367.
3. See pp. 93–4, and cf. the revolution of 1910, pp. 191–2.

After the downfall of Santa Anna it was decreed that the military and ecclesiastical courts were no longer entitled to deal with civil cases. A law of 1856 required the Church and all civil corporations to sell most of their landed property, but as usual the intended restoration of land to the Indians was not in fact effected. The Church lands were bought by rich *criollos*; the Indian villages (technically 'civil corporations') lost the communal lands which had belonged to them under the Aztecs and which the Spaniards, calling them *ejidos*, to some extent had recognized; and so the status of the Indian peasants was unchanged – only they now laboured for other overlords. When in 1857 a liberal Congress drafted a Constitution which confirmed the reforms, conservatives, military officers, and the Church naturally combined to oppose the Constitution, and in the civil war which then broke out, the conservatives gained control of the capital; the liberal leader, Juárez, withdrew to the provinces.

Benito Juárez – justly revered by Mexicans as one of their most honourable heroes – was born in 1806 in the state of Oaxaca. The son of Indian peasants, he was educated by a friendly Franciscan, studied law, and then as a lawyer defended the rights of poor Indians. He became governor of his native state, and distinguished himself by the honesty of his administration. In the civil war that followed the drafting of the Constitution, Juárez established his base at Veracruz; and when his generals finally captured Mexico City (1860), this squat, dark-skinned, stubborn man, wearing the black suit of a lawyer, re-entered the capital. As President of an ostensibly united country, he proclaimed the freedom of speech and of the press, whereupon his enemies made good use of the opportunity to denounce and abuse him.

The national finances had been ruined by many years of war and misgovernment. When Juárez in 1861 considered it necessary to suspend payments on the foreign debt, the country again became the victim of intervention. France in particular was indignant at the default, and Napoleon III decided that it provided him with an excuse for acquiring an American empire. A French expeditionary force landed at Veracruz in 1862 and entered Mexico City in the following year. When Juárez retreated to the north the conservatives, supported by French soldiers, were again in control of the capital. Meanwhile Napoleon III searched for a Catholic European prince whom he could set up as Emperor of Mexico, and in 1864 his choice, the Archduke Maximilian of Austria, arrived in Mexico City to found a hereditary dynasty. A weak, well-meaning, and good-natured young man, Maximilian tried to govern in the interests of the Mexican people, but he was inexperienced in government, totally unacquainted with local conditions, and discouraged by the confusion and corruption that surrounded him. Confirming the liberal Constitution, he alienated his reactionary supporters without gaining the sympathies of the liberals. It was a hopeless task. In 1867 he was captured by Juárez's troops, court-martialled, and shot.

Juárez returned once more to the capital and was re-elected president; but his guerrilla fighters, now disbanded, roamed the country, creating chaos. Banditry was everywhere; revolts were constant; and the electoral franchise was manipulated by unscrupulous politicians. In a desperate endeavour to impose his authority and carry out his reforms, Juárez assumed dictatorial powers, and finding it necessary to be a *caudillo* of the traditional type, he maintained himself in office by means of high-handed decrees and electoral fraud. Disillusioned and ill, he died in 1872. His career had been a practical failure, but he bequeathed to the Mexican people the liberal ideals for which he had worked so hard.

The next Mexican dictator, a *mestizo*, Porfírio Díaz, was a new type of *caudillo*, because his long dictatorship (1876–1911) rested not only upon the support of the military and the landed aristocracy, but also upon business interests.[1] This new phase in *caudillismo* will be considered in Chapter 13.

ARGENTINA

Opposition between the capital city and the provinces was a characteristic of the life of most of the newly formed Spanish American republics. In Argentina, indeed, this was the central

1. Humphreys, *Soldiers and Governments*, p. 158.

theme in the country's early history. It has been suggested that the history of the Spanish American republics generally can be reduced to the biographies of their prominent men. In Argentina, Rosas, a prosperous landowner from the province of Buenos Aires, and Sarmiento, a liberal and an educator, were truly representative of the two opposed trends.

When Spanish authority was overthrown in the area which now constitutes the Argentina Republic, two incompatible types of society existed side by side: on the one hand, in the city of Buenos Aires, and to a much less degree, in a few provincial towns, there was a civilization of the Spanish and European kind; on the other hand, there were the wild, untutored, and lawless gauchos. The gaucho, the South American cowboy, was, so to say, the human expression of the vast and desolate pampa. His way of living was determined by the presence of the herds of cattle and horses which roamed over the unfenced plains. He was of mixed Spanish and Indian blood, accustomed to attack by Indian raiders, indifferent to his neighbour's life, and constantly risking his own. In that era of meat and leather the gaucho had no wants that the animals of the *pampa* could not provide. 'Vain is the endeavour to explain to him the luxuries and blessings of a more civilized life,' wrote one English traveller. 'His ideas are, that the noblest effort of man is to raise himself off the ground and ride instead of walk; that no rich garments or variety of food can atone for the want of a horse; and that the print of the human foot on the ground is the symbol of uncivilization.'[1] When the *criollo* intellectuals and merchants of Buenos Aires began to try to put the country in order, 'the gaucho became the right hand of the petty chiefs of party faction, ever joining the side in conflict with the ruling power. The words law and order signified for him oppression and servitude.'[2] In political terms, the incompatibility between the *porteños* (the people of the port of Buenos Aires) and the gauchos was a conflict between *Unitarios* and *Federales*. The *Unitarios* were those who wished to have a strong central

1. William MacCann, *Two Thousand Miles' Ride through the Argentine Provinces*, London, 1853, Vol. I, pp. 102–3.

2. Herbert Gibson, quoted in Gordon Ross, *Argentina and Uruguay*, London, 1917, p. 171.

government at Buenos Aires dominating the whole country. The *Federales*, living outside the city, had no desire to be ruled by men who wore frock-coats instead of *ponchos*.

Attempts to impose a 'unitarian' pattern on the country produced only anarchy, so that in 1829 the Buenos Aires authorities appealed to a *Federal* – Juan Manuel Rosas – to help them out of their difficulties. This decision meant that a provincial leader had the opportunity to become Argentina's first national *caudillo*.

Rosas was an *estanciero*, the owner of a valuable meat-salting plant and of ships in which he exported the salted meat. But he was also a child of the *pampa*. He had won the devotion of gauchos and Indians by his equestrian skill, and had gathered them together in a militia of his own. From 1835 to 1852 he ruled from Buenos Aires, still styling himself a *Federal*; but, paradoxically, no more 'unitarian' régime than his can be imagined. Everyone in Buenos Aires was obliged to wear as a sign of loyalty a red ribbon inscribed with a denunciation of the '*saluajes Unitarios*'. Even the ladies of the aristocracy did not dare to be seen in the street without their red ribbon sash. Doña Encarnación, Rosas's wife and ardent assistant, wore evening dresses of scarlet satin. *Estancieros* wore scarlet *ponchos*.

The dictator's spies and secret police intimidated and assassinated his enemies. His portrait was exhibited throughout the city, and was even displayed on the altars in the churches; intellectual activity was discouraged; schools were closed.

Rosas quarrelled with France, and the French fleet – later joined by the British – blockaded Buenos Aires, causing disaster to local commerce; he prohibited traffic up the river to Paraguay, in an unsuccessful attempt to bring that country under Argentine domination; and for nine years – unsuccessfully, also – he laid siege to Montevideo, where many of his opponents had sought refuge. Rebellions by provincial *caudillos* were ruthlessly crushed, the leaders being decapitated and their heads exhibited in public. Then one of the provincial *caudillos*, whom the dictator imagined that he had permanently tamed, led an army against him. In 1852 Rosas was beaten in battle. He went to live in exile in England, near Southampton, where he died.

Exile, and death in exile, has been the fate of many of Spanish America's great men; and although Rosas cannot stand comparison with San Martín, he was a formidable figure. He did not finally subdue the provinces (the central authority still needed railways for the completion of that task) but, using tyrannical methods, he did contribute to the unification of the republic.

After the downfall of Rosas, the resistance to Buenos Aires rule continued in many parts of the country; but the townsmen – *porteños, Unitarios,* liberals, many of whom had been in exile during the tyranny – did control at least the central government. And even liberals could produce *caudillos.* For example – and he was the outstanding example – there was Domingo Faustino Sarmiento.

Sarmiento had travelled in Europe and the United States, and had marvelled at the cultural and material achievements of the people of those regions. During years abroad he drew up plans for reforming every branch of the national life on the model of the countries that he visited. In the victorious campaign of 1852 against Rosas, he followed the army with a printing press in a cart and poured forth a stream of bulletins and broadsheets denouncing the tyrant. He wore a full European uniform, because clothes were the symbol of culture, and if his compatriots were to be civilized they must be compelled to change the *poncho* for European clothing. He explained: 'My saddle, spurs, polished sword, buttoned coat, gloves, French képi, and overcoat, everything was a protest against the gauchesque spirit. ... This seems like a small thing, but it was a part of my campaign against Rosas and the caudillos.'[1] Sarmiento was elected President of Argentina in 1868, and during his presidency he continued to sponsor all manner of reforms – agricultural, educational, and political. Time after time provincial *caudillos* took up arms against him, and he had to send troops into the interior to put down the revolts. He encouraged the extension of railways over the *pampa* and the ever wider settlement of European immigrants across the plains, thus pushing forward the frontier of civilization. Sarmien-

1. A. W. Bunkley, *The Life of Sarmiento*, Princeton University Press, 1952, p. 335.

to virtually completed the subjugation of the gaucho chieftains, but in the process, his rule grew increasingly 'personalist'. He never realized that he himself was a *caudillo* at heart. All his life he had denounced *caudillismo* as 'barbaric'; but in imposing his own ideas of civilization on the country he was barbarously intransigent. An English traveller who admired Sarmiento's honesty of purpose and his belief in progress, recorded that he was referred to in Buenos Aires as 'Don Yo', 'Mr I'.[1] Although his aim still was to introduce government by law, he frequently governed by decree, so as to bypass parliamentary opposition. He did not scruple to use his presidential powers of intervention to remove provincial authorities who obstructed his policies.

At last, in 1880, Buenos Aires became the acknowledged capital of the Argentine Republic. The *Unitarios* had won the contest; the provinces were doomed thenceforth to be the satellites of the *porteño* metropolis. Sarmiento's constructive work was carried forward by successive governments, but so were his 'personalist' methods. It became a normal practice for Argentina's Presidents to respect only such parts of the Constitution as they found to be convenient. An Argentine historian has written:

> The presidency absorbed and centralized all the power of the democracy, in such a manner that the fortunes of the candidates did not depend upon the electoral struggle of political parties but upon the wish of the President.[2]

1. Sir Richard Burton, *Letters from the Battle-fields of Paraguay*, London, 1870, p. 164. Burton dedicated his book to Sarmiento.
2. Ricardo Levene, *A History of Argentina*, University of North Carolina Press, 1937, p. 489.

11

Economic Transformation

THE EUROPEAN CONTRIBUTION

'CAUDILLOS' and Constitutions, even if the latter were only
partly observed,[1] contributed to the gradual formation of more
coherent nations in Spanish America; but economic development
was the greatest stabilizing factor. Soon, indeed, among leading
criollos 'economic solutions were elevated above political ones as
the panacea'.[2] Juan Bautista Alberdi, an enlightened and influential Argentine publicist, declared that the real obstacle to
progress was not *caudillos* such as Rosas, but 'distance'. Railways
must be built across the continent; telegraph lines must join the
towns; steam-boats must ply up and down the big rivers; ports
must be improved so as to facilitate communication with
industrial Europe. It was Alberdi, too, who said that 'to govern,
is to populate'. Immigrants must be brought from Europe, to
fill the great gaps that separated the existing centres of population.

From the 1850s onwards a large part of Spanish America
underwent an economic transformation. This was achieved in
spite of the inability of the local people to subscribe more than a
small fraction of the necessary capital, the absence of coal (except
in southern Chile), and the lack of technical skill. Such deficiencies
were overcome because at the crucial moment western Europe –
and Great Britain in particular – happened to be equipped to
supply just what was needed and happened to need what Spanish
America could provide in exchange. Britain's fast-expanding
industries could supply an immense variety of manufactures;
she had coal in plenty; and British citizens had capital to invest,
and a taste for gambling. The overcrowding of British industrial
towns stimulated emigration, and although in the course of the

1. See Chapter 10.
2. John J. Johnson, *Political Change in Latin America*, Stanford University Press, 1958, p. 27.

century emigrants from Britain to Spanish America were very greatly outnumbered by those who sailed from Italy and Spain, many of the Englishmen and Scotsmen were experienced engineers or skilled in useful crafts, and so made an especially valuable contribution. At the same time Britain and France required new sources of raw materials for their industries and of cheap food for their workers. In 1876–7 French inventors proved, by the experimental voyages of a small refrigerator ship – *Le Frigorifique* – that it was possible to transport South American meat across the tropics and to deliver it in the Old World in edible condition.[1]

Political disturbances continued, and governments defaulted on their loans. Emigrants sent home the news that riches were not so easily acquired in El Dorado as they had been led to believe. Furthermore, although Spanish America had an abundance of land, in general (Costa Rica was the outstanding exception[2]) the prevalence of great landholdings restricted the possibilities of settlement and maintained the status of the agricultural labourer far below that prevailing in most European countries or in the United States. ('The movement of capital and people to the Mississippi valley and South America was part and parcel of the same great process, the rising importance of the Atlantic basin, but at no time did migration to Latin America equal the great migration to the United States.'[3])

From the beginning, too, some of the prejudices and customs of the South Americans displeased the European newcomers. The people of Buenos Aires refused to have chimneys in their houses, for fear that they would bring in the wet and the cold. In Lima the men did not shave regularly, and they spat on the floor; while the ladies – so beautiful, and so elegantly dressed in the evening – were far from elegant at home during the daytime:

Indoors the ladies are very untidy; in the morning I have found them, what in England would be called very slovenly and dirty, lolling on a sofa, with a morning gown carelessly put on. They never wear stays, and their front hair would be in paper, hanging down behind in one or

1. The Argentine word *frigorifico*, meaning a packing-plant for meat, comes from the name of this ship.
2. See p. 161.   3. Humphreys, *Evolution*, pp. 54–6.

two long tails. On their feet a pair of dirty faded silk stockings, with a pair of dirty fine old satin shoes down at heel. In this costume they loiter away the whole day, never dressing till evening, which is their time for receiving visitors or going shopping.[1]

The Europeans were shocked by the universal habit of smoking:

The friars and priests smoke while clad in their vestments and surplices before the door of the convent or church. The gentlemen smoke, in white gloves, while escorting ladies in evening clothes. The waiters march in smoking – and go out smoking – their cigars. Ladies find nothing better to do than to imitate [their menfolk]. . . . In Chile everyone smokes on getting up, on going to bed, during dinner, and all day long.[2]

And so on. But although the newcomers experienced many disappointments and found much to disapprove of, they belonged to a robust age (the daughter of Francis Place, the London tailor and social reformer, thought nothing of crossing the *cordillera* of the Andes on muleback[3]), and they made their mark on the cities and the land.

ARGENTINA

After the downfall of Rosas in 1852, the Spanish American area chiefly affected by the influx of foreigners and foreign capital was the Río de la Plata, which, because it had no precious metals, had been largely neglected by the Spaniards. The Chilean coast also attracted mercantile adventurers. Brazil will be referred to in a later chapter.[4]

Argentina's first railroad, inaugurated in 1857, was no more than six miles in length, running south-westwards from Buenos Aires. Financed originally by local capital and constructed under

1. Lieut. Charles Brand, *Journal of a Voyage to Peru*, London, 1828, pp. 184–5.
2. From the Belgian Consular Reports of the 1860s quoted in Tom B. Jones, *South America Rediscovered*, University of Minnesota Press, 1949, p. 136.
3. See John Miers, *Travels in Chile and La Plata*, London, 1826.
4. See pp. 151 and 157–8.

the supervision of a British engineer, with 160 skilled British workmen, it was later sold to a British company.[1] For the construction of most of the later railways Great Britain supplied the capital, the technicians, and the equipment; and the fuel was British coal. By 1890 Argentina had 5,848 miles of railway; in 1900, 10,269 miles; in 1912, 20,400 miles. By the end of the nineteenth century the *pampa* had been tamed, organized, and virtually harnessed to the economy of Great Britain. Argentine cattle-raisers were importing from Britain pedigree stock which provided the kind of meat preferred by British consumers; so that the breeding and feeding of the animals could be controlled, the *estancieros* went to the expense of erecting barbed-wire fencing (likewise purchased from Britain) to divide their wide territories into manageable segments; the British-owned railways transported the produce of the *pampa* to the port of Buenos Aires, which, with the aid of British capital and 'know-how', had been equipped to deal with the traffic; by 1887 fifty-seven refrigerator ships were in regular service between Buenos Aires and the British Isles, and 278 by the end of the century.

The opening up of the interior of southern South America increased the need for immigrant labour, and as political conditions became more stable the tide of immigration rose rapidly. The total population of Argentina in 1895 numbered 3,955,000, of whom one million were foreigners. About eighty per cent of the immigrants in the latter half of the nineteenth century were Italians and Spaniards. It was in particular the Italian peasants – in combination with railways, wire fencing, and steamships – that transformed the *pampa*. The native Argentine horsemen still considered agricultural labour an indignity. The Italians, working as tenant farmers, converted vast tracts where previously the cattle had grazed on wild grasses. An Englishman who had the opportunity to observe the effects of the new immigration wrote:

The estanciero worked the stock with his staff of natives – of the old gaucho class – while the Italians, a race apart, drew their profit out of

1. See George Pendle, 'Railways in Argentina' in *History Today*, February 1958.

the soil in maize, wheat, and linseed, paying their rent in kind, and, when they moved on, left the land transformed and fit for sheep or cattle of the best breeds.[1]

The landowners needed agricultural labourers to prepare the land for the planting of *alfalfa* for their high-grade beef animals, and the most effective way to do this was to rent it for a period of four or five years to tenants and to permit them, for a share in the crop, to raise grain. Thereby, in addition to increasing their *alfalfa* acreage, the *estancieros* were provided with a profitable by-product in the form of their share in the crops of wheat, maize, and linseed. The contracts obliged the tenants to plant the land with *alfalfa* and to move away after a specified number of years. The *alfalfa* fields yielded well for five or ten years, after which time new tenants would be secured, and the cycle repeated. Between 1869 and 1914 the area of land under tillage increased from 0·13 of an acre *per capita* to 7·7 acres, which compared with 1·5 acres in France and 4·8 acres in the United States. In 1875 Argentina still imported grain; but in 1887 exports of wheat amounted to 237,000 tons.

The *pampa* was not the only part of Argentina to experience the economic change: for instance, far away in the north the sugar industry had languished because of the high cost of transport by ox-cart to Buenos Aires, but in 1876 the railway arrived, with the result that six years later the sugar fields had doubled in area, and iron machinery had been installed.

In spite of the new means of transport and the new machinery and techniques, the standard of living of the pastoral and agricultural workers was almost unchanged. But the *estancieros* amassed great fortunes and built extravagant mansions for themselves in Buenos Aires. So the economic development emphasized the contrast between the conditions prevailing in the capital city and the interior. *Porteño* businessmen prospered on the import-export trade and on the growth of local industries manufacturing textiles, shoes, etc. for the general populace. The urban middle class became increasingly numerous and substantial. A large proportion of the merchants and shopkeepers were of European

1. Walter Larden, *Argentine Plains and Andine Glaciers*, London, Fisher Unwin, 1911, p. 80.

birth, or were the sons of immigrant parents. They began to demand honest elections, and thereby a share in government.

Buenos Aires – like other capital cities in Latin America – was a place apart. From the English, her inhabitants learned how to heat their houses in winter. The French were the chief influence in literature. Whereas the provincial ate his beef without bread or vegetables and drank the local rum (*caña*), the *porteño* ate bread, fruit, and vegetables as well as the finest beef, and drank the best wines that France and Spain had to offer. In the city the poor might dress like the gauchos, but the *estanciero* and the merchant class wore European woollens and silks.[1]

During the 1880s Buenos Aires experienced a building fever, in the course of which most of the Spanish colonial architecture was replaced by imitation Parisian. There were now tramways and parks. It was a time of the utmost optimism. Banks and companies were organized without capital, speculators being confident that future profits would cover their obligations, and credit was freely granted by the mortgage banks, because everyone believed that the value of property would continue to rise at the same speed indefinitely. To finance its own lavish undertakings, the Government borrowed excessively from abroad and printed paper money quite recklessly. Inflation grew out of control, and the value of the paper peso fell correspondingly. As the *estancieros* sold their meat and grain for British sterling and French francs, they welcomed the depreciation of the Argentine currency, which meant that they received a higher peso income for their exports. On the other hand, the inflation brought bankruptcy to the Buenos Aires merchants, who had to pay at soaring peso rates for the manufactured goods, the wines, and the olive oil that they imported from the British Isles and Europe. The crash occurred in 1890–1. Business firms suspended payment; banks closed; export earnings of foreign exchange declined and were insufficient to finance the nation's debt-service charges; and the London house of Baring, which had lent millions to Argentina, collapsed.

1. Ysabel F. Rennie, *The Argentine Republic*, New York, Macmillan, 1945, pp. 19–20.

Argentina's recovery was rapid. A great increase in the production of cereals, meat, and wool soon enabled her to pay her foreign debts with export earnings. In the last decade of the nineteenth century British capital invested in Argentina rose by about £15 millions, to a total of approximately £190 millions. (It is considered probable, however, that from the 1890s British willingness to enter new and risky fields of enterprise was on the decline, and that initiative was passing to the Germans and North Americans.[1]) As a result of her extraordinary economic development, by 1900 Argentina was pre-eminent among the republics of Latin America.

CHILE

Meanwhile Chile had become the leading power on the Pacific coast. A much smaller country than Argentina, consisting of a flinty desert in the north, rain-soaked forests in the south, and in the middle a series of fertile valleys mostly needing irrigation and owned by a few conservative families, Chile was not such an attractive land as Argentina for colonists; but some immigration did occur. In particular, in the late 1840s and the 1850s a considerable number of German immigrants – farmers and peasants – came to make their homes in the forests of Valdivia, where people of German descent still live today. British mercantile pioneers settled mainly in the port of Valparaíso, and although they were not numerous in relation to the total population of the country, they exerted an important influence on its development.

In one respect at least Chile had a notable advantage: her fight for independence from Spain had caused less dislocation than that which most of the Spanish American countries experienced, and the subsequent period of political disorder was correspondingly much shorter. The landowning oligarchy soon took charge, and in 1833 they secured the promulgation of a Constitution which confirmed their position. The Constitution excluded the landless and the illiterate – that is to say, the greater part of the population – from the franchise, and it granted virtually absolute power to the President of the Republic, who of

1. H. S. Ferns, *Britain and Argentina in the Nineteenth Century*, Oxford, Clarendon Press, 1960, p. 486.

course was the landowners' nominee. The President not only directed the administration of the country, but controlled the congressional elections and appointed his successor. The courts of justice, the army, the navy, and all public functionaries in the capital and the provinces depended directly on him. So he held the entire nation in one single net of authority. Until the outbreak of a brief civil war in 1891, Chilean presidents ruled autocratically; but they differed from many of the *caudillos* in other Spanish American republics because in a sense they were representative: they represented a social class, the landowning oligarchy. Although this system of government was very far from being a parliamentary democracy – and even farther from that 'adorable equality', which O'Higgins had hoped for – it was realistic and efficient. Thus Chile enjoyed a relatively high degree of internal stability almost until the end of the nineteenth century; and even when, as a result of the civil war of 1891, the President's personal authority was curtailed and he became responsible to Congress, the landowners still controlled Congress. Not only was Chile's stability helpful to economic progress, it enabled her to carry out successfully a policy of territorial expansion.

Chile's economic transformation, like Argentina's, was achieved by the exploitation, with foreign aid, of natural resources which hitherto had been neglected. But in Chile, unlike Argentina, the farming techniques on the big estates were not improved. Indeed, agriculture continued to be so backward that Chile had to become an importer of agricultural produce, and she long remained so. Instead of meat, cereals, and wool, it was the minerals of the deserts and mountains – nitrate, and then copper – that were the basis of the new prosperity.

Many of the most enterprising contributors to the transformation were British, and much of the capital was British. United States ships were active up and down the coast, but during the nineteenth century the North Americans were occupied in opening up and organizing their own lands, and it was not until the 1890s that they had accumulated enough capital to look abroad to any considerable extent or that their industries needed foreign markets. It is true that one of the most active promoters in Chile, William Wheelwright, was a native of Massachusetts, but it was in England that he raised the funds for his projects, and his business was mainly between Valparaíso and London. He provided Valparaíso with a lighthouse and other port facilities, a gas supply, and waterworks. In 1840 he obtained a British charter to found the Pacific Steam Navigation Company, whose vessels would link the ports of Chile with those of Peru and Panama and Europe. In 1849–52 he built the first of the several short railways which now join the inland mines to the coast, and he planned – though he never completed it – a trans-Andine railway between Chile and Argentina. In 1850 Wheelwright gave Chile the first telegraph line.

Chile has been an outstanding example (Brazil is another) of a country which has relied on the export of one chief product at a time. During the latter part of the nineteenth century this was nitrate, extracted from the northern desert. (It is at first sight remarkable that one of the most arid areas on earth should be the world's greatest source of nitrogenous fertilizer. Lack of water is the cause both of the aridity and of the existence of the nitrate deposits: rain would have washed the salts away.) The Spaniards had been aware of the existence of nitrate in the Atacama Desert and had used it in the making of gunpowder, and for the fireworks which enliven Spanish American fiestas; but a very long time passed before its value as a fertilizer was appreciated. Then, suddenly, the desert was a very interesting proposition indeed, and disputes began over the ownership of its northern regions, where the international frontiers had never been clearly defined. In 1879 a Chilean naval squadron appeared off the nitrate port of Antofagasta, which at that time was without doubt a Bolivian town, although largely inhabited by Chileans. And so 'a dispute about manure, more precious than gold or silver',[1] started one of the great wars that have been waged between Latin American nations.

Chilean troops quickly occupied Antofagasta and soon commanded the whole of Bolivia's Pacific shore, while the navy (which, still in the tradition of O'Higgins and Cochrane, was well-disciplined and courageous) sailed northwards to blockade the Peruvian port of Iquique. By the early months of 1880 Peru's

1. Kirkpatrick, *Latin America*, p. 228.

principal warships had been destroyed or captured, and Chilean soldiers were able to take possession of the coast as far north as Arica. The Chileans then attacked Lima, which they entered in 1881 and occupied for nearly three years. Peace was signed in 1883. In consequence of her defeat, Peru had to cede to Chile Arica and her entire territory to the south of that small town. Bolivia was deprived of Antofagasta and her littoral, thus becoming a land-locked country confined among the Andean heights – but Chile undertook to construct a railway from Arica up the western escarpments to La Paz, and agreed to allow the passage of Bolivian goods by that route without payment of Chilean customs duties.

Chile emerged from the War of the Pacific greatly enriched by the sources of mineral wealth that she had seized. The 'Age of Manure' then began in earnest. Adventurers and labourers from other countries and from southern Chile hurried to the desolate little desert ports. Nitrate was shipped in ever-increasing quantities to fertilize the farmlands of Europe and the United States. A spate of publicity persuaded people in Great Britain to invest in the new speculation, and they eagerly (and profitably) did so. The industry was financed mainly by foreign investors. The first, the most successful, and the most picturesque of all promoters was John Thomas North, an Englishman, known in the 1880s as the 'Nitrate King'.[1] North arrived in Chile as a young man, obtained a job on one of the railways, quickly proved his organizing ability, was offered the management of a nitrate plant or *oficina*, and soon was trading on his own account. All his schemes prospered. In Iquique (which became his headquarters in Chile) water was as expensive as wine, so North bought two tankers to carry water from the river at faraway Arica and sold a regular supply to the inhabitants of the town. He built his own fleet of lighters for loading nitrate into the ships anchored in the bay. He went to England to conduct a propaganda campaign to increase the demand for the fertilizer in European markets. Being by nature a man who 'breathed security and sympathy', he easily obtained support for the companies that he was constantly

1. For an entertaining account of North's career, see Enrique Bunster, *Bombardeo de Valparaíso*, Santiago, Ziz-Zag, 1948.

launching. One of these acquired agricultural land and flour mills in southern Chile, to supply food to the workers in the arid north. Other investments were in the desert railways (which North extended), and in a southern coal mine, so that the Nitrate King might have his own source of fuel for his ships, his railways, and his *oficinas*. On his visits to England North now mixed with members of the Royal Family and the Government. In January 1889, before setting out from London on his last journey to Chile, he gave a fancy-dress ball at the Metropole Hotel. The guests – a very distinguished company – numbered 900, and the cost of the party was £10,000. The host reserved 120 bedrooms for any who might wish to stay for the night. The walls of the ballroom and dining-rooms were decorated with palms, ferns, and flowers. The columns were covered with white chrysan-themums, with a large red 'N' in the centre. ('N' for North and for Nitrate too.) North – a large and portly figure, with side whiskers – was dressed as Henry VIII, his wife as Madame Pompadour. On the final voyage to Chile he was accompanied by a numerous retinue, among whom were three of the most famous English journalists of the time. He took with him a fire-engine (complete with hoses and firemen's uniforms) for the fire brigade of Iquique, and two thoroughbred horses as a gift for the Chilean President. North – who never learned to speak Spanish – was given a royal welcome by the people of Chile as he made his way from his southern possessions to Santiago and then onwards to the desert. His journalist companions sent home their reports of his progress.

The nitrate boom lasted until the First World War. The principal desert ports grew in size, flourished, and were the scene of extraordinary extravagance. Everything in the towns was imported – building materials (there were no trees, of course, for timber), furniture and clothes, diamond jewellery, champagne, and cigars. Celebrated singers from Europe performed in the theatre at Iquique. But the 1914–18 war showed how precarious is a nation's economy when it depends on the export of one commodity. Germany, needing nitrate for the manufacture of explosives and prevented from obtaining it from overseas, per-fected methods of producing a synthetic substitute which, like the natural nitrate, could be used as a fertilizer. After the war other nations followed Germany's example, so that Chile lost her dominant position in the world market for fertilizers; but the mining of copper – financed by United States companies – took the place of nitrate.

The development of the Chilean nitrate and copper industries brought into existence a new working class. The miners and factory hands lived in conditions quite different from those that prevailed on the large agricultural estates, where the relations between the landowners and their labourers continued to be almost feudal. Moreover, the towns were expanding, and the ever-growing urban populations were likewise outside the old-fashioned conservative way of life. Political power was still in the hands of the landowning aristocracy, but the new urban middle-class and industrial proletariat began to press for democratic, parliamentary government and welfare legislation. In Chile, as in Argentina, steady progress was made in popular education, and the challenge to the traditional order was thereby rendered more articulate.

During the second half of the nineteenth century, none of the other Spanish American republics experienced an economic transformation at all comparable with that which occurred in Argentina, or such stability and increased prosperity as were enjoyed by Chile. As we have seen, neither Argentina nor Chile had been devastated by wars for independence, and their land-owning classes were particularly well established and in command of the situation. The consequent relative stability attracted not only capital, but also technicians and entrepreneurs from Britain and (to a less extent) continental Europe, for whom the temperate climate of the central zones of both countries was congenial. These conditions did not prevail to the same degree elsewhere.

The next Spanish American country to be given a period of internal peace and economic modernization was Mexico, where Porfírio Díaz began his long and efficient dictatorship in 1876.[1]

1. See pp. 162–4.

12

Brazil: from Empire to Republic

EMPIRE

WHEREAS Spain's American Empire split into nineteen republics, the provinces of Portuguese Brazil – in spite of the huge area over which they were spread[1] – did not break apart, but survived as one nation. Brazil was spared the ravages of war and the need to satisfy the ambitions of national liberators.[2]

The transference of the Portuguese Court from Lisbon to Brazil in 1808[3] preserved the historical continuity, and the Crown exerted a unifying influence. In the early decades unrest occurred in the provinces of the far north (Pará and Pernambuco) and the extreme south (Rio Grande do Sul), where local leaders wished for greater autonomy; but from 1848, for some forty years, the country enjoyed internal peace under one Emperor. And although during his long personal rule (1847–89)[4] Dom Pedro II governed autocratically, he always observed the formalities of the Constitution and, by allowing Congress to meet regularly, he afforded the upper classes, for two generations, valuable experience in the practice of politics. He gave to Brazil as much democracy as she could absorb at that time and prepared her for greater democratic responsibilities in the future.

In the Constitution of the Brazilian Empire the ideals of democracy were recognized – and so were the realities of the situation. The Chamber of Deputies was elected by popular vote, but the illiterate masses were denied the franchise. The Senators proposed candidates for membership of the Senate, but it was the Emperor who made the final choice. The Emperor appointed the senior national and provincial officials. Such

1. Brazil's area is greater than that of continental U.S.A. without Alaska.
2. Jorrín, p. 356.   3. See p. 120.
4. Pedro II was only five years old when he succeeded his father in 1831; he began to rule effectively after his coming of age in 1847.

150

powers could easily have been abused by a ruler less disinterested than Pedro II. So sincere was the Emperor's respect for the freedom of speech that he allowed the liberals to campaign for the curtailment of his own authority and the advocates of republicanism to canvass support for their cause.

Under Pedro II Brazil advanced economically. The wealthy *fazendeiros* – owners of sugar and cotton plantations in the north-east, coffee-planters in the south-east, and cattle proprietors in Rio Grande do Sul – still dominated social and economic life. The production of their estates increased, and between 1849 and 1856 foreign trade doubled. But, as in Argentina and Chile, new factors – the construction of railways and roads, the use of steamships and the telegraph, the founding of banks – now helped the development. The chief promoter of economic expansion was a native of Rio Grande do Sul, the Baron of Mauá, who saw the disadvantages of the country's total dependence on the export of primary products (the so-called 'colonial' form of economy), argued in favour of industrialization, and proposed that local industry should be protected by tariffs. Mauá, indeed, was the forerunner of a new generation whose interests would lie in industry, commerce, and finance, as well as in land, and whose rise would eventually weaken the predominance of the old oligarchy of *fazendeiros*.[1]

Brazil's internal strength – like Chile's – bred self-assurance and made possible the carrying out of an assertive and expansionist foreign policy.

With the conclusion of the colonial era Brazil and Argentina had inherited the rivalry of Portugal and Spain – and particularly in regard to the possession of the eastern bank, the so-called *banda oriental*, of the Río de la Plata, the region which today forms the Republic of Uruguay.[2] The Portuguese had always cherished the ambition of extending their territory southwards beyond the borders of Rio Grande do Sul to the shores of the Plata. As early as the year 1680 they had set up an encampment

1. Humphreys, *New Cambridge Modern History*, Vol. X, p. 662.
2. The official title of the republic still is República Oriental del Uruguay.

A History of Latin America

beside the river on the site of the present Uruguayan town of Colonia, whence they were soon expelled by Spanish forces dispatched from Buenos Aires. In 1726, to counteract Portuguese encroachment, the Spaniards built a fortified outpost at the point where Montevideo now stands; and when the Spanish Viceroyalty of the Río de la Plata was created in 1776[1] it included the Banda Oriental. In the midst of the chaos that prevailed during the Uruguayans' exhausting fight for independence from Spain, the Portuguese invaded the Banda and then annexed it to Brazil. Portuguese-Brazilian rule was tolerant and lax; British visitors to Montevideo in the 1820s noted the abandoned condition of the buildings and streets, the stench of the putrefying carcasses of horses and cattle that lay around the outskirts of the city, and the lack of agriculture. (Montevideo imported its flour from the United States, ate a mixture of marrow and beef suet as a substitute for butter, and used bones and hoofs for fuel.) When in 1825 a few Uruguayan patriots roused their fellow countrymen against the alien government, they received military aid from Buenos Aires. Thus a situation developed which the British Foreign Office had long foreseen and feared: hostilities over the Banda broke out between Brazil and Buenos Aires, the Brazilian navy blockaded the Plata, and Britain's trade was disrupted. It was as a result of skilful and patient British mediation, designed to re-open and safeguard the trade route, that in 1828 a treaty was signed whereby Brazil and Buenos Aires formally recognized Uruguay as an independent buffer state between them. But this marked neither the beginning of internal peace in Uruguay nor the end of foreign intervention. The Uruguayans were now divided into two factions, and while the Argentine dictator Rosas[2] gave his support to one party, Brazil backed the other.

By 1850, when the last of Brazil's provincial troubles had been settled, Pedro II felt strong enough to strike. There were some 3,000 Brazilians in the army which overthrew Rosas on Argentine soil in 1852. Thereafter Brazilian troops in Uruguay helped the local ruling faction to maintain themselves in power, however uneasily. Brazilian businessmen who owned property in Uruguay encouraged the lawless cowboys of Rio Grande do Sul to raid

1. See p. 68.   2. See p. 135.

152

over the frontier, in the hope that they would further extend Brazil's sphere of influence.

The constant Brazilian interference in Uruguayan affairs precipitated the greatest international war in Latin American history. This was the War of the Triple Alliance (1865–70) wherein the Paraguayan dictator, Solano López, drove his people to fight against the combined forces of Brazil, Uruguay, and Argentina. López – a proud and wilful man – had intended that Paraguay should become a major power in the region of the Paraná and Plata rivers, which were that landlocked country's only means of communication with the outside world. The southward pressure of such a great nation as Brazil threatened the fulfilment of López's plan, so he sent a Paraguayan army across the Argentine province of Corrientes in a desperate and hopeless attempt to force the Brazilians to evacuate Uruguay. During the monstrous war which followed, virtually the whole of Paraguay's able-bodied male population was eliminated. The fighting ended only when López had been cornered and killed by Brazilian cavalry. To the victory of the Triple Alliance, Brazil had made the main contribution, and by the peace settlement she received a large increase to her territory at Paraguay's expense, as well as gaining some prestige. Her military leaders, inflated by success, returned home to play a more important role in politics than previously.

The efforts of Pedro II to ensure that the Brazilian Empire should be accorded the respect due to it were not confined to his dealings with South American nations: he had inherited a close relationship with Great Britain which brought many benefits (during the nineteenth century Brazil was the favourite Latin American country for British investment), but also excessive supervision by H.M. Government.

Britain had transported the Portuguese Court to Brazil in 1808,[1] and continued to treat the empire almost as though it were a British protectorate. As a part of the price of the recognition of Brazil's independence from Portugal, H.M. Government in 1826 had obtained an undertaking that the special economic privileges

1. See pp. 120–1.

that Britain had enjoyed from the Portuguese would thenceforth be granted equally by the Brazilians; moreover the British negotiators demanded and obtained a promise that Brazil within a period of three years would ensure the abolition of the slave trade. (That is to say, the prohibition of the bringing in of cargoes of Negroes from Africa for sale. The convention of 1826 did not refer to slaves who were already in the country.) H.M. Government had long been committed to the international suppression of the trade.

The subject was one in which almost the whole British nation had become interested. It could not be ignored. To the leaders of the movement no sacrifice appeared too great to secure the complete cessation of the abominable traffic. They insisted that it should be put in the forefront of every diplomatic transaction.[1]

There were, too, economic motives: for example, sugar interests in the West Indies were menaced by the increasing output of the slave-worked Brazilian plantations. As a maritime power Britain in the nineteenth century was so predominant that no nation – and certainly not Brazil – could successfully thwart her determination that the trade should stop.

Brazilian attempts to suppress the slave trade in accordance with the 1826 convention were half-hearted and ineffectual. Indeed, the traffic grew. From 1824 to 1827 the average importation into Rio de Janeiro, apart from imports into the northern regions of the country, had been about 25,000 Negroes. In 1828 the number landed at Rio was 47,450; in 1829, 57,100; in 1830 (the year for the agreed cessation of the traffic), 32,200. Importations continued after 1830, amounting to about 20,000 in the year 1845. The Brazilian landowners needed labourers, and had always relied on the African trade to supply them. They were unaffected by the religious appeal of abolitionism, which exercised such a deep impression on the British public. However cruel the importing of Negroes might be, the *fazendeiros* did not consider their treatment of slave labourers inhumane. Whereas the use of slaves was new to the colonists in North America, the Brazilians

1. C. K. Webster, quoted in A. K. Manchester, *British Pre-eminence in Brazil: its Rise and Decline*, p. 162. Manchester gives a detailed account of the British–Brazilian controversy over the slave trade.

had been familiar with the idea and practice of slavery for generations. The North Americans looked upon their slaves as chattels;
for the Brazilians they had become members of the community,
of the *fazenda*. The feelings of outrage at British high-handedness
were aggravated in 1845 when Britain, by the passing of the
Aberdeen Act, declared her intention of seizing and treating as
pirates all Brazilian slavers encountered at sea. Rio de Janeiro
retaliated by refusing to enter into any further discussions with
Britain concerning the means of stopping the traffic. For the next
five years the British repeatedly seized ships loaded with slaves
for Brazil and rejected all claims for damages. British warships
even entered Brazilian harbours – such as Paranaguá, a notorious
rendezvous of traders of all nations – and captured or scuttled
the slave-ships they found there.

Brazil could not withstand such forceful intervention as this;
but when, in 1850, the Parliament at Rio at last passed a drastic
law for the suppression of the slave trade, the action was taken
unilaterally, not as the implementation of any agreement with
Britain. Liberal-minded Pedro II had always disapproved of both
the slave trade and slavery, and by 1850 his government had sufficient control over the country to be able to enforce the new
measures. The slave trade was completely stopped by 1853 or so.
Thereby Brazil gained in dignity, and further British breaches of
her national sovereignty were forestalled. British interest in
Brazil persisted, but Britain would never again exercise the same
degree of political influence.

While Pedro II worked unselfishly for his country, the forces
that would cause the downfall of the monarchy were gathering
momentum. To the younger generations of the middle class,
growing in number in the towns, the existence of a monarchical
government in the New World seemed an anachronism. The
Church, whose natural inclination had been to support the
Emperor, was offended by his liberal sentiments. Slavery (which
had not ceased with the cessation of the importing of slaves) had
become increasingly repellent to public-minded citizens and
especially to the new urban classes and the European immigrants,
who had never employed slave labour. In 1888, when Parliament

passed a law freeing all the slaves in the country, Pedro was travelling in Europe, but the *fazendeiro* slaveholders – traditionally conservative monarchists – knew that it would have his approval, and so he shared the blame. Matters were brought to a head by the army officers who, since their homecoming from the war in Paraguay, had been resisting discipline by the civilian authorities and fraternizing with the republicans because they knew that under a republican government they would have greater opportunities for their political ambitions.

When Pedro returned from Europe in 1888 he characteristically made no attempt to suppress his critics and opponents. In 1889 a typical Latin American military uprising caused his abdication. He departed quietly, to settle in France. Like other Latin American leaders mentioned in this book, he died in exile and afterwards was greatly honoured in his own land.

REPUBLIC

With the collapse of the Empire in 1889, the Brazilians had to begin working out for themselves a new form of government. The republicans of course expected the new system to be republican and democratic; the provincial leaders demanded greater freedom in the management of local affairs; and the military officers who overthrew Pedro II had no intention of abandoning political control. Thus did Brazil, whose position until now had been unique, prepare to join the main stream of Latin American history.

A republican Constitution was duly promulgated in 1891, but the military continued to rule. The Constitution was democratic and federal but, like the Spanish American constitutions, it granted to the national President the power to suspend constitutional guarantees and to 'intervene' in the provinces – or 'states', as they now became. Insurrections occurred in several of the states – notably in remote Rio Grande do Sul, the land of the Brazilian gauchos and always a stubborn region. In 1894 a civilian was allowed to assume the presidency, but the military did not cease to regard themselves as the defenders – and indeed as the only true interpreters – of the Constitution, a pretension which has been frequently revived even in recent years.[1] Fundamentally the struggle was one of trying to adapt imported democratic theories to the realities of an enormous, largely virgin country whose diverse, illiterate populations were scattered along tropical coasts, upon isolated plateaus and distant plains, and, even more sparsely, in the jungles of the Amazon and Mato Grosso. In such circumstances orthodox parliamentary processes were impossible. But, as was demonstrated during the Empire, the Brazilians had a genius for compromise. They still have it today.

Brazil, during the civilian and so-called 'liberal' period of 1898–1910, did not conform to the European or United States theory of what a parliamentary democracy should be. Generally, however, the ruling oligarchy did serve the national interests. Political power was in the hands of the leading families of São Paulo and Minas Gerais, and the national Presidents came from those states alternately. A President usually nominated his successor, after reaching an understanding with the Governors of the states. The system worked effectively. It suited the Governors to keep on good terms with the federal executive at Rio de Janeiro. Men of ability and integrity rose to the top. And under the Republic, as under the Empire, the nation held together.

The monarchy had served its purpose, that of uniting and stabilizing; and by abolishing slavery, as its last great act, it opened the way for Brazil's entry into the modern economic era. As a wage system replaced the slave system, the need to find other sources of labour led to schemes for the encouragement of European immigration. Moreover, the immigrants developed new branches of the economy, since they did not go to the sugar and cotton plantations of the north but to the coffee and cattle regions of the south. More than a million and a quarter immigrants – predominantly Italians and Portuguese – arrived between

1. For example, in August–September 1961 the armed forces, disapproving of the political affiliations of the legitimate successor to the presidency, João Goulart, refused to permit his inauguration until he had agreed to an alteration of the Constitution which would deprive the President of most of his power.

1888 and 1898. The Italians went in particular to the coffee *fazendas* of São Paulo, where they fulfilled a function similar to that which other Italians had already performed in Argentina,[1] and by the end of the nineteenth century Brazil was supplying more than seventy-five per cent of the world's coffee. Further to the south, in the states of Rio Grande do Sul, Santa Catarina, and Paraná German pioneers were the chief transforming influence, and their agricultural communities, situated so far from the central government, long retained a high degree of German nationality.

Meanwhile technical innovations in the United States and Europe had provided Brazil with a great new speculative opportunity. The discovery of vulcanization and of new uses for rubber for waterproofing, the manufacture of motor-car tyres, and electrical insulation, created a tremendous market for rubber; and the world's chief source of latex was in the rain forests of the Amazon. So Brazilian speculators scrambled to purchase land in the regions of Belém and Manaus, and many thousands of impoverished labourers came to the area from tne semi-arid and periodically drought-stricken *sertão* of north-eastern Brazil. The labourers were sent up the rivers and into the forests to seek out and tap the rubber trees. They lived in the most primitive conditions and suffered appallingly from tropical diseases; but at least the owners supplied them with food, even if always at prices that were slightly more than they could afford, so that they were permanently in debt. The owners prospered exceedingly. The ramshackle settlement of Manaus, situated in the jungle 1,000 miles up-stream from the Atlantic Ocean, rapidly became a city. A theatre was erected, and famous singers from Europe performed there. (As you approach Manuas today, you can see the green and orange dome of the Teatro Amazonas rising above the trees.) Steamers chugged up the river bringing champagne, *pâté de foie gras*, and other luxuries from France. Money was so plentiful that the wealthy citizens – as we are led to believe was the normal practice in nineteenth-century boom towns – used banknotes to light their cigars. In 1900 Brazil was supplying almost all the world's rubber, and as late as 1914 Theodore

1. See pp. 141–2.

Roosevelt described Manaus as a big, handsome, up-to-date city, with tramways, good hotels, and fine squares and public buildings.[1]

The Brazilians, having had a virtual monopoly of rubber, imagined that the prosperity would last for ever. But in 1876 an Englishman, Henry Wickham, had smuggled some rubber seeds out from Belém and taken them to London, where they were planted in Kew Gardens. The young plants were sent to Ceylon, and from them the great rubber plantations of the Far East originated. In Brazil the rubber industry was one of 'destructive exploitation' of the wild trees; and the labourers were exposed to all the dangers and hardships of those regions. In the Far East, on the other hand, the plantations were supervised by experts; and the workers were carefully housed and given medical attention. Under these conditions the production per tree and per man was far greater and the quality of the rubber much purer than the Brazilian. By 1912 the Far East had replaced Brazil as the world's principal supplier. The whole structure of Brazilian rubber speculation fell in ruins, and the Amazonian labourers were reduced to a state of poverty from which they have not yet emerged. Another of Brazil's economic cycles had closed.

Coffee of course survived rubber as a mainstay of the economy – indeed, Brazil now became too dependent on it. As the European and United States markets expanded, immigrants spread over the rich red soil of the state of São Paulo, planting more and more coffee. They drew a meagre reward; but the *fazendeiros*' profits were fabulous, and their land rose spectacularly in value. Once again, few Brazilians foresaw that a crash might come. But it was not only in Brazil that world demand stimulated coffee planting – gradually Central America, Colombia, Venezuela, Africa, and the East Indies became serious competitors. Still the Brazilians continued planting, in spite of the government's attempts to restrain them. Over-production reached such proportions that when the world-wide economic crisis occurred in 1930, the slump in coffee prices caused a national upheaval.[2]

1. Theodore Roosevelt, *Through the Brazilian Wilderness*, New York, 1914, pp. 333–4.
2. See below on Vargas, pp. 198–9.

So the change in Brazil's political organization – from empire to republic – was matched by a change in economic life. The nation's economic centre moved southwards, the sugar and plantation economy of Bahia and Pernambuco was replaced by the coffee economy of the São Paulo region, and the growth of population and wealth in São Paulo brought into existence Latin America's greatest industrial city.

Brazil's economic history offers a notable illustration of the consequences of an excessive dependence on the export of raw materials. But the country has a natural exuberance, and its people are happy to believe that 'God is Brazilian'. Nor is their optimism unjustified. For one reason or another – such as the outbreak of war in Europe, or in the Far East – the price of one or other of their staple products will suddenly rise from the depths to the heights. So Brazil has survived economic crises, maladministration, and corruption. The Brazilians say that their country grows at night, while the politicians are asleep.

13

'Caudillos' and Business

'CAUDILLOS' AND FOREIGN INVESTORS

By the end of the nineteenth century the leading Latin American republics – Argentina, Brazil, and Chile – had attained a considerable degree of political stability, though this did not mean that they were free from electoral fraud or that their further development would be uninterrupted by revolution. From the turn of the century three other countries – Colombia, Costa Rica, and Uruguay – also evolved democratic or quasi-democratic institutions. Personalities still were more important than political parties (personalities counted for less in Costa Rica, a very politically-conscious country, than elsewhere); but *caudillos* now preferred to prolong their power by 'constitutional' means – that is to say, by amending the Constitution to suit their ambitions, rather than by overriding it.

In most parts of Latin America *caudillismo* did not end with the nineteenth century: *caudillos* simply adjusted themselves to changing conditions. Military backing was still necessary, and care was still taken to satisfy the landowners: but business interests – particularly foreign interests – were cultivated too. Presidential autocrats discovered that one of the surest supports for their régimes was the favour of foreign investors and commercial enterprises. Foreign money enabled the *caudillo* to enrich his friends and to win over some at least of his enemies.

Until recently, and in many countries even now, well-to-do Latin Americans – a relatively small class – were generally reluctant to invest in public utility services, and even in local industry, finding it more profitable to buy real estate in the cities or safer to place their money in Europe or the United States, or preferring to spend their surplus funds on their own personal comforts. Governments, moreover, did not dare to impose heavy taxation on the wealthy class, or to take strong measures to prevent tax evasion, with the result that budget surpluses available for capital expenditure were small. In these circumstances it was the foreigner who supplied a large part of the capital for economic development and who took the greatest risks. In 1914 the total nominal value of foreign investments in Latin America was U.S. $8,500 million, of which about one third was in Argentina, about a fourth in Brazil, and a similar amount in Mexico. Up to that date the chief lending country was Great Britain, but the United States gradually became the principal investor.

Foreign investors naturally chose the countries where conditions were most stable, not caring whether the local ruler was elected by free ballot (an extreme rarity) or had seized power by fraud and force and was maintaining order by the same means.

Of course the foreigner and the foreign-domiciled company bore the main burden of increases in wages and social benefits; but after the Second World War, with the new trend towards nationalization and domestic ownership, this responsibility was largely shifted to the local governments and local capitalists, who then began to insist that the public good required greater production before higher wages.

MEXICO

An early example of how *caudillismo* could be adjusted to take advantage of new economic opportunities appeared in Mexico, where Porfirio Díaz founded his long dictatorship (1876–1911) on business interests as well as landed interests.

Díaz was a *mestizo*, born in 1830 of a poor working family in Oaxaca. He became a professional soldier and was a fine soldierly figure of a man, kept in training by an abstemious and active life; 'of an integrity rare among Mexican politicians; but no more scrupulous than other Ibero-American dictators in methods of keeping the peace.'[1] He had fought against Santa Anna, and had been Juárez's[2] most successful general – though later he was his most dangerous opponent. In 1876, having organized a rebel army in the United States, Díaz marched upon Mexico City, overthrew

1. Kirkpatrick, *Latin America*, p. 342.   2. See pp. 132–3.

Juárez's successor, and took charge of the lawless and impoverished nation. He created order by force and bribery. His well-paid mounted police, the *rurales*, some of whom were ex-bandits, suppressed banditry in the country districts. Conspirators disappeared, their disappearance being accounted for by the so-called *ley de fuga*, 'the prisoner, trying to escape, was shot'. Regional *caudillos* who were too powerful to be disposed of by these means were won over by flattery and honours or by gifts from the national treasury. The landowners were grateful for the unaccustomed security: Díaz enabled them to add to their already vast estates, and his railway programme increased the value of their properties. In the towns most of the critics of the régime preferred to keep quiet, rather than go to prison. Elections were held, but Congress was packed with Díaz's nominees; he himself appointed all the public officials; and he had able men as his senior administrators. Military officers were handsomely rewarded – though the generals were constantly moved from place to place, to prevent them from gathering a local following and plotting rebellion. The Catholic hierarchy were flattered and were allowed greater freedom – but, anti-clericalism always being sound politics in Mexico, previous measures restricting landholding by the Church were reaffirmed. The formula of *pan o palo*, 'bread or the club', was impressively effective.

Stability and security prepared the way for economic development, which was Díaz's particular concern. By meticulously paying the nation's debts, he established Mexico's credit in the eyes of the world. Mexican laws were modified in favour of the foreigner, and capital poured into the country. Huge concessions were granted to United States and British companies for the exploitation of the newly discovered oil resources, and in the first decade of the present century Mexico became one of the world's principal exporters of petroleum, production rising from 10,000 barrels in 1901 to 13,000,000 barrels in 1911.

During the so-called *Pax Porfiriana* foreigners attained a position of such importance that they dominated the Mexican economy, and they were duly appreciative of the régime that so favoured them. United States and British investors owned the oilfields, the mines, and the public utilities, and U.S. citizens acquired millions of acres in the north of the country.[1] It has been said that the Díaz administration was 'mother of the foreigner and stepmother of the Mexican'. Certainly the mass of the people derived little benefit from the dictator's economic achievements, and his courting of the outsider was to be the cause of the violent storm of xenophobia which broke out after his downfall. It is possible that towards the end of his rule Díaz himself may have felt that he had gone too far: he is supposed to have exclaimed: '*Pobre Méjico, tan lejos de Dios, y tan cerca de los Estados Unidos!*' ('Poor Mexico, so far from God, and so near the United States!')

Díaz clung to power too long. His cast-iron rule, which had crushed anarchy, was obsolete in a pacified and partly industrialized Mexico. While young intellectuals agitated against the dictatorship, Indian peasants who had been deprived of their land began to attack the owners who held them virtually in slavery. When Díaz prepared to have himself 'elected' for yet another period of office in 1910, the movement against him grew rapidly, and in 1911 the mob in the streets compelled him to resign. Like so many other Latin American leaders, he went into exile; but the uprising which overthrew Díaz was unusual in that it developed into Latin America's first truly *social* revolution.[2] He died in Paris in 1915.

VENEZUELA

Venezuela had suffered more than any other country from the wars of independence. Not only did her patriots – and, on the other side, Venezuelan supporters of Spanish rule – fight on their own soil,[3] many Venezuelans fought also in the armies that Bolívar led into Colombia and down the Pacific coast. It is estimated that one quarter of the country's population died in

1. 'Between 1883 and 1894, Díaz and his obedient Congress gave away to foreign speculators and personal friends one-fifth of the entire area of the Republic. By 1910 less than ten per cent of the Indian communities had any land whatever.' Lewis Hanke, *Mexico and the Caribbean*, New York, Van Nostrand, 1959, p. 71.

2. See pp. 191–7.   3. See pp. 98–101.

those wars. Thereafter, despotism and anarchy alternated. The economy was in ruins, and corruption existed on a scale rarely equalled and certainly never exceeded in other parts of Latin America. Furthermore, there were international complications: in 1895–6 a long dispute with Great Britain over the frontier with British Guiana reached its climax,[1] and in 1902 British, German, and Italian warships blockaded the Venezuelan ports to press their nations' financial claims.

Then Venezuela, like Mexico, produced a *caudillo* who saw the advantages of being allied with foreign big business and who, by imposing peace at home and punctiliously paying the country's debts abroad, won foreign esteem and financial backing.

Juan Vicente Gómez, like other Venezuelan 'strong men', came from the Andes. Born in 1857, he was a *mestizo*. He had almost no schooling, worked as a cattle-hand, and became a successful landowner before entering politics. A biographer, rather in the manner of a novelist, has tried to recapture the quality of this hard, wily mountaineer with the closely cropped head and the long moustaches:

He has the slow energy of the animals of the cat family, of snakes and bull-fighters. Heavy-lidded eyes, almost asleep, face and body immobile; then suddenly, lightning action; and then repose again, lethargy, and there is nothing there but the results. . . .

The Indians say that he reads your mind, that he is a *brujo*, a witch-doctor. They tell of how he remembers everything, how he remembers every man and animal that he ever saw. . . . They tell of his disregard for the priests and the Mass, his contempt for religion. They tell of his preoccupation with numbers and dates.

He attracted men. He didn't arouse their affections, he was too cold for that, but he drew them to him by the reputation he had for uncanny discernment. His men feared him and followed him. He knew how to get the best from them. Often he would say: 'You, *compadre*, you undertake this mission, for you do things well and you are not afraid of anything.'[2]

Gómez lived frugally and worked assiduously. He never

1. See p. 172.
2. Thomas Rourke [D. J. Clinton], *Gómez, Tyrant of the Andes*, New York, William Morrow, 1936, pp. 56–7, 94, 108.

married, but he was the father of more than a hundred sons and daughters, and provided for all of them.[1]

Gómez seized power in 1908 and remained in complete control of the country for twenty-seven years. His dictatorship was much more savage than that of Porfírio Díaz in Mexico, but was just as competent and was likewise dependent on a well-equipped army. Even in unpropitious times his administration would have been successful, but it so happened that circumstances favoured him abundantly, for petroleum was discovered in Venezuela early in his rule; and after the fall of Díaz in Mexico in 1911, foreign investors were increasingly attracted to the Venezuelan oilfields. From 1918 United States, British, and Dutch companies competed for Venezuelan concessions, and Gómez – who collected his own share on all government transactions – proved himself a shrewd bargainer. There is disagreement regarding the extent to which he gave in to the foreigners. His biographer, who recognized all his faults, wrote however that it was due to 'the perception of this mountain illiterate in grasping the problems of a vast industry, his cleverness in utilizing the talents of educated advisers, his cunning in avoiding the tricks of the foreign legal minds that a good, fair law was finally worked out which assured the nation a proper percentage of the profits without discouraging foreign exploitation'.[2] On the other hand, the author of a history of the Venezuelan oil industry has declared that 'in 1918 Gómez allowed the companies to draft the kind of legislation under which they would be willing to operate, and then decreed it the law of the land'.[3] In any case, the outcome was the realistic Petroleum Law of 1920, which provided that the companies should pay substantial taxes and ensured that the nation would retain ample oil reserves for the future. By 1928 Venezuela – having been an insignificant oil producer at the end of the First World War – was the world's second producer and foremost exporter.

The extraordinary income from oil enabled Gómez to pay off the whole of Venezuela's foreign debt, and most of the internal debt, by 1930. The 'philosophy' of the régime – which was written

1. Edwin Lieuwen, *Venezuela*, O.U.P. for R.I.I.A., 1961, p. 46.
2. Rourke, pp. 170–1.   3. Lieuwen, pp. 47–8.

and published – explained that as the Venezuelans were a primitive race living in a backward, pastoral economy, military dictatorship was the best form of government for them. The benevolent despot, it was said, really represented the unconscious desire of the people for order to be maintained, and for the national economy to be developed by more advanced and technologically superior foreigners.

The discovery of oil was not an unmixed blessing, for it meant that other branches of the economy – notably agriculture and stock-raising – declined. Food had to be imported, and prices rose. In spite of the opulence of the state, the living standards of the mass of the population remained miserably low, and health and education were neglected. Furthermore, a large part of the oil revenue was used to improve the efficiency of the instruments of repression – the army and police. The demands of students of the University of Caracas for a relaxation of the dictatorship, and complaints that Gómez had surrendered the Venezuelan economy to foreign interests, were treated as subversion. Argumentative students were rounded up and put to work on the roads. So Gómez remained the master of the situation till his death, from natural causes, in 1935.

As the news spread that the old man had died, the mob went through the streets of Caracas sacking the houses of his relatives and collaborators. At Lake Maracaibo the wives and children of the foreign oil men were rushed to safety because rioters threatened to set fire to the wells. But no social upheaval such as that which followed the downfall of Díaz in Mexico occurred in Venezuela. The oligarchy – military officers, wealthy land-owners – took charge.[1] Petroleum continued to be king, and the rest of the national economy languished.

It is true that in 1945 a coterie of junior officers carried out a *coup d'état* to bring to an end the ascendency of the elderly generals who had survived from the Gómez era, and – being aware of the growing popular dissatisfaction with military rule – put a civilian government in power. But the democratic experiment only lasted from October 1945 to November 1948.

1. ibid., pp. 50–1.

The leaders of the 1945–8 non-military régime were Rómulo Betancourt, founder of the left-wing party Acción Democrática, and Rómulo Gallegos, author of one of Latin America's most famous novels, *Doña Bárbara*, which is the story of barbaric life as lived on the Venezuelan plains. The new, inexperienced government, in its haste to convert Venezuela into a 'welfare state', quickly alienated those who had vested interests in the old order. Venezuelan businessmen and foreign oil companies alike were alarmed to see their costs rising as a result of the pro-labour policies. The oil companies were obliged to pay a larger part of their profits to the national treasury. The landowners were shocked by the government's plan to distribute uncultivated land to the peasants. Finally, by its endeavours to exclude the army from politics, the government lost the support of the very officers who had put it in power.

In November 1948 the junior officers seized power for themselves. Betancourt and Gallegos went into exile again. The businessmen, oil companies, and landowners were relieved of their anxiety. Venezuela reverted to being what Simón Bolívar, over a century before, had declared her to be, 'a barracks'.

By 1950, and until January 1958, the man in control was a military *caudillo*, Colonel Marcos Pérez Jiménez, of whom Gómez would have whole-heartedly approved. Like Gómez himself, Pérez Jiménez was born and raised at Táchira, in the mountains. His enemies claimed that his dictatorship was just as brutal as that of Gómez, and he certainly crushed all opposition ruthlessly. The Gómez 'philosophy' of the people's inability to govern themselves was re-stated: Venezuela, said Pérez Jiménez, must be rid of politics and devote herself exclusively to material progress. Here was another *caudillo* who knew how to flatter big business. The revenue still came, of course, from oil; and under Pérez Jiménez it increased enormously. Foreign companies, heartened by the government's rejection of the workers' demands and by its friendly attitude towards the employers, invested in new concessions.

Official policy was proclaimed to be that of ploughing back the oil royalties – *sembrar el petróleo*, was the phrase – into public works and industries that would help to diversify the economy, thereby reducing the country's dependence on a single product. The detractors of Pérez Jiménez rightly maintain that he and his clique put vast sums of public money into their own pockets and that there was much wasteful expenditure on such unnecessary projects as the construction of the luxurious officers' club in Caracas and the ostentatious hotel on the top of Mount Ávila. Nevertheless, much useful work was pushed forward – for example, the building of large blocks of workers' flats in the suburbs of the capital. During the Pérez Jiménez régime rapid progress was made in the construction of the important power and steel plant on the Caroni river, and the great irrigation dam on the Guárico was completed. Foreign ownership continued to increase. United State investors – who accounted for sixty-five per cent of foreign investment in Venezuela – owned more than three fifths of the petroleum industry, all of the new iron-mining enterprises, and a large share of local manufacturing industry, commerce, banking, utilities, and insurance.[1] The dictator, by his success in maintaining order and by his lenient tax policies, won high regard in the United States. President Eisenhower conferred upon him the order of the Legion of Merit.

Over the years, however, opposition to Pérez Jiménez developed at home. To some, the spectacular buildings in Caracas seemed a poor substitute for political liberty and a better general standard of living. Another generation of officers of lesser rank grew resentful of their superiors' monopoly of privilege. The air force and navy in particular became restless under a régime run largely by and for the army. (Many young officers in those forces had received training in the United States, where they were influenced by democratic ideas and learned to recognize the value of responsible government for a nation's well-being.) In January 1958 the groups of military and civilian conspirators combined, and Pérez Jiménez was driven into exile.

Betancourt, who was elected to the presidency in December 1958, did not carry on the fallen dictator's solicitous policy towards big business. But, knowing that he had acted too impetuously during the 1945–8 period, he now behaved with

1. ibid., p. 136.

caution. To foster cordial relations with the armed forces, he approved high defence budgets and frequently referred to the important role of the military in defending the country's borders and preserving internal order. Betancourt – always a social reformer at heart – was faced with the problem that has baffled many democratic Latin American leaders: how can social reforms be effected by parliamentary methods when the armed forces disapprove?

14

The United States Rises to Pre-eminence

THE CHALLENGE TO BRITISH PRESTIGE

UNITED STATES investment in Mexico and Venezuela, referred to in the last chapter, was of course just one sign of that nation's increasing interest in Latin America generally. By the 1890s practically the whole territory of the United States from Maine to California had been explored and occupied, and the nation was ready to extend its power abroad. United States industry had developed to a point at which it needed foreign markets, and capital was becoming available for investment in other lands. Hitherto British prestige in Latin America had been unrivalled, but now it was to be challenged, and eventually out-matched. U.S. and German manufacturers and shipping had begun to compete with the British. In 1884 a British consul reported from Brazil that the United States had supplied some rolling stock for the new railways, while her farm machinery was receiving attention.[1] In terms which remind us of present-day official chidings, British consuls warned manufacturers at home that their U.S. and German rivals were more attentive to local requirements and preferences. For example, they introduced 'lighter, more novel, more attractive' styles of glassware and crockery, while the British continued to offer articles of 'old-fashioned solidity'. Whereas U.S. and German travellers spoke Spanish or Portuguese and distributed catalogues printed in those languages, the British only spoke English and their advertising literature was in English. In 1898 a British consul wrote that U.S. and German firms were content with smaller profits, if they could secure the market for their goods.[2] Before the end of the nineteenth century the United States had become the largest foreign buyer of Brazilian products – and she has remained so ever since.

1. A. K. Manchester, *British Pre-eminence in Brazil*, p. 328.
2. ibid., pp. 330–1.

In the 1890s the United States grew increasingly assertive politically as well as economically. Until that date the Monroe Doctrine[1] had not been rigorously applied. The 'new imperial mood of the United States'[2] first became apparent in 1895 in connexion with the British dispute with Venezuela over the western boundary of British Guiana, which Great Britain had long wished to establish far enough to the north-west to incorporate the southern bank of the Orinoco in the colony. The Venezuelans appealed to the United States for arbitration, and in 1895 the U.S. government decided to invoke the Monroe Doctrine to prevent further British expansion in that direction. In a dispatch addressed to Britain, the Secretary of State, Richard Olney, declared:

Today the United States is practically sovereign on this continent, and its fiat is law upon the subjects to which it confines its interposition.[3]

The British Government, unwilling to enter into a major conflict over the boundary question, agreed that it should be submitted to an international arbitration tribunal, where it was settled until its revival by the Venezuelans in November 1962. The Orinoco was of course, and rightly, accorded to Venezuela. Why, it has been asked, did the British public quietly acquiesce in their statesmen's acceptance of the U.S. intervention? There are perhaps three reasons: most people in Britain did not even know that a dispute with Venezuela existed, and the news of it took them by surprise; when they did hear of it, they were distressed – not angered – to discover that the United States considered the British attitude unjust; and, finally, they were more interested in the crisis that was developing in South Africa.

CUBA

After the year 1895 United States intervention in Latin America became more and more forceful and attention was now turned towards Cuba. For reasons already explained,[4] Cuba did not

1. See pp. 113–14.   2. Herring, p. 757.
3. Dexter Perkins, *Hands Off: A History of the Monroe Doctrine*, Boston, 1943, p. 173.
4. See pp. 118–19.

attain independence from Spain at the same time as the other Spanish-American colonies, and in the nineteenth century she experienced the corruption and ineptitude of colonial government at its worst. As a result, in the later decades of the century numerous unsuccessful insurrections against Spanish rule occurred, and a special Cuban revolutionary technique was developed. Rebels would go to the nearby American mainland, where they plotted their campaigns, collecting money from sympathizers, enlisting soldier-adventurers, and buying munitions. Then they would sail in one or two small ships, disembark on Cuba's eastern shore (that is to say, at the point most remote from the capital, Havana), and disappear into the rugged, forested mountains of the Sierra Maestra. The most famous of patriots was the poet and journalist José Martí – Cuba's national hero – who inspired the most effective, and the last, revolutionary movement against the Spaniards. For criticizing the Spanish administration and stirring up opposition to it, Martí had been sent into exile. He lived in the United States, Mexico, Guatemala, Venezuela, and elsewhere, raising funds by persuasive speaking and writing. In 1895 he and his party landed near Santiago, at Cuba's south-eastern extremity. Martí was killed in a skirmish with the Spaniards soon afterwards, but his companions, having established themselves in the mountains, went forth on guerrilla forays, destroying anything that could be of use to the enemy. (In the 1950s this same technique of preparation and attack was practised by Fidel Castro, who arrived in and operated from the same district against the dictator Batista.)

The sympathy of the United States was naturally with the Cuban patriots in their fight for freedom from Spain; and many North Americans took it for granted that when the island was liberated it would become a U.S. dependency. Martí's expedition happened to occur at the very time when many people in the United States were looking beyond the national borders for profitable enterprises in which to invest. Moreover, the United States needed sugar, and Cuba not only had perfect conditions for tropical agriculture, but could provide cheap Negro labour. Last, but not least, the United States was interested in Cuba for strategic reasons. It was recognized that the United States must control the Panama Canal, the construction of which was becoming imminent; and to control the canal it seemed essential to acquire what Senator Lodge called the 'outworks'.

U.S. relations with Spain deteriorated; the U.S. public were shocked to hear of the savagery with which the Spanish authorities treated Cuban rebels; and then, early in 1898, news was received that the U.S. warship *Maine* (which had been sent to Cuba to safeguard U.S. citizens in case of emergency) had blown up in Havana harbour with the loss of two hundred and sixty men. How the catastrophe occurred, whether it was an accidental explosion or caused by a mine, is still unknown today; but U.S. newspapers placed the blame on the Spaniards and called for retaliation. In consequence of the popular clamour and of the growing belief that it was the 'manifest destiny' of the United States to supervise the welfare of the hemisphere, the U.S. Congress passed a resolution declaring Cuba to be independent, demanding that Spain withdraw from the island, and directing the President to use the army and navy to that end. The so-called Spanish American war of 1898 lasted only three months. The U.S. navy promptly sank the antiquated Spanish fleet. An expeditionary force – which included Theodore Roosevelt's volunteer regiment of 'Rough Riders' – landed at Santiago and, with few casualties, overcame the Spaniards, whose army greatly outnumbered them. The U.S. public agreed that it had been 'a splendid little war'. The Spaniards evacuated Cuba, and also Puerto Rico. From 1898 to 1902 Cuba was under U.S. military rule, which was enlightened and efficient. Puerto Rico became a U.S. possession.

The avowed purpose of the U.S. invasion of Cuba had been to secure the island's independence, but Washington was determined that the new Cuba should be 'a safe and tractable neighbour'.[1] With that aim the Cubans in 1901 were persuaded to accept the terms of a U.S. dictate – the Platt Amendment – whereby, among other things, they agreed to lease naval stations to the United States and to recognize the right of the United States to intervene in the island whenever there was danger to life, property, and individual freedom or if Cuban independence

1. Herring, p. 404.

should be threatened. From 1902 the Cubans were free to elect their own presidents; but local conditions became so disordered and violent that in accordance with the Platt Amendment (which remained in force until 1934) the United States repeatedly intervened.

Throughout this period U.S. investment was welcomed and encouraged by Cuban politicians and businessmen, until a great part of the best land in the island was owned or controlled by U.S. citizens or by corporations of absentee shareholders managed by boards in New York. The large U.S.-owned sugar-mills brought a rise in material prosperity, a quickening of the tempo of economic activity; but in the process Cuba came to be dominated by U.S. interests. And when U.S. Marines were stationed in Cuba to impose and maintain order, the consequent relative stability encouraged even further U.S. investment.[1]

The history of U.S. relations with Cuba – and with other Latin American republics too – is a story, on the U.S. side, of good intentions and self-righteousness, idealism and self-interest, jingoism and exuberant commercialism; and on the other side of inexperience, poverty, and corruption, the desire to have U.S. aid, and the fear of U.S. domination.

Cuba's political heritage was so entirely different from that of the United States that the orderly processes of democratic government, confidently expected by Washington, never materialized. ... Either the United States had to support corrupt governments in office, or permit revolutions that were bound to cause suffering to the population, financial depression, and eventually the establishment of another government, probably no less corrupt than the one it had supplanted. With some headshaking, the United States chose the first of these two unpleasant alternatives, knowing that whatever it did was sure to be wrong. ... if the United States is to blame for conditions in Cuba, it is for not having intervened more often, for having been too frightened of the stigma of imperialism.[2]

1. Lowry Nelson, *Rural Cuba*, University of Minnesota Press, 1950, p. 94.
2. Arnold Whitridge, 'Cuba's Role in American History', *History Today*, June 1961.

THE PANAMA CANAL

With the victory over the Spaniards in Cuba, the United States became conscious of being a world power. As such, she needed to be able to move her fleet between the Pacific and Atlantic oceans by a quicker route than the long southern passage of the Strait of Magellan, or Cape Horn. The cutting of a canal through the isthmus of Panama would solve the problem.

Of course the isthmus had always been the shortest *land* route between the two oceans. In colonial times all of Spain's traffic with Peru crossed the continent by that way.[1] During the gold rush to California which began in 1848 thousands of adventurers from the eastern regions of the United States sailed down the Atlantic side of the continent to the isthmus, went overland through the Panamanian jungles to the Pacific shore, and then, on the last stage of their journey, travelled northwards by sea to San Francisco.

Already in the sixteenth century the Spaniards had considered the possibility of cutting a canal from coast to coast. Eventually in the 1880s Ferdinand de Lesseps, who in 1869 had completed the construction of the Suez Canal, attempted to repeat that achievement in Panama, but he had to abandon the project after thousands of his workmen had died of yellow fever and malaria.

In 1903 President Theodore Roosevelt decided that the United States must construct the canal without delay. At that time Panama was a part of the South American republic of Colombia, but she was separated from the main bulk of Colombia by impenetrable jungle, and she had always managed – or mismanaged – her affairs with little effective control from the faraway highland capital, Bogotá. Indeed, the national authorities could only reach Panama by sea. The geographical separation was Colombia's misfortune, but it gave Roosevelt his opportunity. In 1903 the Colombian Congress at Bogotá refused to lease to the United States the strip that she required across the isthmus. In November of that year a small revolt broke out in Panama

1. See p. 63.

City; an independent republic of Panama was proclaimed; and U.S. warships obstructed the landing of Colombian troops sent to suppress the insurrection. Washington at once recognized the independence of Panama, and two weeks later the new republic signed a treaty granting to the United States quasi-sovereign rights over a coast-to-coast corridor, ten miles in width, through its territory. In exchange the United States undertook to pay $10 million in gold and an annuity of $250,000.

Before the construction of the canal could begin, measures had to be taken to protect the health of the labourers who would be engaged in the task. It was now known that the tropical fevers were spread by mosquitoes, and so an American sanitary expert, Colonel Gorgas, set to work to clean up Panama. His men even went into the churches to remove the holy water from the fonts, where mosquitoes often bred. At very great cost to the U.S. taxpayer, yellow fever was eliminated from Panama, and malaria was almost stamped out.

The first ship passed through the canal on 3 August 1914.

Since its creation as an independent nation, the republic of Panama has existed only because of the canal, from which it earns its livelihood. With the growth of nationalism in the republic, the United States has been from time to time obliged to make concessions – such as agreeing to increases in the yearly payment to the Panamanian government, and providing better conditions for Panamanians employed in the canal zone.

Encouraged by his success in bringing the republic of Panama into existence (an operation which had taken only three weeks), President Theodore Roosevelt soon asserted himself again. In 1904, in his annual message to the U.S. Congress, he formulated what came to be known as the Roosevelt Corollary to the Monroe Doctrine. Chronic wrong-doing or the lack of order in any country, he declared, called for the intervention of civilized states, 'and in the western hemisphere the adherence of the United States to the Monroe Doctrine may force the United States, however reluctantly, in flagrant cases of such wrongdoing or impotence, to the exercise of an international police power'.

The 'Roosevelt Corollary', which produced much ill-feeling

towards the United States throughout Latin America, was first applied in 1905, when Washington, to forestall European nations (notably Germany) who were threatening to collect their debts by force, appointed a U.S. official to take charge of all customs houses in the Dominican Republic, to receive the duties, and to distribute fifty-five per cent of the proceeds among that country's foreign creditors. In 1916, political conditions having become chaotic, U.S. Marines were sent to the Dominican Republic to impose order, and they remained there for eight years, during which time they trained and armed a local body of national guards. The Marines were withdrawn in 1924. Six years later Rafael Leonidas Trujillo, the head of the *guardia nacional* which the U.S. had prepared and equipped so well, seized power. He ruled the country as an efficient and ruthless dictator until his assassination in 1961.

Disorder was so constant and violent in Haiti that in 1915 the U.S. government applied the Roosevelt Corollary to that nation also. United States Marines occupied Haiti for nineteen years.

Nicaragua, on the Central American mainland, was no less turbulent than the island republics. U.S. Marines landed there in 1912, and they stayed, with a brief interval, until 1933. In Nicaragua, as in the Dominican Republic, the U.S. Marines trained a *guardia nacional*. After the U.S. withdrawal from the country it was the head of the *guardia*, General Anastasio Somoza, who took over the government. Somoza, one of Latin America's most competent dictators, ruled Nicaragua as his personal estate until he was assassinated in 1956.

Naturally the United States policy of the 'big stick' ('speak softly and carry a big stick' was Theodore Roosevelt's characteristic advice) aroused bitter resentment in all the Latin American republics, and Washington was accused of using U.S. guns to further the advance of 'dollar imperialism'. Certainly the protection and advancement of commercial interests were major aims of U.S. policy. It was by the big stick that the United States acquired the Panama canal zone, and the possession of the

Panama canal made the continued use of the big stick necessary.

Henry L. Stimson – President Coolidge's envoy to Nicaragua in 1927 – gave a classic explanation of his government's motives.

> There are certain geographical considerations which impose upon us a very special interest as to how certain Latin American nations fulfil the responsibilities which go with sovereignty and independence. I refer to those nations whose territory lies adjacent to and in a naval sense commands the great sea route from our eastern to our western states via the Caribbean Sea and the Panama Canal. This situation does not arise out of the Monroe Doctrine but from certain broad principles of self-defence which govern the policy of all nations which are in any way dependent upon the sea. ... Out of the principle of national self-preservation follows the corollary of our interest in the stability of the independent governments resting along the borders of the Caribbean and the Pacific. If those independent governments do not adequately fulfil the responsibility of independence; if they fail to safeguard foreign life within their borders; if they repudiate lawful debts to foreign creditors; if they permit the confiscation within their borders of lawful foreign property – then, under the common usages of international life, the foreign nations are likely to intervene for the legitimate protection of their rights. The failure therefore of one of the Latin American republics to maintain the responsibilities which go with independence may lead directly to a situation imperilling the vital interest of the United States in its sea-going route through the Panama Canal.

Stimson's conclusion was quite straightforward and logical:

> If we, the United States, will not permit European nations to protect their customary rights within this zone, we must, to a certain extent, make ourselves responsible for this protection.[1]

Stimson in 1927 referred to the Caribbean policy of the United States as 'perhaps the most sensitive and generally held policy that we have'. Later events confirmed that opinion. For example, when in 1954 the U.S. government actively assisted in the overthrow by force of President Arbenz of Guatemala, claiming that Arbenz's communist connexions constituted a threat to sovereignty and political independence in the Americas, the majority of U.S. citizens approved of this intervention as being in the true tradition. Likewise when in 1960–1 the U.S. authorities, for

1. Henry L. Stimson, *American Policy in Nicaragua*, New York, Scribner, 1927, pp. 104–11.

similar reasons, began in earnest to work for the overthrow of Fidel Castro of Cuba, the U.S. public generally looked upon this as normal U.S. policy.

Theodore Roosevelt's Panama policy was blatant imperialism – there was no pretence that the United States acted for the welfare of the Panamanians – but when U.S. officials and Marines took charge of Caribbean islands and intervened in Central America, the U.S. public sincerely believed that they were serving the best interests of the local people. It was hoped that the U.S. occupation would prepare the way for honest elections and parliamentary government. In fact, however, when the Marines withdrew the countries reverted to their former political habits.[1]

RESISTANCE IN THE SOUTH

Resentment against U.S. interference has not prevented Latin Americans from being attracted by the U.S. way of life, and since 1900 'anti-Yanquiism' and its opposite have existed side by side in every one of the republics. By her prodigious development during the last years of the nineteenth century, and her easy victory over Spain in Cuba in 1898, the United States had won many admirers. 'Admiration leads to imitation, and a number of the admirers of success dreamed of a Latin America entirely given over to "practical" pursuits. There was a budding Nordomania.'[2] Then in 1900, when U.S. interventionist intentions in the Caribbean were becoming plain for all to see, a Uruguayan essayist, José Enrique Rodó, published *Ariel*, the most influential book ever written by a Latin American author. In *Ariel* – which is still considered by many to be Latin America's ethical Bible – Rodó admonished the imitators of the United States and called for an intellectual aristocracy to withstand the materialistic impact. Rodó had no political motives; he urged that the two Americas (North and South) could and should cooperate and

1. 'Our measures did not result in any very sweeping change in their political habits or in the secure establishment of popular rule.' (Dexter Perkins, *The United States and Latin America*, Baton Rouge, Louisiana State University Press, 1961.)
2. Henríquez Ureña, p. 179.

180

complement each other; but his book stimulated anti-U.S. feeling among young Latin American intellectuals, particularly in countries situated south of the Panama Canal. The chief of those countries was Argentina.

The Argentines had long looked upon themselves as the natural and rightful leaders of the South American family of nations. As early as 1864 the Argentine jurist Carlos Calvo had written, with typical Argentine self-assurance, that his country was 'called upon to be, within half a century, if we have peace, as considerable a power in South America as are the United States in the North'.[1] By 1900 Argentina was indeed very far ahead of the other Latin American republics in economic development and prestige. It was not unreasonable that she should look upon herself as the 'Colossus of the South'. Nor was it unnatural that she should be suspicious of U.S. ambitions in the countries that she herself aspired to lead.

In 1908 a distinguished U.S. visitor to South America observed that 'the Argentino' (unlike the Brazilian) 'likes to exhibit a "chip on the shoulder" attitude to the citizens of the United States'.[2] Argentina's foreign links were with Great Britain, who bought her meat.

In Buenos Aires [in 1908] one looks in vain for an American bank or an agency of any well-known Wall Street house. American financial institutions are like the American merchant steamers, conspicuous by their absence. The Anglo-Saxons that you see briskly walking along the sidewalks are not Americans, but clean-shaven, red-cheeked, vigorous Britishers.

In England they talk familiarly of 'B.A.' and the 'River Plate', disdaining to use the Spanish words. To hear them you might suppose they were speaking of something they owned, and you would not be so very far from the truth. British capitalists have not been slow to realize the possibilities of this great agricultural region. They know its potentiality as a food-producer, and they have covered it with a net-work of railways. Thousands of energetic young Englishmen, backed by this enormous British capital, have aided in the extraordinary progress that Argentina has made.

1. See George Pendle, *Argentina*, O.U.P., third edition, 1963, p. 178.
2. Hiram Bingham, *Across South America*, Boston, Houghton Mifflin, 1911, p. 15.

The Englishman has made many native Argentinos wealthy beyond the dreams of avarice.[1]

The British in Argentina were well aware that U.S. competition threatened their own position, and they welcomed any signs of 'anti-Yanquiism'. But in spite of the fairly prevalent dislike of U.S. pressure, and although the Argentine landowning oligarchy – the real rulers of the country – clung tenaciously to their British connexion, the United States continued to acquire an ever greater share of Argentina's foreign trade. During the two world wars, when Great Britain was unable to supply the goods that Argentina traditionally obtained from her, the United States took Britain's place to a considerable degree, and the Argentines further reduced the dependence on British industry by developing the domestic manufacture of textiles and other articles which they had previously to a large extent imported.

Great Britain followed a tacit policy of discouraging Argentina from whole-hearted participation in the Pan American movement, and this was in harmony with Argentina's lack of enthusiasm for any international organization that was dominated by Washington. By 1943 Argentina had ratified only six of the ninety conventions concluded since 1890 by the Pan American Union, but her attempts to set up a bloc of southern nations under her own leadership were always coolly received by her neighbours.

It is true that the United States experienced a setback in 1933. For some three years Argentina had been suffering from the effects of the world-wide economic depression. In Argentina the crisis took the form which has been customary in all Latin American republics in periods of world depression: exports declined; the price of local products fell; farmers were faced with the foreclosure of their mortgages; and the currency depreciated. Then by the Ottawa agreements of 1932 Great Britain undertook to give preferential treatment to the produce of the British Empire. The Argentine landowners became so alarmed that the Government sent Vice-President Roca to London to negotiate with the Board of Trade, whose president then was Runciman. The Roca–Runciman Treaty was signed in 1933. Its main provisions were that Britain would maintain her imports of Argentine

1. Bingham., pp. 32–3.

chilled beef at the 1932 quantity; that the sterling earned from Argentine exports to Britain would be reserved for remittances to Britain; and that duties on British goods would be reduced. Furthermore, Argentina undertook to accord benevolent treatment to British investors, especially in public utilities such as the tramways and railways.

The United States denounced the treaty as an act of discrimination against her own trade, thereby of course aggravating Argentine resentment towards the United States. But the treaty also brought home to the Argentine public the excessive extent to which their economy was subservient to Britain. In retrospect, Argentine nationalists might look upon the Roca–Runciman Treaty as doubly beneficial: first, it helped to save the cattle industry and the balance of trade in a moment of grave crisis; second, it stimulated the popular desire for 'economic independence'.[1] In any case, the Argentine economy, with its natural resilience, made a rapid recovery; and when the crisis was past, it was evident that U.S. interests had not been permanently affected.

During the Second World War the United States constantly prodded Argentina to declare war on the Axis, but Great Britain was less exigent. Indeed, Argentine neutrality was probably to Britain's advantage, as the shipping of meat from a belligerent Argentina would have been fraught with additional dangers. In any case the British, with an eye to post-war trade, were not displeased that Argentina should be in disagreement with the United States. In 1944, when the outcome of the war was plain, the Argentine Government at last severed diplomatic relations with Germany and Japan. Argentina finally declared war in March 1945, being the last Latin American republic to do so.

In Latin America the United States has gained the pre-eminence that she sought, but with an uneasy conscience. In 1928 a U.S. Under-Secretary of State, J. Reuben Clark, wrote a memorandum in which the Roosevelt Corollary was repudiated as being 'unjustified by the terms of the Monroe Doctrine, however much it may be justified by the application of the doctrine of

1. cf. Pendle, *Argentina*, pp. 77–80

self-preservation'.[1] In his inaugural address of 1933 President Franklin D. Roosevelt introduced his Good Neighbour Policy, in which he dedicated the United States 'to respect the rights of others'.[2] In more recent years there have been countless endeavours to reconcile U.S. self-preservation with good-neighbourliness. Under various auspices, many talented U.S. men and women have gone to the Latin American republics to help them in improving their agricultural and industrial methods, to advise them on health services and education, and to suggest how they should put their national finances in order.

Nevertheless, the United States, to her credit, still feels that she has not been as good a neighbour as she might have been.

When deliberating whether to recognize revolutionary and undemocratic régimes in Latin America, the governments of the United States have sometimes adopted the policy which President Jefferson established in 1793, and at other times that which was enunciated by President Wilson one hundred and twenty years later.

Jefferson wrote:

We surely cannot deny to any nation that right whereon our own government is founded – that every one may govern itself according to whatever form it pleases, and change these forms at its own will; and that it may transact its business with foreign nations through whatever organ it thinks proper, whether king, convention, assembly, committee, president, or anything else it may choose. The will of the nation is the only thing essential to be regarded.

Wilson in 1913 introduced the perhaps rather schoolmasterish idea that it was wrong and even wicked to recognize a government that had seized power by unconstitutional means. 'We hold,' he wrote, 'that just government rests always upon the consent of the governed, and that there can be no freedom without order based upon law and upon public conscience and approval'; and being at that time faced with the immediate necessity of deciding whether to recognize the government of General

1. *An Encyclopaedia of Latin American History*, New York, Abelard-Schuman, 1956, p. 109.
2. Herring, pp. 761–2.

Huerta,[1] who had seized power by force in Mexico, he sent a message to all U.S. diplomatic missions stating that 'usurpations like that of General Huerta menace the peace and development of America as nothing else could. ... It is the purpose of the United States, therefore, to discredit and defeat such usurpations wherever they occur.'

In 1931 H. L. Stimson, then Secretary of State under President Hoover, rejected Wilson's contention that the recognition of a foreign government should be granted or withheld as a reward or a punishment:

The present Administration has refused to follow the policy of Mr Wilson and has followed [the policy of Jefferson]. As soon as it was reported to us, through our diplomatic representatives, that the new governments in Bolivia, Peru, Argentina, Brazil, and Panama were in control of the administrative machinery of the state, with the apparent acquiescence of their people, and that they were willing and apparently able to discharge their international and conventional obligations, they were recognized by our Government.

In 1962 President Kennedy, when confronted with military *coups d'état* in Argentina and Peru, adopted alternately the 'Jefferson-Stimson' policy and the 'Wilson' policy, and on each occasion he was criticized in the United States and in Latin America for having acted improperly.[2]

1. See p. 192.
2. cf. James Reston in the *New York Times*, 27 July 1962.

15

Social Reform and Revolution

THE TRADITIONAL SOCIAL STRUCTURE

MANY of those who inspired the movement for liberation from Spain hoped for something more than national independence: they envisaged reforms on democratic lines – the recognition that all men were equal before the law, that all were entitled to be represented in parliament by persons of their own choosing, that every child had a right to education. Throughout the nineteenth century liberal ideals continued to be held by enlightened minorities, but in general they met resistance that was almost – and often completely – overwhelming.

Until the second decade of the twentieth century there was little change in the social or political structure of any of the Latin American countries, the mass of the people continuing to regard government as not for them. (In many regions even now the majority, if they had the chance to express a choice, would prefer to support an effective dictatorship rather than to entrust their fate to party politicians.) Wealth and power generally remained in the hands of the landowning oligarchy and their military allies, with the addition of a new class, the leaders of business, whose interests sometimes conflicted with those of the landowning families but whose views on labour were usually just as conservative. In many of the republics the introduction of foreign capital and the coming of foreign immigrants had a profound effect on economic development; but the foreign investors and settlers naturally had a horror of any kind of social upheaval, and so their sympathies were with the local groups that resisted social change.

By the beginning of the present century 'reform' had begun to acquire a more radical meaning. Equality in law, free elections, and universal education would not be enough. There was a growing demand for the redistribution of land, and then for the fixing of minimum wages, and for social insurance. Reformers were becoming increasingly insistent, too, that the hold of the foreigner on the national economy must be broken. Indeed – as in other parts of the world during periods of social change – nationalist feelings frequently predominated.

As a matter of historical fact, xenophobic nationalism has been the most important motive force in the transition from traditional to modern societies – vastly more important than the profit motive. Men have been willing to uproot traditional societies primarily not to make more money, but because the traditional society failed, or threatened to fail, to protect them from humiliation by foreigners.[1]

In most of the republics, the carrying out of radical reforms could not be effected by parliamentary means, so the reformers had to resort to force (as they did in Mexico, and later in Bolivia and Cuba), or they allowed an ambitious *caudillo* to assume the championship of their cause (as in Argentina). Getúlio Vargas, who became the pioneer of Brazil's movement for reform, was placed in power by a *coup d'état*.

Many Latin American reformers have spent years in exile. The Peruvian socialist Haya de la Torre was such anathema to Peru's oligarchy and to the succession of dictators who represented their interests, that he was banished or had to seek refuge again and again. In 1924 (while in exile) Haya founded the Alianza Popular Revolucionaria Americana, known as A P R A, which has thought in terms of Indo-America rather than of Spanish or Latin America, thus evolving 'the most remarkable political philosophy that Latin America has produced'.[2] The *Apristas*, or members of A P R A, advocated the return of the land to the Indian communities, an economic programme that would lift the Indian farmers out of purely subsistence agriculture, a campaign to eliminate illiteracy among the Indians, and progressive labour legislation. The principal aim was to enable the Indians to become truly a part of the Peruvian nation. It is not surprising that this intention should have alarmed the oligarchy. In 1949 Haya, hounded by the police, sought asylum in the Colombian Embassy in Lima. He was unable to leave the Embassy until *five years*

1. W. W. Rostow in *The Economist*, 15 August 1959.
2. Humphreys, *Evolution*, p. 23.

later, when the Peruvian authorities granted him a safe conduct to go abroad.

In 1962, after having suffered persecution for three decades, Haya – who now declared himself to be anti-Communist and in favour of foreign investment and U.S. aid – was at last allowed to stand as a candidate for the presidency. He headed the poll, with a slight majority, but the military leaders annulled the results of the elections.

URUGUAY

In the nineteenth century Uruguay provided an example of how an enlightened minority could keep the liberal ideals alive in spite of *caudillos*, permanent political chaos, and civil war. Throughout the century Uruguay was one of the most turbulent of Latin American countries – so much so that in 1880 a military dictator, Latorre, resigned, declaring that the people were 'ungovernable'.

Then the Uruguayans surprisingly and rapidly diverged from the general norm of Latin American political behaviour: they discovered that they could maintain order in their country by democratic means.

Uruguay is a small and compact land (no mountains or jungles); her population are almost entirely of European descent (no Indians); there has never been such a great gap between the owners of sheep and cattle and the mass of the population as between rich and poor in other republics. Those were favourable circumstances, but they are not sufficient to explain how it was that by 1920 Uruguay had become Latin America's first 'welfare state'.

The way was prepared in the second half of the nineteenth century. In that period elections were of course manipulated by the ruling faction. Only one child in fifty attended school. Shocked by the state of affairs, a group of young enthusiasts discussed how to create a more civilized nation. Prominent among them was José Pedro Varela, who in 1867 visited the United States, where he met Horace Mann and became the disciple of Sarmiento (at that time Argentine Minister in Washington).

No sooner had he returned to Montevideo than Varela was demanding the introduction of universal free education. He argued that until primary education was properly organized, Uruguay could not evolve into an orderly democracy. Surprisingly, his ideas attracted the attention of the dictator Latorre, who in 1877 issued a decree whereby the whole Varela plan became law. The reforms had been opposed by doctors of the university, who had a vested interest in the old order, and, because of their liberal and secular character, by the Catholic Church. In the opinion of one well-known Uruguayan writer, the opposition was so powerful that Varela's proposals might never have been passed by a democratic Congress. Thus, on one occasion at least military dictatorship operated in the service of democracy. Varela remarked:

> Tyranny is not the creation of Latorre: it is the natural result of the country's social state. The surest way to fight dictatorship is by transforming intellectual and moral conditions, and this can only be done in the schools. And as the people will not entrust me with the direction of education, I must receive it from whomever will do so, no matter who he may be. I shall not destroy today's dictatorship, but I shall prevent dictatorships in the future.[1]

By 1900 the effects of the educational reforms had been felt only in the capital city, and over one half of the Uruguayan population were still illiterate. But Varela had helped to create conditions in which it would be possible for a socially advanced democracy to come into being.

Meanwhile another young reformer was rising to a position of even greater influence. This was José Batlle y Ordóñez, a burly, thoughtful, and extremely energetic political journalist. In 1886 Batlle had founded his own newspaper, *El Día*, in whose columns he diagnosed his country's ills and proposed remedies for them. He became the leader of the principal political party, the Colorados, and was twice elected president of the republic.

Early in his first period in the presidency (1903–7) Batlle crushed a revolution by force of arms. The victory was decisive: thereafter his ascendancy was undisputed and he could follow

1. Alberto Zum Felde, *Proceso intelectual del Uruguay*, Montevideo, Editorial Claridad, 1941, pp. 134–6.

the course that he had mapped out for the nation. On the expiry of his first term of office he made an unprecedented announcement, which was in keeping with his principles: he declared that he would observe the habitually ignored clause of the Constitution which prohibited a president from succeeding himself. Batlle then sailed for Europe, where he remained for the next four years studying the Swiss and other methods of government. When he returned to Uruguay, to become president for the second time (1911–15), the ideas which he had developed experimentally in *El Día* were mature. He now demanded the establishment by law of an eight-hour working day, old-age pensions, and other welfare measures. He introduced legislation to permit divorce at the will of the wife and to abolish capital punishment and bullfighting. He advocated that the public services and basic industries should be state-owned. Batlle's many innovations outraged the conservatives, some of whom went so far as to declare that he was insane; but no one ever suggested that his policy was dictated by any motive other than sincere conviction.

Batlle's measures would not have been practical if he had not at the same time changed the whole climate of government. He believed that the disorders of the nineteenth century were largely due to corrupt elections and excessive presidential power. By persuading the Colorado Party that they must make themselves worthy of popular support, he secured reasonably honest elections, thereby removing one of the main causes of revolution. Next he proposed that the office of president should be abolished and that executive power should be vested instead in a national council, on the Swiss model. He was unable to have this project fully carried out before his death in 1929. But Batlle's influence did not cease on his death. In 1951 a Constitution was drawn up on the lines that he had suggested. The new Constitution, which came into force in 1952, replaced the presidency by a National Council of Government of nine members, six of whom were to come from the political group that received the greatest number of votes at the elections, and the other three from the second largest party. Members of the majority party were to take it in turns to occupy the presidency of the Council. The Council were to nominate the Cabinet. The same two-party system was to be observed, moreover, in provincial government and in the administration of the State-owned financial institutions, public services, and industries. (State-owned enterprises included the principal banks, insurance, railways, electricity and telephones, the refining of petroleum, the manufacture of alcohol and cement, meatpacking, and the processing of fish.)

The new Constitution protected the nation from the abuse of power by an individual ruler. It is true that government by committee was not always notable for efficiency, but it was undeniably democratic.

So Uruguay became rather an exception among Latin American republics. A diplomat from the Spain of General Franco expressed disgust that the Uruguayans had no compulsory military service; that they had only a tiny professional army, and no respect whatever for their army officers; that they had long ago given up the manly sport of bullfighting; and that Catholic teaching was not provided in the schools.[1]

MEXICO

During the years when Uruguay was being peacefully reformed by Batlle y Ordóñez, Mexico experienced violent revolution. In Mexico the gap between rich and poor was very great – more than three quarters of the people lived off the land, yet ninety-five per cent of these were landless and in a state of virtual serfdom.

Far back in 1810 Father Hidalgo had roused the Mexican Indian peasants, urging them to regain the land that had been taken from them,[2] and in the 1850s Benito Juárez had tried to carry out a more equitable distribution of land by legal means.[3] Both attempts failed, but the ideas did not die.

Paradoxically, Francisco Madero, who unintentionally set the spark to Mexico's great conflagration, was a member of a wealthy landowning family. He was an intellectual, a nervous, black-bearded, sallow little man – the face of a 'Messiah', it was said – a

1. Ernesto la Orden, *Uruguay: el Benjamín de España*, Madrid, 1949.
2. See pp. 93–4.   3. See pp. 132–3.

vegetarian and a spiritualist.[1] His eloquent and vigorous campaign to prevent the 're-election' of Porfírio Díaz[2] in 1910 stimulated political agitation in the capital, but the peasants of the interior also were incited to take up arms, and when Díaz was deposed and Madero took the oath as president in his stead, the peasant revolt continued. Madero, the political theorist, did not understand the people's hunger for land – and for food – and he was too weak and vacillating to be able to control the wild forces that had been let loose.

Soon Zapata, the most powerful peasant leader, was denouncing Madero as 'inept, a traitor, and a tyrant', and from his rural headquarters he issued a manifesto which gave the revolution its true direction. Zapata declared, first, that villages or citizens deprived of lands to which they held titles should at once reoccupy those lands and defend them to the utmost with arms; and, second, that one third part of every great estate should be expropriated, with indemnity, to provide lands for the villages and citizens of Mexico. Virtually the whole rural population was now up in arms, and General Huerta, as head of the central government (Madero had been deposed and murdered), launched a war of extermination against them.

Civil war raged, with only brief interruption, for many years. Armies roamed across the country. In this turmoil some 250,000 people perished; villages were destroyed and cities ruined; factories and farms went up in flames. It is as unnecessary to describe as it would be wearisome to read of the rivalries of the *caudillos*, the betrayals, and the brutalities.

Gradually a so-called 'Constitutionalist' movement developed and gained in strength and, during a period of relative calm (1916–17), a new Constitution was drawn up. This Constitution of 1917 contained three notable clauses. Article 27, which dealt with property, announced that the ownership of lands and waters was vested in the nation, which had the right to transmit title thereto to private persons; the nation had at all times the right

1. Kirkpatrick, *Latin America*, p. 345. For portraits of Madero and other Mexican leaders see Diego Rivera's mural 'Sueño de una tarde dominical en el Alameda Central'.

2. See pp. 162–4.

to impose upon private property such restrictions as the public interest might require for the conservation and equitable distribution of the public wealth; the direct ownership of all minerals in the subsoil, solid mineral fuels, petroleum, etc. was vested inalienably in the nation. Article 123 was an advanced labour code similar to that which Batlle y Ordóñez had been introducing in Uruguay. Article 130 excluded the Church from any share in public education, made marriage a civil contract, and limited the activities of priests.

The ruling autocracy paid little attention to the constitution. Nevertheless, while generals and provincial *caudillos* enriched themselves and ruthlessly repressed all attempts at opposition, the aims of the Revolution (which must henceforth be spelt with a capital 'R') were not forgotten. President Alvaro Obregón (1920–4) ruled as dictatorially as Porfírio Díaz, and believed that the breaking up of the big *haciendas* would mean economic ruin for Mexico, but during his presidency some progress was made with the distribution of land to the villages. (The results were frequently disappointing, because the peasants would lack seeds, implements, credit facilities, and scientific training; village politicians on the committees which were elected to supervise the communal cultivation of the land on the old *ejido* system[1] would often become village tyrants, living at their ease while their neighbours worked for them; and the peasants would be virtually the serfs of those who provided them with loans, or they would drift back to work on the *haciendas*.[2]) Obregón encouraged protection of labour by trade union means; and he appointed as his Minister of Education one of Latin America's outstanding intellectual figures, José Vasconcelos. Not only did Vasconcelos establish hundreds of schools in rural villages, he broadened the scope of education by adding the arts and vocational training to the curriculum, and he engaged a group of young artists to paint upon the walls of public buildings their interpretations of Mexican history. By reviving mural painting – which had been one of the chief art forms in Aztec times – Vasconcelos gave to

1. See p. 132.
2. Henry Bamford Parkes, *A History of Mexico*, London, Eyre & Spottiswoode, third edition, 1962, p. 318.

young men such as Diego Rivera, José Clemento Orozco, and David Alfaro Siqueiros their great opportunity. They attained world-wide fame.

Like so much else that has happened in Mexico in recent decades, the revival of mural art was a part of the continuing Revolution. Jean Charlot explained in Mexican terms how it occurred.

The Revolution was a cog, the piece of machinery needed to bring together ancient walls and young muralists. As it happened, ca. 1920, the upper dog *politicos* were desirous to ram down the throats of the bourgeois the consciousness of defeat and a squirming sense of their social predicament. Bohemians in their 20s, at most their 30s, were given public walls to paint as other men had been given palaces to sack.

The frescoes – depicting the Mexican people's struggle for liberty, their constant desire to regain the land that had been taken from them by the Spanish *conquistadores*, the Church, local *caudillos*, and Porfírio Díaz's foreign backers – were roundly condemned by the conservative classes, but eventually, as their merit was acknowledged abroad, they became a source of national pride.

Under Obregón's immediate successor, President Plutarco Elías Calles (1924–8) the Revolution was carried a stage farther. As a step towards fulfilling the constitutional Article 27, which vested all the country's mineral resources in the State, a law was passed in 1925 ordering the owners of oilfields – which meant the U.S. and British oil companies – to exchange their titles for fifty-year leases. Calles continued the agrarian reform programme, and although much of the expropriated land went to his friends, many peasants did find themselves owning their plots of maize. In consequence of his determination to enforce Article 130 of the Constitution, which denied the Catholic Church the right to take part in public education and instructed priests to register with the civil authorities, a violent conflict developed between the Government and the *Cristeros* (the followers of *Cristo Rey*, Christ the King); Calles closed the clerical primary schools; and in 1926 the priests went on strike, so that for the first time since the arrival of the Spaniards in 1519 no public Mass was celebrated in all Mexico, though the churches remained open.[1] *Cristeros* burned government schools, and there were three years of banditry and murderous retaliation before a compromise was reached and the priests returned to their churches. The three-year strike by the priests had been a failure.

The Indian peasantry were devoutly religious, but their religion was still – after four hundred years – more pagan than Christian. ... As long as the churches remained open, as long as the Indians could burn candles and celebrate dances and *fiestas* in honour of their local saints, they could dispense with the services of the priests.[2]

The Church could not approve of the Revolution, which was undermining its authority, while from the point of view of the Revolution, the Church was still identified with the Spanish conquest and all that the colonial system represented. In the event, however, both the Church and the Revolution proved to be realistic and flexible, and a war to the death was avoided. The Revolution was powerful, but so was the Church. When the clergy were on strike, Calles's wife was one of many women who admitted a priest to her home secretly to celebrate the Mass.

During the presidency of Calles the Revolution became an institution. In 1929 Calles formed an official party – the Partido Nacional Revolucionario (PNR) – to bind together the numerous regional political organizations and bosses, so that a small, central group might arrange the presidential succession and write the laws for the approval of Congress.[3] Reform now progressed more slowly, for the old revolutionaries were the new conservatives.

In both his strength and his weaknesses Calles was typical of the Mexican revolutionary movement. He had once been a teacher in a primary school, but he could scarcely be classified as an educated person; he was a military chieftain rather than an intellectual. He called himself a socialist; but this did not prevent him from becoming himself a wealthy landowner or from allowing his colleagues to develop into capitalists. ... Calles [was an] example of the ease with which the

1. Herring, p. 369.   2. Parkes, p. 327.
3. Lewis Hanke, *Mexico and the Caribbean*, New York, Van Nostrand, 1959, p. 76.

crude and confused idealism of the Mexican Revolution could be transmuted into conscious self-seeking. [1]

By 1934 it seemed that reform had almost come to a halt – yet it was in that year that the Revolution entered on its most vigorously constructive phase.

In 1934 Calles, to pacify the left wing of the PNR, chose as his successor in the presidency General Lázaro Cárdenas, a Zapotec Indian who had joined the revolutionary ranks at the age of sixteen, had taken part in the Revolution in all its stages, and had always remained in close contact with the humble people throughout the country. Cárdenas proved to be the outstanding figure of the Revolution, whose ideals he worked seriously and disinterestedly to fulfil: unlike so many other revolutionary leaders he lived simply, almost puritanically, showed no desire to enrich himself, and did not indulge in oratory. The strongest support for his régime came from labour: when there was a wave of strikes in 1935, he expressed sympathy with them; he gave encouragement to the Confederation of Labour, whose secretary was Lombardo Toledano, a Marxist (but Cárdenas himself disapproved of the Soviet system of government); in 1937 he nationalized the railways, which were largely foreign-owned; in that same year, following a sharp rise in the cost of living in the oil regions, he ordered U.S. and British oil companies to pay substantial wage increases and to train Mexican employees for promotion to responsible managerial posts: in 1938 as the companies refused to comply with all of his terms, he expelled them from Mexico and seized their properties (compensation was eventually agreed). By 1940 Cárdenas had distributed forty-five million acres of land (more than twice as much as the amount distributed by all previous governments combined) among three quarters of a million peasant families located in nearly twelve thousand villages, and he had experimented with a new type of *ejido*. Hitherto politicians had usually looked upon the *ejido* as a device for calming the land hunger of militant peasants; under Cárdenas, however, agrarian reform included not merely the distribution of plots of ground upon which peasants could grow enough maize for their own needs, but also the organization of large cooperative

1. Parkes, p. 324.

farms for the production of commercial crops such as cotton and henequén on a profit-sharing basis; seeds and machinery were supplied to the cooperatives, and loans were made by a new National Bank of Ejido Credit. Even most of those who disapproved of Cárdenas's policies respected him for his sincerity and integrity, his genuine devotion to the people's welfare, and his extraordinary energy.[1]

Cárdenas was followed in the presidency by men of less radical tendencies, but they all came from within the official party. Greater attention was now given to industrial development than to social reform, and during the Second World War the United States helped Mexico (the Mexican government declared war on the Axis in 1942) to modernize and enlarge her industries and public services and to improve her agriculture. Thus Mexico attained a degree of stability in strong contrast with her violent past and rare among Latin American nations.

Mexico continues to be a one-party state, but her people enjoy the civil liberties; 'only the right to successful revolution [with a small 'r'] is limited'.[2] Since 1934 the official Party has embraced almost all shades of political opinion. Other political organizations are tolerated, but they do not present a serious challenge. When a president nears the end of his term of office, he consults prominent members of the Partido de la Revolución Institucional (as the party is now named), and then nominates his successor. The party's monolithic character has enabled Mexico to make a remarkable advance towards the solution of the basic Latin American problem of establishing a 'state idea' sufficiently powerful to command the support of the great majority of the people.[3]

BRAZIL

Until the outbreak of the Mexican revolution in 1910, 'revolution' in Latin America meant little more than the substitution of the 'outs' for the 'ins' in government: the life of the mass of the

1. Parkes, pp. 340–8.
2. H. F. Cline, *The United States and Mexico*, Harvard University Press, 1953, p. 198.   3. Preston James, p. 654.

population was not greatly affected. Since 1910, however, revolutionary movements have often had a profound social significance. The acquisition of power by Vargas in Brazil in 1930 and by Perón in Argentina in 1945–6 accelerated the rise of social and political forces, hitherto submerged, which could never again be ignored. The revolution which brought Paz Estenssoro to power in Bolivia in 1952 and the victory of Fidel Castro over Batista in Cuba in 1958–9 introduced régimes which altered the whole social and economic structure of these two countries.

Caudillos of the new type have relied on the backing, not of landowners, nor of the foreign investors (as did Porfírio Díaz, Juan Vicente Gómez, and Batista), but of the workers – particularly the rapidly expanding class of urban industrial workers in Argentina and Brazil, the miners in Bolivia, and the rural labourers in Cuba. In addition, the new *caudillos*, like their predecessors, have needed the support of a powerful section of the nation's armed forces, or they have been backed by a working-class militia, as in Bolivia and Cuba; but force now serves political theory, nationalism, socialism, as well as personalities.

After Mexico, Brazil – in her more gentle fashion – set an example in the adaptation of *caudillismo* to twentieth-century circumstances. In 1930 – a critical year in which Latin America felt the effects of the world-wide depression and Brazil was encumbered with a vast unsold stock of coffee – a body of army officers and disaffected politicians moved upon Rio de Janeiro and placed Getúlio Vargas, governor of the southern state of Rio Grande do Sul, in the presidential palace. For fifteen years Vargas ruled Brazil as a benevolent dictator.

Vargas (b. 1883) was a competent, amiable little man. Rio Grande do Sul is Brazil's pastoral *gaucho* state, and Vargas had something of the *gaucho* in his character. But Gilberto Freyre wrote that the people of the south – being in part the descendants of Indians who had been educated by Spanish Jesuits – were not typical *gauchos*, in the Río de la Plata meaning of the term.

The men of Rio Grande do Sul are instinctive, fatalistic, proud, dramatic, almost tragic in their reactions to crises. Getúlio Vargas seems to be a sort of Dr Jekyll and Mr Hyde in that he has something of the Jesuit but something also of the Indian. He is avid for power and domination, but he has also stood for the common people and for revolt against sterile conventions and powerful plutocratic groups. Characteristically he gave his first child the name of Luther; and the first thing he ever wrote as a young man was an article in defence of Zola.[1]

In 1942 a U.S. journalist described Vargas as 'able, friendly, slippery ... He seldom disagrees with anyone. He may delay or equivocate, but he almost never says an outright No. He has very few enemies, and he seldom bears grudges. No dictator is so little vengeful.'[2]

The Vargas dictatorship was a period of exuberance and progress. In 1943 an enlightened labour code was enacted which largely prevented the ruthless exploitation of workers in the urban industries. The government initiated many public works, which were of lasting benefit. They encouraged the expansion of Brazil's important steel industry at Volta Redonda and, with the help of U.S. loans, kept steel production in Brazilian hands. During the Second World War (Brazil declared war on the Axis in 1942) many other industries – notably the manufacture of textiles, paper, and chemicals – expanded enormously.

It was during this period, too, that Brazil's modern architectural movement began. The starting-point was in 1936, when the French architect Le Corbusier, at the invitation of Vargas's Minister of Education, travelled (by Zeppelin) to Rio de Janeiro to give advice on the layout of a university city and on the design for new headquarters for the Ministry of Education. It was a momentous visit, for its influence is apparent today in the clean, light, colourful modern buildings of all Brazil's cities – and, indeed, of most of the chief cities of Latin America.

This was just the right moment for the birth of an imaginative architecture. Brazil was developing economically, and the Brazilians were aware more than ever before of their country's potentialities. Also Brazil is a prolific land, where the climate

1. Gilberto Freyre, *Brazil: An Interpretation*, New York, Knopf, 1951, p. 87.

2. John Gunther, *Inside Latin America*, London, Hamish Hamilton, 1942, pp. 281, 291.

favours the good life and requires the minimum of technological assistance.

Le Corbusier worked in Brazil for several weeks with the leading Brazilian architect, Lúcio Costa, and a small group of younger men – among them Oscar Niemeyer. Under Niemeyer's direction the Ministry of Education building was finished in 1943. Still the most distinguished building in the centre of Rio de Janeiro, it incorporates several of Le Corbusier's favourite devices, such as *brise-soleil* (louvred screens to protect the windows from the glare of the sun) and *pilotis* (pillars on which the whole building is raised off the ground). These devices, or variations of them, have now been used widely in Brazil. Sun glare is one of the main difficulties which every Brazilian architect has to contend with, and *pilotis* have also served a practical local purpose, because in Rio de Janeiro the by-laws governing the height of buildings have permitted an extra floor to be added if the ground floor is left open. The high cost of building sites encouraged developers to take advantage of this regulation.[1] Le Corbusier reminded the Brazilians of the existence and modern possibilities of the *azulejo* – the Portuguese blue ceramic tile which at that time was identified only with old colonial buildings. 'The two decades that followed Le Corbusier's visit were imbued with the most ardent architectural optimism, a kind of creative lust which permeated Brazil's architects, clients, public administrators, and the man in the street.'[2] Brasília – Brazil's modern capital city, inaugurated in 1960 – is the movement's most spectacular product.

Under Vargas there was a substantial improvement in education – achieved as a result of strengthening federal authority at the expense of the provincial states – and in the medical services.

Brazilians, however, are attached to the forms of constitutionalism, and Vargas's dictatorial methods offended their dignity. By 1945 discontent had grown so strong that the army compelled him to resign, and he retired quietly to his cattle ranch in Rio Grande do Sul.

Nevertheless Vargas remained popular with the masses, and in

1. *The Times* Supplement on Latin America, 8 June 1959.
2. Stamo Papadaki, *Oscar Niemeyer*, London, Mayflower, 1960, p. 11.

1950 he returned to the presidency by free election. This second period in power was an anti-climax. Vargas's vigour and ability were in decline; his entourage were incompetent and corrupt; and in 1954, discouraged, he committed suicide.

Social change was not a major issue in Brazil during the 1950s. The Brazilians' 'El Dorado spirit', however, was unquenched. President Kubitschek (1956–61) went ahead vigorously with a plan (it was far from being an original plan, but his predecessors had always let it lie dormant) for transferring the national capital from the overcrowded coast of Rio de Janeiro to a more central, higher, and more healthy position, the ultimate object being to attract younger generations towards the development of the republic's almost unpopulated interior regions. The new capital, Brasília, was inaugurated before the end of Kubitschek's term of office. The government's lavish expenditure on this and other projects aggravated the already chronic inflation; but although people complained of the ever-rising cost of living, many, with typical optimism, were persuaded that continued inflation could be a means of financing economic expansion, rather than a cause of eventual bankruptcy. When in 1959 Kubitschek applied for a large loan from the United States, and was told by the U.S. authorities that he must first give an assurance that he would put into operation the austerity programme normally prescribed by the International Monetary Fund for such cases, he replied indignantly that those conditions were an insult to Brazil's pride and amounted to interference in the nation's internal affairs. The Brazilian ambassador to Great Britain endeavoured to explain his countrymen's temperament: 'We are extroverts, impetuous, tropical. We like to march towards the unknown without considering latitudes.'

After the end of Kubitschek's presidency the military hierarchy resisted the revival of social revolutionary movements.

ARGENTINA

In Argentina, as elsewhere, new classes arose and began to demand a share in government. Classes, and class interests, overlapped. Sons of *estancieros* settled in town as businessmen, or as members of the professions, and sometimes became enthusiasts for liberal reform.

By the end of the nineteenth century it was evident that the urban middle class could not be permanently denied participation in the management of the republic, but the financial crash of 1890[1] did not lead to any immediate change. Young men of the middle class agitated for honest elections and founded an opposition party, the Radical Party, but the conservatives remained in power.

It became fashionable in Argentine nationalist circles in the early decades of the present century to argue that the rule of the conservative oligarchy was contrary to the nation's real interests. That criticism was unjust: the majority of landowners doubtless were lacking in public spirit; but the rapidity of Argentina's economic development during the second half of the nineteenth century proves that their rule cannot have been wholly incompetent, or their own financial interests entirely at variance with those of the nation. Faced by a seemingly endless influx of immigrants of diverse nationalities and a locally born population which for the most part was illiterate and which, anyway, was quite inexperienced in public affairs, the oligarchs, whatever their defects, performed a useful function. And the patriarchal community of the *estancia* was humane. Most people were poor so that the few might be rich; but the poor had all that they needed for their simple lives, and bore no resentment against their masters, who, when they visited their estates, showed a fatherly pride in the *peones*' loyalty and equestrian skill.

It was in fact a member of the oligarchy, Roque Sáenz Peña, who in 1912 pushed through Congress electoral reforms which, four years later, enabled the Argentines for the first time to choose their own government.

In 1916 the first Radical president, Hipólito Irigoyen, was elected. He received the votes of the middle class and also of the poorer people, who regarded him as their champion, a saintly figure. By present-day standards, Irigoyen's attempts at social

1. See pp. 143–4.

reform were timid; but during his presidency proposals for legislation on minimum wages, maximum working hours, and so on were sent to Congress, and they were a novelty in a country whose rulers until then had given no thought to such matters. Irigoyen was muddle-headed, and as autocratic as any other *caudillo*. He repeatedly 'intervened' in the provinces; he showed no respect for Congress; and the crowd of hangers-on whom he appointed to administrative posts were allowed to indulge in an orgy of corruption. In 1930 Irigoyen (then in his second term as president) was seen to be quite incapable of dealing with the problems arising from the world-wide economic depression. There was no serious opposition to the military *coup d'état* which, in September 1930, put the conservatives back in office.

Not only had the Radicals wasted their opportunity, they had shown that, in spite of their name, they had little desire to carry out radical reforms. In reality, the interests of the commercial class who formed the backbone of the Radical Party were not so different from those of the conservatives as had been generally supposed.

The urban workers were now ready for more forceful leadership.

Principally it was national pride that drove a group of military officers to overthrow the conservative régime in 1943. If Argentina was to become the Colossus of the South, as the officers intended, she would have to modernize her government. By 1943 more workers were employed in industry than in cattle-raising and agriculture. The landed aristocracy's monopoly of power was out of date.

One officer, Colonel Juan D. Perón – who had experience of Mussolini's Italy, where he served as military attaché – realized more clearly than anyone else that a new type of *caudillo* was now required. He must be the *caudillo* of the trade unions, of industrialization, nationalization, and Five-Year Economic Plans. To obtain the votes of the neglected masses, the new *caudillo* would really have to improve their living conditions. (In the military régime of 1943 Perón chose for himself the post of head of the then unimportant Secretariat of Labour, a job which no one else wanted.) Also, of course, even the newest *caudillo* would still need to be a man endowed with the traditional *caudillo* qualities: masculine charm, dash, and eloquence (all of which Perón abundantly possessed). Perón was up to date even in his public-relations technique. Friendly with a glamorous radio actress, Eva Duarte, he appreciated the enormous prestige enjoyed by entertainment stars and sporting aces. He bestowed his patronage on Argentine boxers, racing motorists, swimmers, and footballers, thereby sharing, in some measure, the acclaim that they received.

Under Perón's direction at the Secretariat of Labour, many long-overdue reforms were effected. Perón encouraged the development of trade unions in the meat-packing plants and other industries where the employers had not allowed them. He contrived that his Secretariat should supervise collective bargaining between workers and employers; that the bargaining should usually result in substantial concessions to the workers; and that the new wage agreements should be given the widest possible publicity, as evidence of his success in defending working-class interests. He also kept a close hold on the trade union movement by ruling that collective contracts would only be recognized as valid if the unions signing them had been officially approved by the Secretariat. During this preparatory period in his rise to power, Perón secured the appropriation of a large sum for the construction of working-class flats. Compulsory holidays with pay were decreed for all wage-earners. It was not surprising, therefore, that when in 1945, jealous of Perón's growing political influence, a military clique arrested him, the trade union leaders – feverishly assisted by Eva Duarte – organized mass demonstrations to demand that he be set free. Men in shirt-sleeves – henceforth to be known as *descamisados* – poured into Buenos Aires from the working-class suburbs. On the famous day of 17 October these *descamisados* were virtually in control of the capital. To appease them, Perón was released. A few days later he and Eva Duarte were married.

After the triumph of 17 October, Perón placed his friends in key positions in the government but did not himself take office: instead, he devoted his energies to preparing for the elections which were to be held in February 1946. His supporters formed a new party, the Partido Laborista, which nominated him as its candidate for the presidency. The party pledged itself to work for the nationalization of the public services (notably the railways), the building of hospitals and homes for the workers, the aged, and the infirm, and the defence of the social gains made while Perón was Secretary of Labour. The hierarchy of the Catholic Church supported Perón. Because he had sympathized with the Germans and Italians during the Second World War, the United States government did their utmost to discredit him. The elections took place under the supervision of the army, and were, by common consent, the cleanest that had ever been held in Argentina. Perón won the presidency for himself, almost two thirds of the seats in the Chamber of Deputies, and all but two of the seats in the Senate. With the rank of brigadier-general, he was inaugurated president of the republic.

The rule of Perón and 'Evita' in the space of a few years brought Argentina right out of the era of the *estanciero* and of upper-class charity for the poor, into the era of urban industry and 'social security'. But while they badgered the landowning oligarchy politically and financially, the Peróns never attempted to nationalize the great estates: they knew that the disruption of the social pattern in the rural areas would have disastrous effects on production.

When Evita died in 1952, still a young woman, the Perón régime had already served its purpose. The Peróns had broken the landowners' monopoly of power, without ruining that class (indeed, the value of land was always rising). For the mass of the population, Peronism had 'lifted the horizon of expectation'.

After Evita's death the régime disintegrated, and its excesses multiplied. The rising cost of living caused widespread discontent. Perón's high-handed methods had always infuriated the upper classes, and they increasingly gave offence to the Church. Corruption in government circles and in the state-owned industries and agencies now exceeded anything that Argentina had endured even under Rosas or Irigoyen. Nationalist-minded military officers were indignant when Perón, with the purpose of reducing the huge cost of importing petroleum, decided to grant concessions in the Patagonian oilfields to a United States company. The situation became more and more troubled, until in September 1955 it was rumoured that Perón intended to distribute arms to the trade unions, with instructions to suppress his enemies. Thereupon the officers commanding the chief provincial garrisons led their troops against Buenos Aires, while the navy, joining the rebellion, blockaded the Plata estuary. Perón sought refuge on a Paraguayan gunboat which was in Buenos Aires harbour. In accordance with Latin American practice, he was granted political asylum, and a fortnight later he was allowed to travel into exile.[1]

So the military right wing were again in charge of the country, and as usual they were confident that they alone knew what was good for the people. They dismissed all Peronistas from the senior ranks of the armed forces, from the federal and provincial administrations, and from the judiciary and the universities; military *interventores* were placed in charge of the trade unions; and when presidential and congressional elections were at last held in 1958, the Peronistas (who comprised at least one third of the electorate) were not allowed to nominate their own candidates.

At the 1958 elections a Radical politician, Arturo Frondizi, won the presidency, with the help of Peronista votes. Frondizi declared that he would govern, not for one party, but for the nation as a whole, and it was evident that he intended to bring the Peronistas back into the community. Soon after assuming office he ordered a general increase in wages, granted an amnesty to all those who were in prison or exile for political offences, and enabled Peronistas to re-enter the public service. The military leaders protested against these concessions, and during the next three years they repeatedly compelled Frondizi to remove from official posts persons of whom they disapproved. At elections for partly renewing Congress and for the provincial governorships in March 1962, Frondizi permitted the Peronistas to vote for their own candidates, and their success at the polls was so overwhelming that the military deposed Frondizi, imprisoned him,

1. For a more detailed account of the Perón régime see George Pendle, *Argentina*.

and annulled the electoral results. The generals and admirals had no clear policy for the nation. Their one aim was to keep the Peronista workers out of politics, to drive them back to where they properly belonged – to the meat-packing plants, the textile factories, etc., whence Perón had so irresponsibly brought them forth.

BOLIVIA

Visitors to the high plateau of Bolivia – the Altiplano – are apt to feel oppressed by the mournfulness of the scenery. Bolivia's history, likewise, has been sad, and the prospects for the mass of the people (of whom sixty per cent are Indians) have often seemed almost hopeless.

In the War of the Pacific (1879–83) Bolivia was deprived of her sea-coast to the west, so becoming a landlocked nation.[1] Her military officers and politicians, frustrated and embittered, then turned their attention eastwards, to the Chaco and the Río Paraguay, envisaging an outlet to the Atlantic. Ambitions in that direction were bound to lead to a clash with the republic of Paraguay, which blocked the way. Paraguay, too, had suffered a military catastrophe in the second half of the nineteenth century.[2] So both countries were recuperating simultaneously; they were both building up new armies which would welcome an opportunity to wipe out the memory of defeat; both considered that they had a historical right to the possession of the Chaco; and both supposed that that desolate region of floods and droughts contained rich deposits of oil.

The Chaco War began in 1932. The Bolivians were confident of rapid victory. They greatly outnumbered the Paraguayans; their army had been trained by a German general; and they had used generous loans from U.S. banks to import military equipment left over from the First World War. The Paraguayans, however, are a warrior race; they had the interior lines and were nearer their base; and they were better acquainted than the Bolivians with the terrain. The Bolivian army consisted mostly of Indians, devoid of patriotism, who had been brought down from

1. See pp. 146–7.
2. The War of the Triple Alliance (1865–70); see p. 153.

the bleak Andean altitudes to fight in the unaccustomed heat of the lowland plain. Casualties in the fighting and from disease were heavy on both sides; but the Paraguayan commander, Colonel Estigarribia, outwitted the enemy by sending his men in small groups or singly behind their lines to cut communications and seize supplies. The Paraguayans steadily advanced. To invade the highlands of Bolivia, however, was beyond their power. So an armistice was agreed to in 1935, and by the subsequent peace treaty Paraguay gained possession of most of the disputed territory.

The strain of the Chaco War had been severe on Bolivia, and political instability and violence followed. The white minority – who were mainly of Spanish descent and were traditionally the employers and the rulers – had always dreaded an Indian rebellion, and in the years after the return of the conscripts from the Chaco conditions seemed to favour a rising of that kind. But, like social revolutions in other countries, the Bolivian revolution which eventually occurred in 1952 did not originate among the masses. It was planned by intellectuals, the chief planner being Víctor Paz Estenssoro, a lawyer and professor of economics, leader of the political party Movimiento Nacional Revolucionario (MNR). Paz's programme was comprehensive. He demanded the granting of the right to vote to illiterates – i.e. the majority of adult Indians. He proposed to nationalize the tin mines, which provided vast wealth to absentee 'tin barons' while the Indian miners lived in degrading poverty. He prepared plans for land reform, the improvement of agricultural methods (about seventy-five per cent of Bolivia's food was imported), the building of roads to open up new areas of the country (notably a road connecting the Altiplano, where most of the people live, with the fertile eastern valleys of Santa Cruz), the diversification of the economy (to reduce the country's excessive dependence on tin), and so on.[1] Such far-reaching proposals naturally frightened the conservative politicians, whose interest was to serve the 'tin barons' and the landowners. Small wonder that when the MNR,

1. cf. Robert J. Alexander, *The Bolivian National Revolution*, Rutgers University Press, 1958.

with the help of more extreme left-wing groups, won the elections in 1951, the conservatives and military prevented them from taking office.

At the time of the elections Paz Estenssoro was in voluntary exile in Buenos Aires (where he found himself in general agreement with the policies of Perón). Although Paz continued to be the brains of the MNR, the revolution now reached the stage where it was the mine-workers who would enable it to become a reality. The mine-workers had arms, and they were led by a forceful man, Juan Lechín. Son of a Syrian father and a Bolivian mother, Lechín was of more than usual height and weight for a Bolivian and was a champion football player. (It is said that he was originally hired by the Patiño tin-mining company so that he could be a member of their football team).[1] In May 1952 the MNR and the mine-workers struck against the ruling military junta. After fierce fighting, the government were defeated. Lechín's mine-workers had proved themselves to be the most powerful force in the country. Paz was now summoned from Buenos Aires to assume the presidency, and he began at once to put into practice his very extensive plans for social reform. Universal suffrage without qualifications of literacy or income was decreed. The tin mines belonging to the three great absentee concerns – Patiño, Hochschild, and Aramayo – were expropriated and nationalized. Agrarian reform laws were promulgated.

Bolivia could not afford the expense of these and other reforms, and she lacked trained technicians to take over the management of the mines. The world price of tin (the nation's main source of income) was in decline, and the best veins of ore had been exhausted. It seemed unlikely that the granting of land to the Indian peasants would stimulate agricultural production. Paz Estenssoro was well aware of such problems, but he knew that the revolution had to be pushed through in its entirety at once, or it would be whittled away. Strangely, it was aid from the United States that enabled him to carry on.

At this point we can appropriately consider the character of

1. ibid., p. 35.

the Indians whom the reformers in Bolivia, Peru, and other Andean countries have been endeavouring to 'integrate' into modern society.

The majority of Andean Indians are still outside the monetary economy. They have been accustomed for generations to an extremely low standard of living and cannot easily be persuaded to grow more food than is necessary for themselves. They have little or no ambition to better their material existence.

When Indians acquire a monetary surplus – as for example from coca growing [in Bolivia's semi-tropical eastern valleys] – they squander it upon their *fiestas*. They are fanatically traditional and highly resistant to culturization – which in the past has always meant for them exploitation. . . . [Generally the Indian desires to] perpetuate the pattern of life which he has lived for generations, to be free from interference and taxation. . . . The advantages of a planned economy supporting an enlightened modern state have no appeal for him and he feels no inducement to produce agricultural surpluses in order to sustain the life of the towns and obtain for himself the conveniences and amenities of factory-produced consumer goods.[1]

For the Indian, agrarian reform is essentially *conservative*. It is a means of preserving, or of reviving, the remnants of an old way of life which the Spaniards almost destroyed and which modern capitalists have treated with equal lack of respect.

But of course the arming of a Bolivian mine-workers' militia and the granting of universal suffrage were two very *un*conservative measures. No one could be sure what the consequences would be.

When Paz Estenssoro returned to Bolivia in 1952 to become President, U.S. diplomats were already aware that he was an earnest and an able man, and before the end of 1953 they had persuaded Washington that if Paz's social revolution failed through lack of financial resources – as at that time appeared very likely – it would be followed by chaos and communism. So –

1. Harold Osborne, *Bolivia: a Land Divided*, R.I.I.A., 1954, pp. 95–7. Osborne remarked in 1954 that the only two products of industrial civilization which had penetrated to any extent to the Indian communities were sewing machines and tin chamber-pots (p. 96).

to the astonishment of the M N R and others, including the North Americans themselves – the U.S. government launched an extensive programme of economic aid which enabled Paz to feed the people of Bolivia's towns and made it possible for him to go ahead with his development projects, education, health services, etc. This was the first occasion on which the U.S. Government showed willingness to cooperate with a progressive Latin American régime even though some of its prominent members were Marxists who denounced 'Yanqui imperialism' and although some of its actions – such as the expropriation of foreign-owned mines – were contrary to U.S. principles.

Various theories have been propounded to explain how the United States came to adopt this unexpected attitude. One U.S. writer suggested that the Bolivian geography may have been partly responsible.

The 12,000-foot altitude of La Paz, the capital, has not made the U.S. Embassy in Bolivia a particularly delectable plum for amateurs in search of a diplomatic post. As a result, the conduct of U.S. relations with Bolivia since the 1952 Revolution has been in the hands of career diplomats, who have had an active sympathy for the aims which the M N R governments have been attempting to achieve.[1]

GUATEMALA

In 1950, when Colonel Jacobo Arbenz became president of Guatemala, the development of the country had long been held back by the feudal form of land ownership which still persisted and the isolation of the Indian communities (the population is overwhelmingly Indian). The nation maintained a favourable balance of trade by exporting coffee and bananas, but produced insufficient food for its own requirements. Thus Guatemala's problems were similar basically to those which Paz Estenssoro was at that time tackling – with U.S. help – in Bolivia. But Guatemala is much nearer the United States than is Bolivia, and agrarian reform at such close range looked suspiciously like communism, which the U.S. Government were doing their best to exclude from the hemisphere and which,

1. Alexander, p. 259.

anyway, they could not tolerate in a country situated so near to the Panama Canal.

To the impartial observer in 1950 it was evident that any conscientious Guatemalan Government, no matter what its political complexion might be, would have to approach in a revolutionary spirit the fundamental questions of land ownership and agriculture, and the closely allied subject of transport. It so happened, however, that not only was a U.S. company – the United Fruit Company of Boston – the biggest single landowner in the country, but that same organization owned the pier and dock installations of the Caribbean port of Puerto Barrios, had a joint interest in the Pacific port of San José, controlled the republic's railways through its stock holdings in the International Railways of Central America and was in control, too, of a considerable part of Caribbean shipping. Approximately four fifths of all electric services in the country were supplied by another U.S. concern, the Empresa Eléctrica, a subsidiary of the American and Foreign Power Company. Therefore any programme for effecting a more just distribution of the country's wealth was bound to be bitterly opposed not only by Guatemalan landowners and businessmen but also by very powerful U.S. interests.

In May 1952 the Guatemalan Congress passed a law which provided for the expropriation of uncultivated land from the large estates and its redistribution among landless peasants. Compensation was to be paid in the form of government bonds. In the following year extensive areas of uncultivated land belonging to United Fruit were expropriated. Strikes by United Fruit workers received the tacit support of the Government. For a while the main motive for public clamour was the excessive power and privileges of the U.S. enterprises, instead of Britain's perfidy in holding Belice (British Honduras).[1]

By the local propertied class, and generally in the United States, the acts of the Arbenz régime were looked upon not as manifestations of economic nationalism but as proof that the

---

1. For the history of the Belice controversy see R. A. Humphreys, *The Diplomatic History of British Honduras*, O.U.P., 1961; and D. A. G. Waddell, *British Honduras*, O.U.P., 1961.

country was becoming a Soviet dependency. It was certainly true that Guatemalan communists – some of whom had made frequent visits to Moscow – were at the head of the trade unions and held influential positions in government departments and the information services. Arbenz himself had no desire to lead Guatemala into the Soviet camp, but, having underestimated the power of local and foreign capitalists, he found himself relying more and more on the help of a small but well-organized and hardworking band of communists, to whom he was obliged to make ever greater concessions. Whereas Paz in Bolivia exercised a modernating influence on left-wing extremists, Arbenz in Guatemala allowed them to become increasingly extreme. While Paz found a way of obtaining U.S. collaboration without greatly modifying his policies, Arbenz made no attempt to reach a compromise. As for the U.S. Government, although they behaved with patience and generosity in Bolivia, they deliberately aggravated the situation in Guatemala by giving their support to an army of Guatemalan exiles, who were trained in Honduras and invaded Guatemala in 1954. As a result of the invasion Arbenz was overthrown, and Guatemala fell under a right-wing dictatorship.

Latin Americans noted that Theodore Roosevelt's 'big stick' had not yet been permanently discarded.

CUBA

Revolutions in Latin America are no longer of merely national significance. Nowadays they are symptoms of – or reactions against – a *continental* movement towards greater economic independence and social justice. Vargas (Brazil) pointed the way for Perón (Argentina), Zapata (Mexico), Paz Estenssoro (Bolivia), and Arbenz (Guatemala) in their different circumstances were just as truly the precursors of Castro as was the Cuban Martí himself.[1] Throughout Latin America the foreign ownership of public utilities and industrial monopolies, which formerly was accepted as contributing to a nation's economic advancement, has come to be regarded as an indignity. Everywhere the peasants'

1. For Martí see p. 173.

cry for land – a cry which was raised in Mexico as long ago as 1810[1] – now sounds modern and realistic.

The United States drove the Spaniards out of Cuba in 1898,[2] but U.S. investors then attained a dominant position in the island, so that Cuba, newly liberated from Spain, lost control of her own economic resources. Moreover, while the production of sugar for the U.S. market was the mainstay of the Cuban economy, it was also largely responsible for the perpetuation of the workers' poverty, because the sugar industry only gave them employment for about four months in the year. So great was the concentration on sugar that Cuba had to import her basic foods; and although the need for cultivating other crops was recognized, little progress was made in the diversification of agriculture.

Demands for reform came, as usual, from university students and intellectuals. Prominent among young political orators in the late 1940s was Fidel Castro. The son of a well-to-do landowner, Castro was already active in politics while a law student at Havana University; in 1953 he led his first, unsuccessful insurrection against the brutal and corrupt dictatorship of Fulgencio Batista; in 1956 he and his bearded guerrillas began the decisive revolutionary movement in the Sierra Maestra, the forested mountains in eastern Cuba which were the traditional base for such operations.

Castro's first aim was to rid the island of Batista; but in 1953 he had announced his further plans: briefly, the revolution would (1) return to the Cuban people their sovereignty and punish those who had betrayed the Constitution; (2) give land to the landless peasants and to those whose holdings were too small, with indemnification for the previous owners; (3) provide non-agricultural workers with a share in all industrial, mercantile, and mining enterprises; (4) grant sugar-workers a proportion of the income from cane; and (5) confiscate all property obtained corruptly by members of previous governments.[3]

The overthrow of Batista on 31 December 1958 brought the revolutionaries into direct contact with the business interests the

1. See p. 93.   2. See p. 174.

3. Robert J. Alexander, *Prophets of the Revolution: Profiles of Latin American Leaders*, New York, Macmillan, 1962, pp. 271–2.

dictator had protected for so long, and many of the estates and factories which Castro then expropriated were U.S. property. Protests and retaliatory action from Washington merely added to the revolutionaries' conviction that Cuba would never be free so long as the United States had a stake in her economy; and it followed that, as Cuban capitalists were so closely associated with U.S. interests, the capitalist system appeared incompatible with the people's freedom. By the end of 1960 the revolutionary Government were in control of virtually all Cuba's resources – land, industry, and commerce – and almost nothing remained of the previously flourishing trade with the United States. To replace the U.S. market, and to obtain essential supplies (such as petroleum, and machinery for his industrialization programme), Castro looked chiefly to the Soviet bloc countries, which also provided technical assistance and the military equipment Castro said he needed for defending the island against invasion. The United States – greatly alarmed by the prospect of having a Soviet outpost ninety miles from the coast of Florida – denounced Castro as a creature of the U.S.S.R. He replied that his form of Marxist-Leninism was 'just as Cuban as palm-trees'.

While the connexion between Cuba and the Soviet bloc grew ever closer, the United States went ahead with plans for overthrowing Castro; U.S. government agencies organized, trained, and equipped an invasion force of anti-Castro Cubans in Central America; and in April 1961 these men were landed on the Cuban shore, where they were soon killed or captured by Castro's militia.

Whereas Theodore Roosevelt would have approved of the manoeuvre which neatly ejected Arbenz from Guatemala, the fiasco of the Cuban invasion would have made him turn in his grave.

By 1962 it was apparent that Cuba had become virtually a Soviet satellite, and a base from which nuclear missiles might be launched against the United States. Suddenly Cuba was a vital factor in the U.S.–U.S.S.R. 'cold war' manoeuvres, with the result that the Cubans themselves had a diminishing influence on the decisions taken in regard to their own island by the two great powers. The naval blockade of Cuba inaugurated by the U.S. president in October 1962 was not primarily a measure against the Cuban government but a strategic act designed to prevent the U.S.S.R. from adding to its military equipment on Cuban soil. And when, a few days later, the Soviet premier undertook to remove his country's offensive weapons from Cuba, Castro had no say in the matter.

16

Conclusion

THERE are occasions when Latin Americans realize that, as Bolívar said, they are a distinct variety of the human species. At other times they are more conscious of differences that exist among them: when a Uruguayan or a Chilean goes to Guatemala he is unable to think of 'those Indians' as being Latin Americans like himself; an Argentine travelling to Paraguay or Brazil (or, indeed, anywhere else) will feel that the local people are of an inferior race; Brazilians visiting the highlands of Bolivia will be courteous to the inhabitants of those bleak regions (as they always are to everyone, wherever they may go), but they will not be conscious of having any special bond with Bolivians. And so on. Each nation is very aware of its own nationality.

It is particularly when Latin Americans meet together *outside* Latin America that they know that they possess some common quality which distinguishes them from the rest of mankind. In spite of the great differences in the geographical, racial, and economic factors which have determined the development of the various regions, there has nevertheless been a general Latin American history. Bolívar and San Martín, Rosas and Santa Anna, Gómez, Vargas, Cárdenas, Perón – each had his own national characteristics, but we recognize them also as *Latin American* figures. Some came from the mountains, others from the plains. Some were much more honourable, some much more ruthless, than others. But only Latin America could have produced them just as they were.

This book, in one sense, is an essay towards an interpretation of Latin American civilization, which is still in formation.

We have noted the appearance of one characteristic of Latin American society as early as the late sixteenth century, when Santa Teresa's brother, returning to Spain from Ecuador, assumed a title which had always been reserved for the nobility.[1]

1. See pp. 17–18.

That was a sign of typical Latin American optimism, self-assurance. Latin Americans have grown up, so to say, in opposition to Europe. They feel that Europe is finished, whereas Latin America is only beginning. They are impatient of European caution, and of the European respect for the law. In colonial times the laws were frequently violated – indeed, colonial legislation governing economic activities was often so ill-conceived and so inimical to the development of natural resources and to the fulfilment of common desires, that its violation became almost a necessity, and contraband was normal. Independence, attained in the nineteenth century, did not change those habits. There remained a general and enduring discrepancy between the law and actual life.

The foundation of the Brazilian character was already laid during the seventeenth century, by which time the Portuguese settlers and their Negro slaves had evolved a way of living in the South American tropics. Tolerance and exploitation have not been incompatible in Brazil, just as parliamentary elections and *caudillismo* have not been mutually exclusive in that and other Latin American countries.

Latin America is so spacious that there is still room for anything and everything. Even the inhabitants of the shanty-towns which now surround most of the large cities can see the beginning of the *pampa* or the jungle, just a few miles away from their miserable shacks. Although they may have put their faith in the city, the knowledge of the existence of so much space around them encourages optimism and a generous outlook.

But of course Latin America is not simply a vast undeveloped New World: it is also a very old world. In Latin America today the pre-Columbian races and, to some extent, their cultures, survive. The 'El Dorado' outlook of the modern Latin American dates from the early colonial era. The old Spanish and Portuguese attitudes to the land, religion, and the family still prevail in an extraordinary degree in this twentieth-century multi-racial society. Therefore, while Latin Americans are attracted by the material achievements of the United States, they nevertheless feel that, as Rodó suggested,[1] they have a more mature judge-

1. See pp. 180–1.

ment, a better grasp of human values, than the North Americans.

One definition of the nature of Latin American culture has been given by a North American long acquainted with the people:

> The world will hardly look to the Latin American for leadership in democracy, in organization, in business, in science, in rigid moral values. On the other hand, Latin America has something to contribute to an industrialized and mechanistic world concerning the value of the individual, the place of friendship, the use of leisure, the art of conversation, the attractions of the intellectual [life], the equality of races, the juridical basis of international life, the place of suffering and contemplation, the value of the impractical, the importance of people over things and rules.[1]

Although the Latin American nations have so much in common, practical cooperation among them has made slow progress since 1826, the year in which Bolívar convened the first American conference at Panama.[2] Tariffs and payment deficiencies have been partly responsible for the fact that the exchange of goods among the republics has usually amounted to only about ten per cent of their total international trade. The chief causes of the smallness of inter-regional trade, however, have been the geographical obstacles and the nature of the republics' products. In the 1950s approximately eighty per cent of the movement of merchandise between the Latin American countries was by sea, and the traffic was unbalanced. It was characteristic of trade between the southern countries that goods going to the Pacific coast (for instance, wool, vegetable oil and meat, cotton and coffee) had a much higher specific value than most of those carried in the opposite direction (cement, nitrate, anthracite, and petroleum). This meant that for the balancing of payments there had necessarily to be inequality in the volume of cargo transported in each direction, and ships sailing from the South Atlantic to the South Pacific would make the journey with half-empty holds. Anyway, the economies of all of the republics depended on their primary products, for which the natural markets were outside Latin America.

1. Samuel Guy Inman quoted in Lewis Hanke, *South America*, New York, Von Nostrand, 1959, p. 10.
2. See p. 114.

Many inter-American conferences have been held. Usually they have ended in declarations of solidarity, etc. without much practical consequence. After the Second World War the United States constantly pressed the members of the Organization of American States[1] to take united action against communism in the hemisphere; but Latin America's rulers – although they would blame 'communist agitators' for any uprisings against their régimes – were not seriously alarmed by the threat of communism in their lands. True, communist parties existed legally or illegally, in all of the republics; but they had a foreign air about them, and it seemed that the communist faith had not undergone the 'sea change' which is necessary before any ideology from abroad can become fertile in Latin America. Then suddenly events in Cuba suggested that a Castro type of communism might spread among the poor, the undernourished, the landless. Castro spoke as a Latin American, and the radio brought his voice and ideas into even the remote villages on the far side of the Andes, breaking through the curtain of illiteracy. A traveller in 1961 remarked that only two faces were universally recognized throughout Latin America: those of the Virgin Mary and Fidel Castro.

It so happened that Castro's rise to power came in the midst of a period when the prices of many of Latin America's major products were in decline and the terms of trade unfavourable. The Latin American governments had long been appealing to the United States for greater financial aid, and as a result of the worsening economic situation most of them now became more willing to adopt the strict economic policies (limitation of money supply, freezing of wages, reduction of imports, etc.) which the United States demanded if further loans were to be granted. The U.S. authorities, for their part, were increasingly apprehensive that, unless the Latin American economies did quickly receive very substantial aid, the conditions likely to breed Castro-communism would grow out of control.

Such was the general atmosphere in 1959–60, when the United

1. The Organization of American States consists of the United States and the independent countries of the Latin American area.

States sponsored the creation of an Inter-American Development Bank and undertook to subscribe to a long-term programme for Latin American development. Those two decisions brought the Latin American governments together on a more practical basis than ever before, to tackle problems more or less common to all of them. All of the republics needed to raise the standard of living of their poorer classes but lacked the financial resources to carry out on an adequate scale the necessary schemes for the construction of public works and low-cost housing, the modernization of agriculture, the improvement of education, etc. In Latin America as a whole the population was increasing so fast that such development and welfare measures as had so far been proposed would scarcely even suffice to maintain the current standard of living of the masses and certainly could not achieve any real betterment *per capita*. The situation was similar to that in *Through the Looking-Glass*, when the Queen explained to Alice: 'Now *here*, it takes all the running you can do, to keep in the same place.' It was estimated that Latin America's 1961 population of about 208 million would double in the next twenty-five years.

The Argentine economist Raúl Prebisch had long foreseen this predicament, and as executive secretary of the United Nations Economic Commission for Latin America (ECLA) he had repeatedly advocated the creation of a Latin American common market. Prebisch argued that even with U.S. aid the republics would not be able to afford to import all of the goods and equipment that an expanding economy required. Therefore they must set up industries to manufacture a much bigger quantity of such things for themselves. But those industries, if they were to develop adequately, would need a larger market than that which any individual Latin American republic could provide. At last in 1960–1 – influenced by the example of the European common market – some of the republics joined together in a Latin American Free Trade Association (LAFTA), and a beginning was made towards the reduction of tariffs.[1] A similar organization,

1. cf. Economic Commission for Latin America, *The Latin American Common Market*, United Nations, 1959. Also Bank of London and South America, *Quarterly Review*, July 1960.

on a smaller scale, had already been formed by four of the Central American republics.[1]

Among other problems that the Latin American republics had in common was that of inducing their ruling classes to acquire a greater sense of public responsibility. In all of the republics the wealthy landowners and the new class of industrialists were unwilling to pay taxes in proportion to their income or to cooperate in agrarian reform. When, early in 1962, disturbances occurred in Brazil's drought-ridden, poverty-stricken north-east and the Brazilian Government sent troops to that region to search for the trouble-makers, a Rio de Janeiro newspaper commented that the real agents of subversion were 'the big landowners who refuse to admit that times have changed'. President Kennedy tried to establish the principle that U.S. aid would be granted only to countries which showed their determination to undertake tax reform and land reform.

So serious was the plight of the rural people that – at least during the initial period of President Kennedy's programme for assisting Latin America – U.S. advisers on foreign aid were inclined to give insufficient attention to the new urban populations, whose living conditions were even more likely to lead to social unrest. One U.S. specialist in economic development gave warning of this danger:

> People are migrating by the millions from the farms and villages to the cities. This gathering of the rural dispossessed and distressed into urban multitudes goes on day after day with no let-up. It is comparable in importance to all the other great movements of human beings in history.

In Colombia, for instance, the Cauca Valley project for controlling floods and generating electricity attracted industry to the town of Cali, with the result that in the surrounding region the people no longer looked exclusively to the land for their future: that future was centred in an expanding Cali – in its industries,[2]

1. cf. 'The Central American Common Market' in the *Quarterly Review*, Bank of London and South America, April 1961.
2. Cali's industrial companies and manufactures include Celanese Colombiana; Cartón de Colombia (an affiliate of the Container Corporation of Chicago); the Goodyear (tyre) Company; textiles, paper by-

and the colourful variety of its streets. In the late 1950s and early 1960s Cali's population increased at the rate of eight per cent a year, with two thirds of the increase the result of migration from the rural districts. Virtually all of the migrants arrived with little more than the clothes on their backs; they lacked any technical skills; and so they worked in the city as common labourers, often for the equivalent of less than a dollar a day.

In all of the principal countries of Latin America the great migration is creating new social tensions.

As the poor move to the cities, they swell the forces of a new urban class. The members of this class may live in shacks; they may lack pure water, medical facilities and schools for their children. If they are lucky, they may have a few of the humbler decencies of life – a tiny plot of land for a house, a weekly visit by a municipal nurse. Whatever their condition, they can measure their own lot against that of others – the ones who own cars and homes, who can afford to eat well, who buy clothing in the stores, whose children are never hungry or poorly clothed and who go to school. Seeing with their own eyes what these other people have thrusts it within reach of their imagination – and their growing capacity for resentment and envy.[1]

Latin Americans share not only problems, but also a robust faith in progress and perfectibility. Their glory is the men who in the nineteenth century dedicated themselves to guiding the people towards a better life. Those great Latin Americans were essentially teachers at heart – even though, like Bolívar, they may have been compelled by circumstances to become soldiers. Whether they wrote a Discourse to the Nation, or a novel, their main purpose was to correct local habits and to re-model society and the state. Sarmiento, José Hernández (author of the epic gaucho poem *Martín Fierro*), Martí, Rodó, Batlle y Ordóñez, and the rest – for them literature was a part of public service.

By 1890 conditions in Latin America had become generally

products, soap, pharmaceuticals, building materials, office equipment, beer, clothing, hats, canned produce, tobacco, and plastics. There are some forty U.S. concerns, and the North American colony numbers about 500.

1. David E. Lilienthal, 'Foreign Aid: the Teeming City' (from a lecture delivered at Rutgers University), *New York Times* (International Edition) 8 September 1962.

more peaceful and, at certain levels, more prosperous. Men of letters now found it possible to devote themselves to intellectual pursuits, abandoning politics to the mere politicians – though, as one shrewd observer remarked, 'nothing was gained by it, quite the contrary'.[1]

Then the social stirrings of the twentieth century attracted the writers back to their old habit of taking part in public affairs. The Mexican revolution of 1910 was preceded by an intellectual movement; agitation for university reform began in Argentina in 1918 and spread to other republics; poets in several lands – notably Pablo Neruda in Chile – taught that communism would do away with poverty; in Argentina during the Perón régime, and afterwards, authors anxiously discussed their country's destiny.

Authors and professional men have become particularly conscious of belonging to a Latin American fraternity. Poets in the various countries have been acquainted with one another's work. Literary critics – and they abound – have helped to make the literature of other Latin American countries familiar. As Latin America has only two literary languages, Spanish and Portuguese, the big publishing houses of Mexico City and Buenos Aires have been able to distribute books in Spanish over a wide area.

The conception of Latin America as a unit has developed, too, among officials of the several international organizations, such as the Organization of American States, the Economic Commission for Latin America, and the Inter-American Development Bank. These officials – especially the economists – have recognized the advantages that might be gained through greater cooperation among the republics. Latin America, organized as a bloc, would be better able than the republics individually to bargain with the United States.

It has been said – and not entirely without reason – that the greatest bond uniting the Latin Americans is their suspicion of the United States. Many Latin Americans have not even considered U.S. financial aid to be an unmixed blessing; while conservatives have been shocked by the United States' demand that their governments should carry out programmes of social reform as a

1. Henríquez Ureña, p. 161.

condition for receiving aid, the left wing have protested that the real purpose of the insistence on reform was to prolong the life of the capitalist system by means of minimum concessions to the needs of the poor.

The Latin American peoples have agreed in not wishing to be involved in the 'cold war', which they have looked upon as a northern hemisphere matter. They would occupy a 'third position', a position which Perón described as being 'somewhere between the materialistic individualism of the United States and the materialistic collectivism of the U.S.S.R.'; Brazilian presidents, in particular, have stressed that, although their sympathies were with the West, they would not necessarily follow the leadership of the United States on all issues.

The U.S.–U.S.S.R. crisis over Cuba in October 1962 caused such alarm among Latin American governments – most of which were middle-class and right-wing, or moderately liberal – that they unanimously supported a U.S. decision that the flow of Soviet offensive weapons into Cuba must be stopped. Several of the republics rejected, however, any proposals which might seem to commit them to support an invasion of the island, if the United States should consider this to be necessary. Prominent Latin American statesmen, such as President López Mateos of Mexico, while approving of U.S. endeavours to get Soviet nuclear missiles removed from Cuba, publicly blamed the United States for having created conditions which had compelled Castro to throw in his lot with the U.S.S.R.

In so far as public affairs are concerned, perhaps the most important Latin American characteristic is the habit of *not cooperating*. This is the continent of 'personalism', and since the early days of independence the various sectors of the population in most of the republics have had an aversion for cooperation: *caudillo* has been against *caudillo*, the capital city against the provinces, the inhabitants of the mountains against those of the lowlands. In 1930 Ortega y Gasset said of the immigrants to Argentina that they were 'men lacking in all interior discipline, men uprooted from their native European societies, where they had lived, without realizing it, morally disciplined by a sort of stabilized and integral collective life'. Emigrating, those people broke away from the collective life and became unattached individuals. The present-day Argentine author, H. A. Murena, has written: 'We behave as if each one of us were unique and as if he were alone.'

So – as they experience simultaneously the effects of the industrial revolution, the modern social revolution, and an extraordinary acceleration in the rate of growth of the population (largely accounted for by modern medicine) – the Latin Americans go ahead in a typically Latin American manner, with little aptitude for parliamentary government, an optimistic preference for consumption rather than for productive investment, and a happy certainty that human beings are more important than 'things and rules'.

Some of the 'traditional' Latin American characteristics may no longer be quite so significant as formerly. Changes of influence have been occurring in public life, such as that resulting from the emergence of the new 'managerial' class of economists, engineers, scientists, who, in several countries, have sometimes seemed to be replacing the political careerists and the military in positions of power; there are signs that this change in national leadership is gaining impetus; but it is still too early to say that a new class has 'taken over' – in Brazil, in May and June 1964, several of the dedicated and capable younger leaders were deprived of their political rights, in the traditional fashion, by the military. At the same time, it is probably true that in many of the republics the composition of the officer corps is also changing; that the officers come increasingly from the 'lower middle sectors', and even from the working class, and that they are therefore inclined to sympathize with plans for social and economic reform – so long, at least, as the reforms are not accompanied by social disorder.[1] And the growth in the proportion of young people in the Latin American population – in 1963 half of the Venezuelan population

1. Cf. John J. Johnson, *The Military and Society in Latin America*, O.U.P., 1964.

was under 18 years of age[1] – is bound to stimulate a new approach to national problems and opportunities.

Nevertheless, in Gertrude Stein's words, 'Anybody is as their land and their air is', or, in those of General de Gaulle, 'No ordeal alters the nature of man, and no crisis alters the nature of States'; at least, the characteristics created by history and environment do not quickly disappear. Although the routine of life for the majority of Latin America's town-dwellers becomes more and more similar to that of people in towns in the more developed countries of the world – the commuting to work by train and bus; lunch at a snack-bar or in a factory canteen; television in the evening; hire-purchase; pensions – there remains a quality that is distinctively Latin American. That quality is still most difficult to define; we can only point to examples – knowing that they are inadequate – such as the survival of the 'rhetorical tradition' in education: as a Venezuelan teacher remarked, in Latin America a schoolboy will still generally be praised for saying something well, rather than for the content of what he has said,[2] and the political implications of this habit are far-reaching. Again, the manner in which Latin America's wealthy employers deal with their workers' demands differs from that which is usual in the more developed countries: 'in their relations with individuals and the government the employers are more personal; matters are more likely to be arranged and compromised, rather than enacted and enforced.'[3]

Eventually there may be little to distinguish the inhabitants of, say, Medellín, or São Paulo, from those of Chicago and Manchester (appalling prospect!), but that day has not yet come.

1. *The Times*, 13 August 1963.
2. The *Saturday Evening Post*, June/July 1963.
3. John Paton Davies in the *New York Times*, 31 August 1963.

Table of Populations

	Millions
ARGENTINA	21
BOLIVIA	3·5
BRAZIL	73
CHILE	7·8
COLOMBIA	14·4
COSTA RICA	1·2
CUBA	6·9
DOMINICAN REPUBLIC	3
ECUADOR	4·4
EL SALVADOR	2·5
GUATEMALA	3·8
HAITI	4·2
HONDURAS	1·8
MEXICO	36
NICARAGUA	1·5
PANAMA	1·1
PARAGUAY	1·8
PERU	10·3
URUGUAY	2·8
VENEZUELA	7·5
	208·5

A Bibliographical Note on Books in English

THE literature in English on Latin America is vast. The best selective bibliography contains more than 2,000 entries. This is R. A. Humphreys's *Latin American History: a Guide to the Literature in English*, Oxford University Press, 1958. Two brief introductions are *Latin America: an Introduction to the Basic Books in English*, London, Hispanic and Luso-Brazilian Councils, 1960, and George Pendle, *South America*, a National Book League 'Reader's Guide', Cambridge University Press, 1957.

A few of the books published in the present century are listed here. They have been chosen for the help of readers who may wish to look further into the history of Latin America or of individual countries.

I. LATIN AMERICA, GENERAL

BENHAM, F., and HOLLEY, H. A., *A Short Introduction to the Economy of Latin America*, O.U.P., 1960. Part I deals with general characteristics. Part II gives an account of recent economic trends in Argentina, Brazil, Chile, Colombia, Mexico, Peru, and Venezuela.

DAVIES, HOWELL (editor), *The South American Handbook*, London, Trade & Travel Publications. A useful guidebook, published annually, and kept more or less up to date. In spite of the title it includes Mexico, Central America, and the Caribbean islands.

Economic Survey of Latin America, New York, the Economic Commission for Latin America of the United Nations Economic and Social Council. Published annually. First appeared in 1949.

HENRÍQUEZ UREÑA, PEDRO *Literary Currents in Hispanic America*, Harvard University Press, 1949. A brilliant survey of Latin American culture from the sixteenth century to the twentieth.

HERRING, HUBERT, *A History of Latin America*, New York, Knopf, 1955. Perhaps the best of the several mammoth histories that have been published in the United States. More than 800 pages.

HUMPHREYS, R. A., *The Evolution of Modern Latin America*, Oxford, Clarendon Press, 1946 – a concise introduction to the modern period, up to the end of the Second World War – and *Liberation in South America*, University of London, Athlone Press, 1952.

JAMES, PRESTON E., *Latin America*, New York, Odyssey Press, third edition, 1959. A standard geographical textbook, which is also a history of the relation of the indigenous races, the European invaders, and the modern Latin Americans to their environment.

MADARIAGA, SALVADOR DE, *The Rise of the Spanish Empire* and *The Fall of the Spanish Empire*, London, Hollis & Carter, 1947. The Spanish author looks upon the Spanish Americans as still being rebels against the mother country.

SCHURZ, WILLIAM LYTLE, *This New World*, London, Allen & Unwin, 1956. A distinguished work, primarily concerned with the three centuries of Spanish colonial rule.

II. PERIODICALS

Fortnightly Review and *Quarterly Review*, London, Bank of London and South America. Mainly financial and economic affairs.

Hispanic American Historical Review, Durham (N.C.), Duke University Press. A scholarly review, published quarterly.

Hispanic American Report, California, Stanford University. A monthly review of current affairs.

Inter-American Economic Affairs, Washington, Institute of Inter-American Studies. Quarterly.

III. INDIVIDUAL COUNTRIES

Argentina

BRIDGES, E. LUCAS, *Uttermost Part of the Earth*, Hodder & Stoughton, 1948. Life in Tierra del Fuego.

BUNKLEY, A. W., *The Life of Sarmiento*, Princeton University Press, 1952. A biography of Argentina's great educator and statesman.

FERNS, H. S., *Britain and Argentina in the Nineteenth Century*, Oxford, Clarendon Press, 1960.

GÜIRALDES, RICARDO, *Don Segundo Sombra*, London, Penguin Books, 1948. A translation of the most famous Argentine novel of gaucho life.

HUDSON, W. H., *Far Away and Long Ago*, London, Dent, 1918. Vivid reminiscences of life in Argentina in the time of Rosas.

PENDLE, GEORGE, *Argentina*, third edition, O.U.P., 1963. One of the series of Chatham House studies of the history, politics, and economics of the Latin American countries.

RENNIE, YSABEL F., *The Argentine Republic*, New York, Macmillan, 1945. Argentine developments, vividly described, up to the arrival of Perón.

Bibliography

Bolivia

ALEXANDER, ROBERT J., *The Bolivian National Revolution*, Rutgers University Press, 1958. The author approves of the Paz Estenssoro régime.

OSBORNE, HAROLD, *Bolivia: a Land Divided*, second edition, London, Royal Institute of International Affairs, 1955.

Brazil

BOXER, C. R., *Salvador de Sá and the Struggle for Brazil and Angola, 1602–86*, London University, 1952; *The Dutch in Brazil, 1624–54*, Oxford, Clarendon Press, 1957; *The Golden Age of Brazil, 1695–1750*; *Growing Pains of a Colonial Society*, University of California Press, 1962. Authoritative studies of the early history of Brazil.

CAMACHO, J. A., *Brazil: an Interim Assessment*, second edition, London, Royal Institute of International Affairs, 1954.

FREYRE, GILBERTO, *The Masters and the Slaves*, New York, Knopf, 1946. A study of the development of Brazilian civilization, with many fascinating details of Portuguese colonial society.

MANCHESTER, A. K., *British Pre-eminence in Brazil: its Rise and Decline*, University of North Carolina Press, 1933.

WAGLEY, CHARLES, *Amazon Town: a Study of Man in the Tropics*, New York, Macmillan, 1952. An anthropologist's account of life in the remote regions of the Amazon valley.

WAGLEY, CHARLES, and others, *Race and Class in Rural Brazil*, Paris, UNESCO, 1952. Field studies of various parts of Brazil.

The Central American republics

MONRO, DANA G., *The Five Republics of Central America*, O.U.P., 1918. A standard work.

PARKER, FRANKLIN D., *Central American Republics*, O.U.P., 1963. A Chatham House study.

Chile

BUTLAND, GILBERT J., *Chile*, third edition, London, Royal Institute of International Affairs, 1956.

CLISSOLD, STEPHEN, *Chilean Scrap-book*, London, Cresset Press, 1952. A charming description of the country, region by region, with the historical background.

McBRIDE, G. M., *Chile: Land and Society*, New York, American Geographical Society, 1936. A masterly analysis of the agrarian problem.

Bibliography

Colombia

GALBRAITH, W. O., *Colombia*, London, Royal Institute of International Affairs, 1953.

MARTZ, JOHN D., *Colombia: a Contemporary Political Survey*, University of North Carolina Press, 1962.

ROMOLI, KATHLEEN, *Colombia*, New York, Doubleday, 1941. A general description of the country.

Cuba

DRAPER, THEODORE, *Castro's Revolution: Myths and Realities*, London, Thames & Hudson, 1962. One of the author's main theses is that Castro betrayed his liberal, democratic supporters when he led his revolution into the 'Marxist-Leninist' camp.

NELSON, LOWRY, *Rural Cuba*, University of Minnesota Press, 1950. This study of the structure and problems of Cuban rural society goes a long way to explaining why the Fidel Castro revolution occurred.

WOLLASTON, NICHOLAS, *Red Rumba*, London, Hodder & Stoughton, 1962. A journey through the Caribbean and Central America in 1961, with special reference to Cuba and the Castro régime.

Ecuador

BEMELMANS, LUDWIG, *The Donkey Inside*, New York, Viking Press, 1941. Amusing impressions.

LINKE, LILO, *Ecuador: Country of Contrasts*, third edition, O.U.P., 1960. One of the best of the Chatham House studies.

Mexico

CLINE, HOWARD F., *Mexico: Revolution to Evolution, 1940-60*, O.U.P., 1962. A Chatham House study.

PARKES, HENRY BAMFORD, *A History of Mexico*, London, Eyre & Spottiswoode, third edition, 1962. A standard history.

Panama

BIESANZ, JOHN and MAVIS, *The People of Panama*, Columbia University Press, 1955. Everyday life in Panama.

Paraguay

CUNNINGHAME GRAHAM, R. B., *A Vanished Arcadia*, London, Heinemann, 1901 – the Jesuit Missions in Paraguay, somewhat idealized; and *Portrait of a Dictator*, London, Heinemann, 1933 – the story of Solano López and his mistress, Madame Lynch.

PENDLE, GEORGE, *Paraguay: a Riverside Nation*, second edition, London, Royal Institute of International Affairs, 1956.

RAINE, PHILIP, *Paraguay*, New Brunswick, N.J., Scarecrow Press, 1956.

SERVICE, ELMAN R. and HELEN S., *Tobatí, Paraguayan Town*, University of Chicago Press, 1954. An interesting study of life in a small town.

WARREN, HARRIS GAYLORD, *Paraguay: an informal History*, University of Oklahoma Press, 1949.

Peru

BINGHAM, HIRAM, *Across South America*, New York, Houghton Mifflin, 1911. A journey from Buenos Aires to Lima, with special attention to the Inca ruins which the author discovered at Machu Picchu.

MASON, J. ALDEN, *The Ancient Civilizations of Peru*, London, Penguin Books, 1957. One of the best introductions to the Incas.

OWENS, R. J., *Peru*, O.U.P., 1963. A Chatham House study.

Uruguay

FITZGIBBON, RUSSELL H., *Uruguay: Portrait of a Democracy*, London, Allen & Unwin, 1956. A comprehensive history.

PENDLE, GEORGE, *Uruguay*, third edition, O.U.P., 1963.

STREET, JOHN, *Artigas and the Emancipation of Uruguay*, O.U.P., 1959. Uruguay's national hero.

Venezuela

LIEUWEN, EDWIN, *Venezuela*, O.U.P., 1961. A Chatham House study.

MASUR, GERHARD, *Simón Bolívar*, University of New Mexico Press, 1948. The most reliable biography, though not the most entertaining.

ROBERTSON, W. S., *The Life of Miranda*, 2 vols., University of North Carolina, 1929. A masterly biography of the great '*precursor*' of Venezuelan independence.

ROURKE, THOMAS [D. J. Clinton], *Gómez, Tyrant of the Andes*, New York, William Morrow, 1936. A vivid and critical, but not unfair, biography.

IV. INTERNATIONAL RELATIONS

There are many books by U.S. authors on Latin America's international relations. Among the most useful are the following:

FENWICK, C. G., *The Inter-American Regional System*, New York, McMullen, 1949.

PERKINS, DEXTER, *A History of the Monroe Doctrine*, Boston, Little Brown, 1955.

RIPPY, J. F., *Latin America in World Politics*, London, Allen & Unwin, 1938.

WHITAKER, A. P., *The United States and South America: the northern republics*, Harvard, 1948, and *The Western Hemisphere Idea*, Cornell University Press, 1954.

ADDENDA

Among notable books published since the first printing of the present book are the following:

FREYRE, GILBERTO, *The Mansions and the Shanties*, New York, Knopf, 1963. Freyre continues his social history of Brazil into the modern era, the rise of the power of the cities.

HANKE, LEWIS, *Do the Americans have a Common History?* New York, Knopf, 1964. An anthology of comments by U.S. and Latin American authors bearing on the idea that the Americas – North and South – have something in common that distinguishes them from other parts of the world.

JOHNSON, JOHN J., *The Military and Society in Latin America*, O.U.P., 1964. Military officers still intervene in politics, but they are now more inclined to recognize the need for social and economic reform.

JOSLIN, DAVID, *A Century of Banking in Latin America*, O.U.P., 1963. A book written to commemorate the centenary of the Bank of London and South America, which is at the same time a history of one hundred years of Britain's economic relations with Latin America.

PETERSON, HAROLD F., *Argentina and the United States*, State University of New York, 1964. A 600-page study of the relations between the two countries from 1810 to 1960.

VAGNER, MILTON I., *José Batlle y Ordóñez*, Harvard U.P., 1963. A masterly history of Batlle's rise to power in Uruguay and his first presidency.

Maps

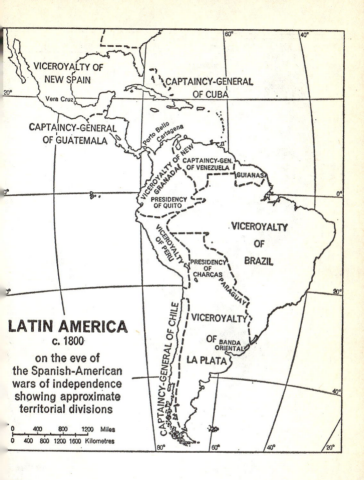

VICEROYALTY OF
NEW SPAIN

Vera Cruz

CAPTAINCY-GENERAL
OF CUBA

CAPTAINCY-GENERAL
OF GUATEMALA

Porto Bello
Cartagena

VICEROYALTY OF NEW
GRANADA

CAPTAINCY-GEN.
OF VENEZUELA

GUIANAS

PRESIDENCY
OF QUITO

VICEROYALTY
OF PERU

VICEROYALTY
OF
BRAZIL

PRESIDENCY
OF
CHARCAS

PARAGUAY

LATIN AMERICA
c. 1800

on the eve of
the Spanish-American
wars of independence
showing approximate
territorial divisions

CAPTAINCY-GENERAL OF CHILE

VICEROYALTY

OF BANDA
ORIENTAL

LA PLATA

```
0    400    800    1200  Miles
0  400  800 1200 1600 Kilometres
```

80° 70° 60° 50° 40°

10°

Panama Canal

Orinoco

Guiana Highlands

Equator 0°

Amazon

Lowlands

Amazon

Mato Grosso Highlands 10°

Lake Titicaca

São Francisco

A n d e s

20

Gran Chaco

Paraguay

Paraná

A n d e s

30°

Argentine Pampa

Río de la Plata

30

SOUTH AMERICA
(Physical)

Patagonian Plateau

0   300   600 Miles
0   400   800 Kilometres

40°

50°

Falkland Is

Tierra del Fuego

Str. of Magellan

Cape Horn

90° 80°

■ High Mountains (Over 15,000 ft.)
▨ Rugged Mountains (5,000-15,000 ft.)
⠿ Plateaus and Uplands (500-5,000 ft.)
☐ Lowlands and Plains (0-500 ft.)

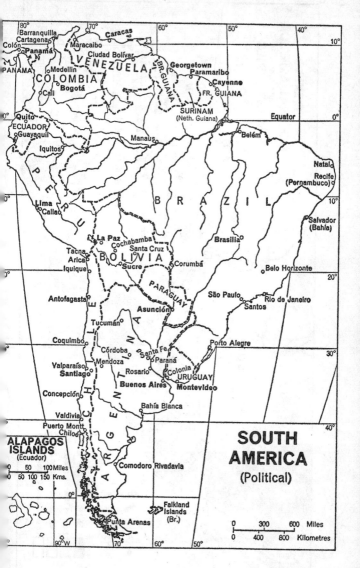

80° Barranquilla
Cartagena
Colón
Panamá
PANAMA
Maracaibo
Caracas
Ciudad Bolívar
V E N E Z U E L A
Georgetown
Paramaribo
Cayenne
FR. GUIANA
BR. GUIANA
Medellin
C O L O M B I A
Bogotá
Cali
Quito
ECUADOR
Guayaquil
Iquitos
SURINAM
(Neth. Guiana)
Equator 0°
Manaus
Belém
P E R U
Natal
Recife
(Pernambuco)
B R A Z I L
Lima
Callao
10°
Salvador
(Bahía)
La Paz
Cochabamba
Santa Cruz
Brasilia
Tacna
Arica
Iquique
B O L I V I A
Sucre
Corumbá
Belo Horizonte
20°
P A R A G U A Y
Antofagasta
São Paulo
Rio de Janeiro
Santos
Asunción
Tucumán
Coquimbo
Córdoba
Mendoza
Santa Fe
Paraná
Porto Alegre
30°
Valparaíso
Santiago
Rosario
Colonia
URUGUAY
Montevideo
Buenos Aires
Concepción
Bahía Blanca
Valdivia
Puerto Montt
Chiloe
40°
ALAPAGOS
ISLANDS
(Ecuador)
50 100 Miles
50 100 150 Kms.
Comodoro Rivadavia
SOUTH
AMERICA
(Political)
Falkland
Islands
(Br.)
Punta Arenas
90° W
70°
60°
50°
0 300 600 Miles
0 400 800 Kilometres

241

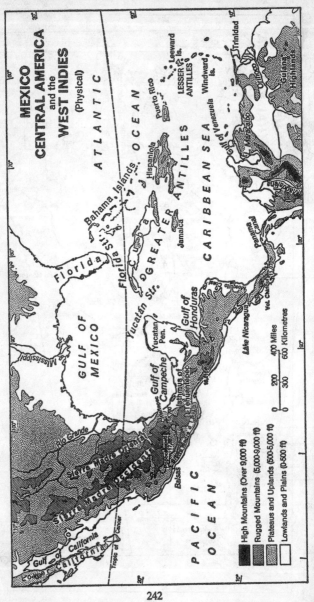

MEXICO CENTRAL AMERICA and the WEST INDIES
(Physical)

ATLANTIC OCEAN

PACIFIC OCEAN

GULF OF MEXICO

CARIBBEAN SEA

Gulf of California

Baja California

Tropic of Cancer

Rio Grande

Mississippi

Florida

Florida Str.

Bahama Islands

GREATER ANTILLES

Cuba

Jamaica

Hispaniola

Puerto Rico

Leeward Is.

LESSER ANTILLES

Windward Is.

Trinidad

Gulf of Venezuela

Maracaibo

Guiana Highland

Panama Canal

Lake Nicaragua

Vol. Chiriquí

Gulf of Honduras

Yucatán Pen.

Yucatán Str.

Gulf of Campeche

Isthmus of Tehuantepec

Balsas

Sierra Madre Occidental

Sierra Madre Oriental

Sierra Madre del Sur

0   200   400 Miles
0   300   600 Kilometres

High Mountains (Over 9,000 ft)

Rugged Mountains (5,000–9,000 ft)

Plateaus and Uplands (500–5,000 ft)

Lowlands and Plains (0–500 ft)

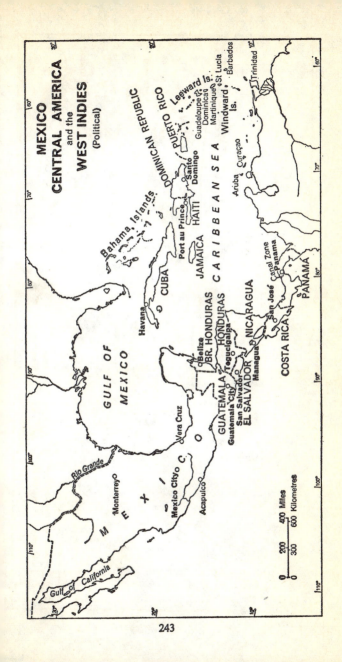

MEXICO
CENTRAL AMERICA
and the
WEST INDIES
(Political)

GULF OF MEXICO

Gulf of California

Rio Grande

Monterrey

Mexico City

Acapulco

Vera Cruz

M E X I C O

Bahama Islands

Havana

CUBA

JAMAICA

Port au Prince

HAITI

DOMINICAN REPUBLIC

Santo Domingo

PUERTO RICO

Leeward Is.

Guadeloupe
Dominica
Martinique
St Lucia
Barbados

Windward
Is.

CARIBBEAN SEA

Aruba Curaçao

Trinidad

Belize

BR. HONDURAS

GUATEMALA

Guatemala City

San Salvador

EL SALVADOR

Tegucigalpa

HONDURAS

Managua

NICARAGUA

San José

COSTA RICA

Canal Zone

Panama

PANAMA

0   200   400 Miles
0   300   600 Kilometres

Index

Index

Some other Pelican books
are described on the
following pages

THE MAKING OF MODERN RUSSIA

Lionel Kochan

'This is a history of Russia from the earliest times up to the outbreak of the Second World War. However, in keeping with his choice of title, Mr Kochan has concentrated on the modern period, devoting about as many pages to the eighty years following the Emancipation of the Serfs in 1861 as to the preceding 800-odd years.... The result is a straightforward account of a complicated story. A successful balance has been held between such conflicting themes as foreign policy ... foreign influences and native intellectual trends. His book could be a valuable introduction to the general reader in search of guidance ... a commendable book' – *Sunday Times*

'He handles his material with skill and sympathy. I cannot think of a better short book for acquainting the general reader with the broad outlines of Russian history. I hope many will read it' – Edward Crankshaw in the *Observer*

'Gives proper weight to economic, geographical, and cultural, as well as political and military factors, and ... while giving long-term trends their place, manages very often to convey a sense of real events happening to real people' – Wright Miller in the *Guardian*

'It reads easily, it is the ideal book for the general reader' – *The Economist*

A HISTORY OF MODERN JAPAN

Richard Storry

The rise, fall, and renaissance of Japan, within the space of less than a hundred years, is one of the most curious and dramatic stories of our time. This history begins by describing the historical background to Japan's emergence as a modern state in the sixties of the last century. It then discusses in detail the stages of Japan's advance as a world power up to the tragedy of the Pacific War. This struggle and its aftermath – the Occupation – are vividly described and analysed. The last chapter, bringing the account right up to the present day, is a fascinating study of the new Japan that has come into being since the San Francisco Peace Treaty of 1951.

A HISTORY OF SPAIN AND PORTUGAL

William C. Atkinson

This book attempts to show as a whole the Peninsula made up of Spain and Portugal, with the slow unfolding of a pattern of society and an attitude to life still subtly distinct from those north of the Pyrenees. The successive occupations of Roman, Visigoth, and Muslim span between them more than a thousand years. The Peninsula's great contribution to the modern age was the opening up of the New World in the west by Spain, and of new routes to the east by Portugal. 'And were there more lands still to discover,' wrote Camoens, 'they would be there too.' Over the last century and a half the history of both peoples provides a case-study in the essential relativity of forms of government. The reader will find here, too, a commentary upon great Spanish and Portuguese literary and artistic figures: Camoens, Cervantes, Lope de Vega, Calderón, Velázquez, Goya, and many more.

A HISTORY OF MODERN FRANCE
IN 3 VOLS
Alfred Cobban

When the first volume of Professor Cobban's new history was published it was generally acclaimed by the critics as a masterly work. In it he covers the eighteenth century, of which he writes: 'The French eighteenth century is not a period of great, dominating political figures. Yet if no one man counted overmuch, more men – and women – counted for something than possibly at any other time. The eighteenth century was ... and above all in France, the nursery of the modern world.'

The second volume begins with the refashioning of French laws and institutions under Napoleon in 1799; the third volume covers the period from the Franco-Prussian war to de Gaulle. Between these years régimes have risen and fallen and governments been set up and overthrown at a dizzy pace. Whilst his work contains an ample supply of factual history, Professor Cobban devotes most attention to the great turning points. His book aims to be not a textbook compilation but an interpretation of French history.